THE ESSENTIALS OF BUDDHIST PHILOSOPHY

BY THE SAME AUTHOR

Editions :

Taishō Shinshū Daizōkyō (Taishō Edition of the Buddhist Tripiṭaka in Chinese), 100 vols.

The Pāli Samanta-pāsādikā, 4 vols. (with S. Nagai)

Hōbōgirin, dictionnaire encyclopédique du bouddhisme d'après les sources chinoises et japonaises, 3 vols., and a supplement (with S. Lévi)

The Sākuntala, a Sanskrit Play by Kālidāsa

Dai Nippon Bukkyō Zensho (The Complete Works of Japanese Buddhism), 160 vols. (with Shinkyō Mochizuki and Seigai Omura)

Works :

Parigo Bukkyō Bungaku Kōhon (Pāli Buddhist Literature)

Indo Tetsugaku Shūkyō Shi (History of Indian Philosophy and Religion) (with T. Kimura).

Shōwa Hōbō Sōmokuroku (Complete Catalogue of the Tripiṭaka), 3 vols.

Indo Bukkyō Shiseki Shajitsu (Records of Indian Buddhism)

" The Date of Vasubandhu, the Great Buddhist Philosopher," *Indian Studies in Honor of Charles Rockwell Lanman*

Translations :

A Record of the Buddhist Religion as Practised in India and Malay Archipelago (A.D. 671-695), by I-tsing (*Gijō Nankai Kiki Den*)

Amitāyur Dhyāna-Sūtra (The Sūtra of the Meditation on Amitāyus) (The Sacred Books of the East, Vol. XLIX) (*Kanmuryōjukyō*)

" The Life of Vasubandhu," by Paramārtha (*T'oung Pao*, 1904)

" The Abhidharma Literature of the Sarvāstivādins " (*Journal of the Pāli Text Society*, 1905)

Upanishatto Zensho (Japanese translations of 108 Upaniṣads), 9 vols. (with others)

Baga Bonka (Japanese translation of the *Bhagavad-gītā*)

Indo Koseika (Japanese translation of the *Ṛg-veda*)

" Le Voyage de Kanshin en Orient (724-754)," par Aomi-no Mabito Genkai (779) (B.E.F.E.O., t. XXVIII et XXIX) (*Kakai Daishi Tōseiden*)

Nanden Daizōkyō (Japanese translation of the Pāli Tripiṭaka and commentaries), 60 vols.

THE ESSENTIALS OF
Buddhist
Philosophy

JUNJIRŌ TAKAKUSU

Edited by
WING-TSIT CHAN
and
CHARLES A. MOORE

MOTILAL BANARSIDASS
Delhi   Varanasi   Patna
Bangalore   Madras

First Edition Published by University of Hawaii, Honolulu, 1947
Second Edition: 1949
Third Edition: Bombay, 1956
Reissued: 1987

M O T I L A L   B A N A R S I D A S S
Bungalow Road, Jawahar Nagar, Delhi 110 007

Branches
Chowk, Varanasi 221 001
Ashok Rajpath, Patna 800 004
24 Race Course Road, Bangalore 560 001
120 Royapettah High Road, Mylapore, Madras 600 004

By arrangement with M/s Asia Publishing House, Bombay

ISBN: 81-208-0429-5

PRINTED IN INDIA
BY JAINENDRA PRAKASH JAIN AT SHRI JAINENDRA PRESS, A-45 NARAINA
INDUSTRIAL AREA, PHASE I, NEW DELHI 110 028 AND PUBLISHED BY
NARENDRA PRAKASH JAIN FOR MOTILAL BANARSIDASS, DELHI 110 007.

PREFACE TO FIRST INDIAN EDITION

It is with great pleasure that we have welcomed the opportunity to offer Dr. Takakusu's study of Buddhism to a new part of the world and to new readers by the publication of this first Indian edition of the book. Since this edition is to be printed by letterpress process, the editors have been enabled to undertake a rather comprehensive re-editing of the volume and to correct a few errors and a number of questionable words or passages and to make other improvements in the text. Chief among these has been the inclusion of all diacritical marks in the text as well as in the index. In the preceding editions diacritical marks for Sanskrit words were omitted from the text and included only in the index. That situation was necessitated by financial limitations; and the editors are happy to have the opportunity to prepare the volume for this edition with complete accuracy in this phase of the work.

The Chinese and Japanese characters which were included in the first two editions of this book so as to give the Chinese and Japanese equivalents of all names and practically all concepts included in the book have been omitted from this edition. It is felt that this is a justifiable modification of Dr. Takakusu's original text because this edition is intended primarily and almost exclusively for those who are acquainted with English and Sanskrit and who have no knowledge of Chinese and Japanese. For this reason the inclusion of Japanese and Chinese characters might well be an inadvisable source of confusion as well as a very great additional expense to the publisher. The previous editions were published primarily for use by those who are acquainted with Chinese and Japanese or both and it was therefore advisable to include the characters so as to clarify the meanings of numerous Sanskrit names and terms in Chinese and/or Japanese equivalents.

While the editors did not assume the liberty of changing many of Dr. Takakusu's words or phrases in the first two editions, it has been considered wise to make some changes in this edition where greater clarity was needed and could be provided by a revision of English terminology and sentence-structure. In no case, however, has Dr. Takakusu's treatment been changed in any substantial way; the book is still fundamentally as Dr. Takakusu wrote it.

One type of correction which was felt to be advisable has not been made, primarily because it would involve many changes in the text and might lead to more confusion than clarity. This has to do with Dr. Takakusu's use of Japanese names for Chinese Buddhist writers and also for schools of Buddhism which were originally developed in China and therefore should probably be cited by their Chinese names.

There are a few places in the text where the precise meaning which Dr. Takakusu intended to express is still somewhat uncertain, but in such cases, because of the doubtful meanings involved and because of the possibility that changes might distort Dr. Takakusu's meaning, no changes have been made.

Dr. Richard A. Gard of the Asia Foundation ; Professor Johannes Rahder of Yale University, and Professor C. W. Taam and Professor Yukuo Uyehara of the University of Hawaii rendered invaluable aid in re-checking this entire volume for its first Indian edition. Deep appreciation is hereby expressed for this invaluable assistance.

WING-TSIT CHAN
CHARLES A. MOORE

Honolulu
January 28, 1956

EDITORS' PREFACE

For several decades prior to Professor Takakusu's death in June, 1945, the English-speaking world knew him as an author, editor, and translator of monumental works on Buddhism. In this book, Dr. Takakusu's only major work in English, the summation of his lifetime study of Buddhist philosophy is presented. Dr. Takakusu prepared the material in Tokyo and in 1938-39 delivered it as a series of lectures at the University of Hawaii, where he was a visiting professor. In the summer of 1939, philosophers from several parts of the world gathered at the University of Hawaii, for an East-West Philosophers' Conference, and they used this text as one of the books in their discussions. The results of this conference are presented in *Philosophy—East and West*, published in 1944 by the Princeton University Press.

Before Professor Takakusu returned to Tokyo, he authorized us to publish this text and to make minor alterations without consulting him. We have made some revisions, but, in order to avoid the possibility of altering the meaning, we have revised the English only where we felt that a change was essential. The text gives basic Buddhist terms in English, Chinese, and Sanskrit, and the index gives the diacritical marks of the Pāli and Sanskrit. Dr. Takakusu employs irregular Sanskrit forms at times in order to avoid confusion on the part of the reader. As an aid to students, we have inserted references to important texts of all major Buddhist philosophical systems.

This work represents the conclusions of a Buddhist scholar whose renown is attested by the academic and honorary degrees and other honors conferred upon him. Among these were: M.A., D.Litt. (Oxon.), Dr. Phil. (Leipzig), D.Litt. (Tokyo), Ehren Dr. Phil. (Heidelberg), Member of the Imperial Academy (Japan), Fellow of the British Academy. At the time of his death he was Professor Emeritus of Sanskrit at Tokyo Imperial University.

Some readers may believe that Japanese Buddhism has been overstressed in this volume, but, as Professor Takakusu states, it is justified—or necessitated—by the fact that in Japan "the whole of Buddhism has been preserved," as well as the fact that, in Japan, Buddhism is the living and active faith of the mass of the people.

As Director of the University's Oriental Institute (now the School of Pacific and Asian Studies), Mr. Gregg M. Sinclair arranged for Dr. Takakusu's engagement as visiting professor at the University of Hawaii, and as President of the University since 1943 he has kept alive the plan for publishing this book at an appropriate time.

The project has received generous financial assistance from Professor Takakusu's friends in Hawaii, especially through the co-operation of Mr. Eimu Miake and the Reverend Kenju Ohtomo. Thanks are also due to Professor Yukuo Uyehara for his assistance in planning and effecting publication of the volume, to Professor Johannes Rahder for invaluable assistance on the proofs and index, and to the Reverend Iwasaburo Yoshikami for help on the index. Special appreciation is hereby expressed to Mr. Richard A. Gard for his very generous assistance in checking the entire manuscript with Professor Takakusu after the latter's return to Japan from Hawaii in 1939, and working out with the author many important changes in the text. Mr. Gard deserves thanks also for similar assistance in connection with Professor Takakusu's chapter in *Philosophy —East and West,* which includes, in essence, the same material as found in Chapter III of this volume.

WING-TSIT CHAN
CHARLES A. MOORE

EDITORS' PREFACE TO SECOND EDITION

The enthusiastic reception of Dr. Takakusu's presentation of the basic principles and schools of Buddhist Philosophy led to the early depletion of the first edition and has been interpreted to mean that the book fills a substantial need in the field of technical secondary literature on the subject. A second edition, therefore, seemed desirable to the editors and to those who first published the book, namely, the University of Hawaii and friends of Dr. Takakusu in Hawaii.

In presenting this second edition, the editors have maintained the policies stated in the preface to the first edition; that is, they have not considered it their privilege to change the text materially. A few changes have been made for the sake of greater clarity, however, and minor errors have been corrected.

The editors wish to express their great appreciation for generous assistance in making these revisions to Professor Johannes Rahder, Yale University; Professor Sitaram Tripathi, Banaras Hindu University; Professor Yukuo Uyehara, University of Hawaii; and Mr. Richard A. Gard, Ontario, California.

WING-TSIT CHAN
CHARLES A. MOORE

Honolulu
May 1, 1949

CONTENTS

I. INTRODUCTION

(1) How to Depict Buddhism

A discourse on Buddhist philosophy is usually begun with the philosophy of Indian Buddhism, and in this respect it is important to trace the development of Buddhist thought in India where it thrived for 1,500 years. It should be remembered, however, that before Buddhism declined in India in the eleventh century its various developments had already spread far into other countries. Hīnayāna Buddhism, or the Small Vehicle, which emphasizes individual salvation, continued in Ceylon, Burma, Siam ànd Cambodia. Mystic or esoteric Buddhism developed as Lamaism in Tibet. Mahāyāna Buddhism, or the Great Vehicle, which emphasizes universal salvation, grew in China where great strides in Buddhist studies were made and the different thoughts in Mahāyāna schools were systematized.

In Japan, however, the whole of Buddhism has been preserved—every doctrine of both the Hīnayāna and Mahāyāna schools. Although Hīnayāna Buddhism does not now exist in Japan as an active faith, its doctrines are still being studied there by Buddhist scholars. Mikkyō, which we may designate as the Esoteric Doctrine or Mysticism, is fully represented in Japan by Tendai mysticism and Tōji mysticism. The point which Japanese mysticism may be proud of is that it does not contain any vulgar elements, as does its counterpart in other countries, but stands on a firm philosophical basis.

The schools which were best developed in China are Hua-yen (Kegon, the 'Wreath' School) and T'ien-t'ai (Tendai, the 'Lotus' School). When the Ch'an (Zen) School is added to these two, the trio represents the highest peak of Buddhism's development. These three flourished in China for a while and then passed away, but in Japan all three are still alive in the people's faiths as well as in academic studies.

A rather novel form of Buddhism is the Amita-pietism. It is found to some extent in China, Tibet, Nepal, Mongolia, Manchuria and Annam; but it flourishes most in Japan where it is followed by more than half of the population.

I believe, therefore, that the only way to exhibit the entire Buddhist philosophy in all its different schools is to give a résumé of Buddhism in Japan. It is in Japan that the entire Buddhist literature, the Tripiṭaka, is preserved and studied.

The great Tripiṭaka Literature,[1] which is chiefly in Chinese translation, was brought to Japan from China in the T'ang (618-907) and Sung (960-1279) periods. It consisted then of 5,048 volumes, all of which have been preserved in Japan although many were lost in China. In Japan, the Tripiṭaka Literature has been published at least four times, *each edition adding new volumes*. Recently it became my responsibility to complete its latest publication, which contains the Chinese and Korean compilations as well as texts newly discovered in Central Asia and Japan—a work of thirteen years—comprising 13,520 *chüans* or parts in 100 bound volumes of about 1,000 pages each.[2]

There is little need of describing the numerous monasteries in Japan, which are seats of Buddhist learning. But I should mention the fact that there are six strong universities of Buddhist affiliations which make the philosophy of Buddhism their chief subject of study. There are also many colleges and schools of Buddhist support, and in five of the governmental universities Buddhist philosophy, Sanskrit and Pāli are studied.

In the present study of Buddhist philosophy the subject will not be presented in its historical sequence but in an ideological sequence. This ideological sequence does not mean a sequence in the development of ideas; it is rather the systemati-

---

[1] This constitutes the basic literature of Buddhism comprising the three divisions of Buddhist doctrine : the Buddha's discourses ; disciplinary rules; and philosophical treatises.

[2] *Taishō Shinshū Daizōkyō* (Taishō Edition of the Tripiṭaka in Chinese). Edited by J. Takakusu, K. Watanabe, and G. Ono. 100 volumes. Tokyo, 1929—. Hereafter cited as *Taishō*.

zation of the different schools of thought for the purpose of easier approach.

Because of my peculiar approach to the subject, I am going to present a classification of Buddhist thought different from that of Professor Stcherbatsky, who made a very masterful presentation of Buddhist ideas in his *Buddhist Logic*.[3] He divided the first 1,500 years of Buddhist history, dating back to 500 B.C., into three periods of five hundred years each, as follows :

First	Middle	Concluding
Pluralism	Monism	Idealism
Pudgala-śūnyatā	Sarva-dharma-śūnyatā	Bāhya-artha-śūnyatā
(Denial of individuality)	(Denial of all elements)	(Denial of the external world)

In his table, Professor Stcherbatsky indicated the extreme and moderate schools in each period.

Historically, Professor Stcherbatsky's table is more accurate, and I am conscious of the fact that the idealism of Asaṅga and Vasubandhu [4] arose in reaction against the extreme passivity of Nāgārjuna's Negativism.[5] However, it being impossible to place Harivarman's Negativism [6] after Nāgārjuna, I have taken the liberty of assuming the following table with the great thinker and writer Vasubandhu as the starting point of the development of all Buddhist thought :

---

[3] Th. Stcherbatsky : *Buddhist Logic*, two volumes (*Bibliotheca Buddhica* Vol. XXVI). Leningrad, 1932 ; Vol. I, p. 14.

[4] c. 410-500 A.D. ; c. 420-500 A.D.

[5] c. 100-200 A.D. See 4th column of the following table.

[6] c. 250-350 A.D. See 2nd column of the following table.

(1) REALISM*	(2) NIHILISM*	(3) IDEALISM*	(4) NEGATIVISM*
Hīnayānistic	Hīnayānistic (Nihilism)	Semi-Mahāyānistic	Mahāyānistic (Nihilism)
Sarvāsti School (holding that everything exists)	*Satyasiddhi School* (holding that truth is attainable by antithetic negation)	*Vijñaptimātra School* (holding that ideation alone exists)	*Mādhyamika School* (holding that truth is attainable by synthetic negation)
Pudgala-śūnyatā (denying individuality)	*Sarva-dharma-śūnyatā* (denying the reality of all—matter and mind)	*Bāhya-artha-śūnyatā* (denying the reality of all external things)	*Sarva-dharma-śūnyatā* (denying the reality of all—matter and mind and all attachments of living beings; thereby striving to reach the "highest" truth [Middle Path] which can be conceived only by synthetic negation or the negation of negation)
Doctrine of *Ens* (being)	Doctrine of *Non-ens* (non-being)	Doctrine of *both* Ens *and* Non-ens	Doctrine of *neither* Ens *nor* Non-ens
Middle Path as the ideal way in practical life; neither optimistic nor pessimistic.	Middle Path or Truth attainable by the recognition of nonentity, admitting neither individuality (*Pudgala*) nor reality of matter and mind (*Dharma*). All end in *Nirvāṇa* (Void). Nihilism as opposed to Realism.	Middle Path or Truth lies neither in recognizing the reality of all things because outer things do not exist, nor in recognizing the non-reality of all things because ideations do exist.	Middle Path or Truth attained by either reciprocal negation or repetitional negation; reciprocal negation being the eightfold denial of phenomena of being, and repetitional negation being the fourfold serial denial of the popular and the higher ideas.
Vasubandhu (c. 420-500 A.D.)	Harivarman (c. 250-350 A.D.) Chinese translation 407 A.D.	Vasubandhu (c. 420-500 A.D.)	Nāgārjuna (c. 100-200 A.D.)

*Each of these schools will be explained in detail later. See Chapters IV (Realism), V (Nihilism), VI (Idealism) and VII (Negativism).

According to my scheme, Nāgārjuna, the earliest Buddhist philosopher, is placed after Harivarman and Vasubandhu, as may be seen in the table. However, when the development of idea is to be fitted into a simple pattern, such a discrepancy is inevitable. In China when a philosopher-priest engages in philosophical studies, he does not usually take up the history of ideas, but he at once goes into the speculation of whichever thought attracts his interest. Therefore, in this respect, there is little advantage in studying Buddhist ideas according to the historical sequence.

(2) BUDDHISM IN THE HISTORY OF CHINA

The history of Buddhist activities in China covers about 1,200 years (A.D. 67-1271) and is practically identical with the history of the Chinese translation of the Buddhist scriptures. During those years 173 Indian and Chinese priests devoted themselves to the laborious work of translation, and the result was the great literature of the Chinese Tripiṭaka.

Careful studies of these translations were continued, and many schools of thought, or religious sects, were established. The most notable of them (fourteen in number) may be picked out for our purpose. Almost all of them were introduced to Japan. But we shall not trouble ourselves with minute accounts of them here, for we shall have to return to them when we study the philosophical tenets of each.

We must remember, however, that the Sui (A.D. 581-618) and the T'ang (A.D. 618-907) dynasties are the age when the sectarian schools were completed and that these schools were founded or originated some time earlier by those able men who translated or introduced the texts. We shall now examine the list of these schools founded and completed on Chinese soil. This list indicates the vast development and systematization of Buddhism in China.

LISTS OF CHINESE SECTS*

A. Foundation (Before Sui and T'ang Dynasties, A.D. 67-581)	B. Final Completion (In the Sui and T'ang Dynasties, A.D. 581-907)
Western Tsin Dynasty (A.D. 265-317)	
1. **P'i-t'an Tsung** (Abhidharma) Hinayāna Formalistic (Transl. Sanghadeva A.D. 383-390)	
Eastern Tsin Dynasty (A.D. 317-420)	
2. **Ch'êng-shih Tsung** (Satyasiddhi) Hinayāna Sautrānta Nihilistic (Transl. Kumārajīva A.D. 417-418)	
3. **San-lun Tsung** (Mādhyamika) Mahāyāna Negativistic (Found. Sêng-chao, pupil of Kumārajīva ; transl. c. A.D. 384-414)	(3) **San-lun Tsung** Mādhyamika Negativism systematized by Chi-tsang, A.D. 549-623.
4. **Lü Tsung** (Vinaya) Hinayāna Disciplinary (Found. Hui-kuang, pupil o. Kumārajīva; transl. c. A.D. 402-412)	(4) **Lü Tsung** Dharmagupta Discipline completed by Tao-hsüan, A.D. 596-667.

* Those sects in Bold Face were introduced into Japan.

LISTS OF CHINESE SECTS* (Continued)

Northern Liang Dynasty (A.D. 397-439)

5. Nieh-p'an Tsung
   (Nirvāṇa)
   Mahāyāna
   Noumenological
   (Transl. Dharmarakṣa A.D. 423)

11. T'ien-t'ai Tsung
    (Puṇḍarīka—The 'Lotus' Doctrine)
    Mahāyāna
    Phenomenological
    Phenomenology completed by Chih-i, A.D. 531-597.

Northern Wei Dynasty (A.D. 386-535)

6. Ti-lun Tsung
   (Daśabhūmi)
   Mahāyāna
   Idealistic
   (Transl. Bodhiruci, c. A.D. 508)

12. Hua-yen Tsung
    (Avataṅsaka, the 'Wreath' Doctrine)
    Mahāyāna
    Totalistic
    Totalism completed by Fa-tsang, A.D. 643-712.

Eastern Wei Dynasty (A.D. 534-550)

Western Wei Dynasty (A.D. 535-557)

7. Ching-t'u Tsung..............
   (Sukhāvatī)
   Mahāyāna
   Pietistic
   (Transl. Bodhiruci, A.D. 529. Found. T'an-luan (A.D. 476-524)

(7) Ching-t'u Tsung
    (Sukhāvatī)
    Mahāyāna
    Pietistic
    Amitābha Pietism completed by Shan-tao, d. A.D. 681.

Southern Liang Dynasty (A.D. 502-557)

8. Ch'an Tsung..............
   (Dhyāna)
   Mahāyāna
   Contemplative

(8) Ch'an Tsung
    (Dhyāna)
    Mahāyāna
    Contemplative

* Those sects in Bold Face were introduced into Japan.

LISTS OF CHINESE SECTS* (Continued)

Ch'ên Dynasty
(A.D. 557-589)

(Found. Bodhidharma, c. A.D. 470-534)

The system of meditation flourished under Hui-nêng (A.D. 638-713), northern school, and Shên-hsiu (A.D. 605-706), southern school.

9. Shé-lun Tsung ....
(Mahāyāna-saṃparigraha)
Mahāyāna
Idealistic
(Transl. Paramārtha, c. A.D. 563)

13. Fa-hsiang Tsung
(Vijñaptimātratā)
Quasi-Mahāyāna
Idealistic
Idealism translated and completed by Hiüen-tsang (Hsüan-tsang, A.D. 596-664) and Kuei, his pupil (K'uei-chi, A.D. 632-682).

10. Chü-shê Tsung
(Abhidharmakośa)
Hīnayāna
Realistic
Similar in tenet to 1 above
(Transl. Paramārtha, A.D. 563-567)

Chü-shê Tsung
(Abhidharmakośa)
Hīnayāna
Realistic
Kosa Realism transmitted by Hiüen-tsang and completed by Kuei, his pupil.

14. Chên-yen Tsung
(Mantrayāna)
Mahāyāna
Mystic
Mysticism transmitted by Subhakarasiṃha. A.D. 637-735, Vajrabodhi, A.D. 663-723, and Amogha-vajra, A.D. 705-774.

* Those sects in Bold Face were introduced into Japan.

Of the above sects, ten (2, 3, 4, 7, 8, 10, 11, 12, 13, 14) were transmitted to Japan, and of them three, i.e., the realistic Chü-shê (10), the nihilistic Ch'êng-shih (2), and the negativistic San-lun (3) schools did not remain in Japan as active sects but are preserved for the purpose of training and preparing the Buddhist mind for higher speculation and criticism.

(3) JAPAN AS THE LAND OF MAHĀYĀNA

Buddhism was officially introduced into Japan in A.D. 552 from Paikche, a kingdom in Korea, but thirty years earlier Buddhist images had been brought to Japan. In 594 the Prince Regent, Shōtoku Taishi (574-622) declared Buddhism the state religion.

Buddhism at this time was quite devoid of the distinction of sects or schools, although the difference of Mahāyāna and Hīnayāna was clearly recognized. The Prince himself strictly adhered to Mahāyāna and wrote commentaries upon three Mahāyāna texts. The fame of these excellent annotations spread abroad, and one of them was chosen as a subject of commentaries by a Chinese savant.

The particular type of Mahāyāna that was adopted by the Prince may be seen from a consideration of the texts which were chosen. The first is the *Lotus of the Good Law*, a text devoted to the Ekayāna (One Vehicle) doctrine, indicating the idea of the good law. The second is the *Discourse on the Ultimate Truth* by Vimalakīrti, a lay *Bodhisattva* of Vaisali, while the third is the *Book of the Earnest Resolve* by Śrīmālā, a woman *Bodhisattva*, the Queen of Ayodhyā.[7] The central idea of this non-sectarian period was the doctrine of the Great Vehicle (Mahāyāna) as expressed in these three texts. This idea has remained the dominating feature of Buddhism throughout its history in Japan.

---

[7] *Saddharma-puṇḍarīka, Taishō* No. 262; *Vimalakīrti-nirdeśa, Taishō* No. 475; *Śrīmālā-devi-simhanāda, Taishō* No. 353.

(4) Japanese Buddhism Philosophically Classified

To depict the whole of Buddhism it will be better, as I have already emphasized, to treat it according to its philosophical development. For the sake of clarity, I shall group the schools under two heads: the Schools of Negative Rationalism, i.e., the Religion of Dialectic Investigation ; and the Schools of Introspective Intuitionism, i.e., the Religion of Meditative Experience.

It is well known that Buddhism lays stress on the Threefold Learning (*siksa*) of Higher Morality, Higher Thought, and Higher Insight. That is to say, without higher morals one cannot get higher thought and without higher thought one cannot attain higher insight. Higher Thought here comprises the results of both analytical investigation and meditative intuition. Buddhism further instructs the aspirants, when they are qualified, in the Threefold Way (*mārga*) of Life-View, Life-Culture and Realization of Life-Ideal. In other words, without a right view of life there will be no culture, and without proper culture there will be no realization of life. Life-Culture here again means the results of right meditation.

The twofold inheritance of the Buddha was Right Reasoning (*nyāya*) and Right Meditating (*dhyāna*). One set of the Buddhist Schools which chiefly dwells on the former method I classify here as Negative Rationalism. It may seem a misnomer to group Realism under Negative Rationalism. However, when we see that it holds the doctrines of selflessness, impermanence, blisslessness, and momentariness of life we cannot assume much of its positive features. As to the rest of the schools, no explanation will be necessary.

The other set of schools I classify as Introspective Intuitionism, because all these are taught according to the result of meditative or introspective activity of the mind and not by dialectical reasoning or simple perception of the senses. The Intuitive Schools are of two kinds : the Undifferentiative and the Differentiative. According to my idea, Buddhism may be classified as follows :

I
SCHOOLS OF NEGATIVE RATIONALISM

1. Realism (Sarvāstivāda, Abhidhārmika), Abhidharmakośa, Chü-shê, or Kusha School [*Ens* School]
2. Nihilism (Sarvaśūnyavāda, Sautrāntika), Satyasiddhi, Ch'êng-shih, or Jōjitsu School [Non-*ens* School]
3. Idealism (Vijñaptimātravāda), Yogācāra, Fa-hsiang, or Hossō School [Both *Ens* and Non-*ens* School]
4. Negativism (Sarvaśūnyavāda), Mādhyamika, San-lun, or San-ron School [Neither *Ens* nor Non-*ens* School]

II
SCHOOLS OF INTROSPECTIVE INTUITIONISM

(A)
Undifferentiated Intuitionism

5. Totalism (Avataṅsaka), Hua-yen, Kegon, or 'Wreath' School
6. Phenomenology (Saddharmapuṇḍarīka, Ekayāna), T'ien-t'ai, Tendai, or 'Lotus' School
7. Mysticism (Mantra), Chên-yen, Shingon, or 'True Word' School
8. Pure Intuitionism (Dhyāna), Ch'an, Zen, or Meditation School
    Four divisions :
    a. Rinzai Sect founded by Eisai [8]
    b. Sōtō Sect founded by Dōgen
    c. Fuke Sect founded by Kakushin in 1255 ; abolished after 1868
    d. Ōbaku Sect founded by Ingen [9]

(B)
Differentiated Intuitionism

9. Amita-pietism (Sukhāvatī), Ching-t'u, Jōdo, or 'Pure

---

[8] 1141-1215.   [9] 1592-1673.

Land' School [Objectively differentiated Intuitionism]
Four divisions :
   a. Jōdo Sect founded by Hōnen [10]
   b. Shin Sect founded by Shinran [11]
   c. Yūzūnembutsu Sect founded by Ryōnin [12]
   d. Ji Sect founded by Ippen [13]
10. Lotus-pietism, Nichiren, or 'New Lotus' School founded by Nichiren [14] [Subjectively Differentiated Intuitionism]
11. Disciplinary Formalism (Vinaya), the New or Reformed Ritsu (Lü) founded by Eison [15] [Subjectively Experienced Intuitionism]

---

[10] 1133-1212.   [11] 1173-1262.   [12] 1071-1132.
[13] 1239-1289.   [14] 1222-1282.   [15] 1201-1290.

II. INDIAN BACKGROUND

(1) BUDDHIST INDIA

The Buddha may or may not have been 'the greatest Aryan of all the Aryans,' or 'the greatest of all philosophers,' as some would call him. It is difficult to determine how such a man as the Buddha, who is so different from the other philosophers and religious men of India, could have appeared there, for he denied entirely the traditional gods, religious beliefs, institutions and customs.

When the Aryans conquered India, they pushed southward in their march of victory until they entered the tropical zone. Then, because of the severe heat, they chose to select their abode among the cool forests of the Black Mountains, which form the smaller range along the foot of the great Himālaya. Gradually they came to regard the forest as their ideal abode, and in time they acquired the habit of meditating with the great Himālaya as the object of their thoughts, for there was Himālaya, eternally magnificent, eternally unapproachable. During mornings and evenings the snows would glow in changing splendor as the rays of the sun struck them ; in winter the glaciers in the valleys were frozen solid; but in summer the glaciers flowed along the winding valleys like giant dragons come to life after a year's sleep. Finally, the Aryans, who had conquered India by force, in turn came to be completely conquered by the mysterious influence of Nature.

In very few words, Brahmanism, the old Indian religion, was a pantheism with *Brahman* (the eternal, absolute, unchanging principle) as the first cause of the universe. The manifestation of this Brahman is sometimes personified and is called Brahmā (God, or the Great Self). Every human being has *ātman* (little self). Brahman and *ātman* are one, and of the same substance. Brahmanism, therefore, is an effort to seek the ultimate principle, Brahman, by studying one's Self, *ātman*.

The Buddha denied the existence of Brahman and *ātman,* and advanced a new theory of *anātman* (no-self), for, he declared, all things are changing and it is unreasonable to look for an absolute unchanging principle or an eternal self.

It is appropriate to speak of the Indian civilization as the civilization of the Forest. Religion, philosophy and literature were all products of the forest. Education was carried on in the sacred depth of the forest. Music, medicine and other branches of civilization were, without exception, cultivated in the forest.

Such theories as those which contend that city life produces civilization or that the origin of civilization is the triumph of man over Nature cannot be acceptable in India. The Indian people believe that the struggle for life is a hindrance to higher civilization. To them civilization means the assimilation of man into Nature ; hence city life is simply the breeding-place of crime.

Brahmanism, the Indian philosophy, and Buddhism may both be called the product of self-culture [1] under Nature. The result of the custom of meditating morning and evening reverently before Nature was *yoga* (concentration of mind) in Brahmanism, and *dhyāna* or *zen* (meditation) in Buddhism. There might be a sect in Brahmanism which does not require *yoga,* but in Buddhism no sect can be without *dhyāna.* At present certain sects in Buddhism do not practice *dhyāna* daily. However, it is a well-known fact that even those sects have their origin in *dhyāna.* This is true with both Hīnayāna and Mahāyāna. For instance, the Three Learnings of Buddhism (*trisik-ṣa*) are discipline, contemplation and wisdom; and one of the Six Perfections (*pāramitā*) is *samādhi* or concentration. Without *samādhi* the attainment of Buddhist knowledge is impossible. In Buddhism to act righteously is to think deeply.

---

[1] The doctrine of *anātman* denies the self as permanent substance or entity. However, Buddhism retains the self as a combination of matter and mind in continuous change. This 'self' is perfected by cultivation. This is what is meant by 'self-culture' or 'self-creation.' See also Section 3 of this chapter.

(2) THE BUDDHA AS A DEEP THINKER

The Buddha (c. 566-486 B.C.) was not satisfied with the ideas of his contemporary thinkers. Those who regard this earthly life as pleasant (optimists) are ignorant of the disappointment and despair which are to come. Those who regard this life as a life of suffering (pessimists) may be tolerated as long as they are simply feeling dissatisfied with this life, but when they begin to give up this life as hopeless and try to escape to a better life by practicing austerities (self-mortification)', then they are to be abhorred. The Buddha taught that the extremes of both hedonism and asceticism are to be avoided and that the middle course should be followed as the ideal. This does not mean that one should simply avoid both extremes and take the middle course as the only remaining course of escape. Rather, one should transcend, not merely escape from, such extremes.

The Buddha's doctrine, in fine, rests on the idea of "knowing and regarding reality as it is." That means one should know the true facts about this earthly life and look at it without making excuses, and regulate one's daily conduct of life according to this knowledge and standpoint.

This idea that there is nothing but hardship in this world —even pleasures end in hardship—is one of the significant points of Buddhism. Someone might say that this idea of recognizing this life as hardship cannot be anything but pessimism. But that is not right. The idea is this : in this present life there are both pleasures and hardships. It is shallow to try to regard it as entirely of pleasure ; what one regards as pleasure will cause suffering when it ceases to exist. In other words we may call it a kind of hardship which appears in the guise of pleasure. Therefore this life must be regarded as consisting entirely of hardship. Yet one must not lament over it. If one is ignorant of the fact that pleasures can cause hardships, one will be disappointed when that fact presents itself. The Buddha teaches that one should regard hardship as hardship, accepting it as a fact and opposing it. Hence his emphasis on perserverance, fortitude, and forbearance, the latter being one of the Six Perfections.

In short, there are both pleasures and hardships in life, but one must not be discouraged when hardship comes, or lose oneself in rapture of joy when pleasure comes. Both pleasure and hardship must be taken alike with caution, and one must attack them with all one's might. For this reason bravery and diligence (*virya*) were included among the Six Perfections.

The middle course does not mean escaping from life but it means invading life, and yet not to become a prisoner of life.

When the Buddha's idea on reality develops further and further along its path, it becomes the Buddhist philosophy. To realize it in the actual life of living men is the religious side of Buddhism

Apart from Buddhism, however, there are efforts on the part of many thinkers to build up their respective thoughts on optimism and pessimism. Ever since before the time of the Buddha there had existed both schools of thought. The optimistic thought has developed into naturalism, hedonism, materialism, mechanism, etc. During the lifetime of the Buddha there existed even stronger materialism than that we see today. Pessimism developed along the line which may be described as more religious. They reasoned that, since our organism (body and mind) is imperfect, we should overcome it by austerities (self-mortification) ; then in the next life we shall attain a perfect heavenly existence. Thus they invented various methods of self-mortification and practiced them. The Buddha abhorred this practice.

Because the Buddha's idea on both optimism and pessimism was very clear, there has never been anyone in Buddhism who strayed into materialism nor has there been anyone who went into the practice of self-mortification. In short, the extremes of both optimism and pessimism were prevented by the moderate doctrine of Buddhism. In a way Buddhism was a scheme against the ravages of both materialism and asceticism.

(3) WHAT IS SELF ?

The Buddha regarded this world as a world of hardship,

and taught the ways to cope with it. Then, what are the reasons which make it a world of hardship ? The first reason, as given by the Buddha is that *all things are selfless or egoless*, which means that no things—men, animals and inanimate objects, both living and not living—have what we may call their original self or real being. Let us consider man. A man does not have a core or a soul which he can consider to be his true self. A man exists; but he cannot grasp his real being—he cannot discover his own core, because the existence of a man is nothing but an "existence depending on a series of causations." Everything that exists is there because of causations ; it will disappear when the effects of the causations cease.

The waves on the water's surface certainly exist, but can it be said that a wave has its own self ? Waves exist only while there is wind or current. Each wave has its own characteristics according to the combination of causations—the intensity of the winds and currents and their directions, etc. But when the effects of the causations cease, the waves are no more. Similarly, there cannot be a self which stands independent of causations.

As long as a man is an existent depending on a series of causations, it is unreasonable for him to try to hold on to himself and to regard all things around him from the self-centered point of view. All men ought to deny their own selves and endeavor to help each other and to look for co-existence, because no man can ever be truly independent.

If all things owe their existence to a series of causations, their existence is a conditional one—there is no one thing in the universe that is permanent or independent. Therefore, the Buddha's theory that selflessness is the nature of all things inevitably leads to the next theory that *all things are impermanent (anitya)*.

Men in general seem to be giving all of their energy to preserving their own existence and their possessions. But in truth it is impossible to discover the core of their own existence, nor is it possible to preserve it forever. Even for one moment nothing can stay unchanged. Not only is it insecure in relation to space but it is also insecure in relation to time. If it were possible to discover a world which is space-less and time-less, that would be a world of true freedom, i.e., Nirvāṇa.

If, as the modern physicists assert, space is curved and time is relative, this world of space and time is our enclosed abode from which there is no escape—we are tied down in the cycles of cause and effect.

As long as men cannot discover a world which is not limited by time and space, men must be creatures of suffering.

To assert that such a state, unlimited in time and space, is attainable by man is the message of Buddhism.

Of course there is no such thing as a limitless space or limitless time. Even modern physical science does not recognize infinity in time and space. However, the Buddha brought forward his ideal, Nirvāṇa (extinction), following his theories of selflessness and impermanence. *Nirvāṇa means extinction of life and death, extinction of worldly desire, and extinction of space and time conditions.* This, in the last analysis, means unfolding a world of perfect freedom.

Selflessness (no substance) and *impermanence* (no duration) are the real state of our existence ; *Nirvāṇa* (negatively extinction ; positively perfection) is our ideal, that is, perfect freedom, quiescence.

(4) THE IDEAL OF BUDDHISM

The special community established by the Buddha was called the *Ārya-saṅgha* (The Assembly of the Nobles), intended to be the cradle of noble persons. Since the Brahmanical tradition had been firmly established, the race distinction was strictly felt. On that account the Buddha often asserted that in his own community there would be no distinction between Brahmans (priests) and warriors or between masters and slaves. Anyone who joined the Brotherhood would have an equal opportunity for learning and training.

Against the asserted superiority of the Aryan race and the appellation of *anārya* (non-Aryan) given to the aborigines or some earlier immigrants, the Buddha often argued that the word *Arya* meant 'noble' and we ought not call a race noble or ignoble for there will be some ignoble persons among the so-called *ārya* and at the same time there will be some noble persons among the so-called *anārya*. When we say noble or ignoble we should be speaking of an individual and not of a race as a whole. It is a question of knowledge or wisdom but not of birth or caste. Thus the object of the Buddha was to create a noble personage (*ārya-pudgala*)—in the sense of a noble life.

The noble community (*ārya-saṅgha*) was founded for that very purpose. The noble ideal (*ārya-dharma*) and the noble discipline (*ārya-vinaya*) were set forth for the aspiring candidates. The path to be pursued by the noble aspirant is the Noble Eightfold Path (*ārya-aṣṭangika-mārga*) and the truth to be believed by the noble is the Noble Fourfold Truth [2] (*catvāri-ārya-satyāni*). The perfections attained by the noble were the four noble fruitions (*ārya-phala*) and the wealth to be possessed by the noble was the noble sevenfold wealth (*sapta-ārya-dhana*), all being spiritual qualifications. The careful application of the word *ārya* to each of the important points of his institution must not be overlooked by a student of Buddhism. The Buddha thus seemed to have endeavored to revive the original meaning of *ārya* in personality and the daily life of his religious community.

Whether the Buddha was an Aryan or not we cannot say. Some consider him to be an Indo-Scythian while others consider him to be an Indo-Sumerian. The question of race has nothing to do with him, who in his idea transcends all racial distinctions.

The ideal set forth by him must be taken to be purely personal. As a man, he teaches men to be perfect men, i.e., men of perfect enlightenment.

(5) What is Truth? What is the Way?

The Buddha organized these ideas into the Fourfold Truth as follows :

  1. That life consists entirely of suffering ;

[2] See next section.

2. That suffering has causes ;
(The above two are the description of reality.)
3. That the causes of suffering can be extinguished ;
4. That there exists a way to extinguish the causes.
(The last two express the ideal.)

These constitute the Fourfold Truth to be believed by the *āriya* or those who pursue the way toward Nirvāṇa. (Hereafter the word *āriya* or *ārya* will be used in preference to its English equivalent 'the noble.' *Āriya* as used in Buddhism includes both those who aspire to become noble and those who are already noble.)

In explanation of the fourth Noble Truth the Buddha taught the Eightfold Way to be pursued by the *āriya* as follows:

1. Right View, by which to see the real state of all things.
2. Right Thought
3. Right Speech
4. Right Action

(Right Thought, Right Speech, Right Action are the elements of human character.)

5. Right Mindfulness
6. Right Endeavor
7. Right Livelihood

(These three are the elements of human life or the dynamic aspects of human character.)

8. Right Concentration, which is the motive power to carry one through all the worlds—this human world of desire, the heaven of (bodily) beings, the higher heaven of formless (bodiless) beings and holy beings (*arhats*)—finally to reach the state of *Parinirvāṇa* (Highest Nirvāṇa), the Buddhahood.

The Eightfold Way may be regarded as the practical ethics of Buddhism for the purpose of building up the human character and improving it, but at the same time it is the way of the holy religion for attaining the highest enlightenment —Buddhahood.

The Worlds of Beings attainable by Progressive Meditation

	Dharma-dhātu-samāpatti (Abstract-meditation on the universal principle, i.e., world) **Buddha**			V.
	Nirodha-samāpatti (Extinction) **Arhats**			IV
	Neither conscious nor unconscious state of the heaven			
Ārūpya-Samāpatti	The heaven of nothingness	Heaven without Form		III.
	The endlessness of mind			
	The endlessness of space			
Rūpa-Samāpatti	Fourth Dhyāna heaven	Heaven with Form		II.
	Third Dhyāna heaven			
	Second Dhyāna heaven			
	First Dhyāna heaven			
	The world of living beings.			I.

The Eightfold Way should not be regarded as a combination of eight different ways. It is a unitary way—the Path of Insight (*Darśana-mārga*)—to lead the *āriya* toward perfection.

The next stage [3] of the path is the Path of Practice and is described as the Seven Branches of Enlightenment (*Bodhi*) as follows:

1. Thorough investigation of the Principle
2. Brave effort
3. Joyous thought
4. Peaceful thought
5. Mindfulness
6. Concentration
7. Equanimity

[3] The Buddha taught a Threefold Path: the Path of Insight (Meditation), the Path of Practice or Culture, the Path of No-More-Learning.

Thus the *āriya* proceeds to the last stage : i.e., the Path of No-More-Learning. Then the firm conviction that he has realized the Fourfold Truth will present itself.

The above three stages are to be passed through in the study of the Fourfold Truth. The Truth is studied and conceived in the first stage by the application of the Eightfold Way (Life-View) ; in the second stage it is investigated more fully and actualized by the practice of the Seven Branches of Enlightenment (Life-Culture) ; and in the last stage the Truth is fully realized in the Path of No-More-Learning (Realization of Life-Ideal).

When the *āriya* reaches this last stage, he becomes an *arhat*. According to the Hīnayānistic view this is the perfect state of enlightenment, but according to the Mahāyānistic view an *arhat* is thought to be only partially enlightened. The purpose of Buddhism is to perfect a man's character, or to let him attain Buddhahood on the basis of perfect wisdom and right cultivation, i.e., the highest personality. Such are the characteristics of Buddhism.

III. FUNDAMENTAL PRINCIPLES OF BUDDHIST PHILOSOPHY

The usual procedure would be to explain the genera principles which are common to all the schools of Buddhism In this section I will not refer to those doctrines which are made the basic principles of the existing sects in Japan, because we shall study them in detail when we come to Buddhism in Japan. At present I will bring out six general principles, common especially to all schools of Mahāyāna :

a. The Principle of Causation
b. The Principle of Indeterminism of the Differentiated
c. The Principle of Reciprocal Identification
d. The Principle of True Reality
e. The Principle of Totality
f. The Principle of Perfect Freedom

(1) THE PRINCIPLE OF CAUSATION

Buddhism does not give importance to the idea of the Root-Principle or the First Cause as other systems of philosophy often do ; nor does it discuss the idea of cosmology. Naturally such a branch of philosophy as theology did not develop in Buddhism. One should not expect any discussion of theology from a Buddhist philosopher. As for the problem of creation, Buddhism is ready to accept any theory that science may advance, for Buddhism does not recognize any conflict between religion [1] and science.

According to Buddhism, human beings and all living things are self-created or self-creating. The universe is not homocentric ; it is a co-creation of all beings. Buddhism does not believe that all things came from one cause, but holds that everything is inevitably created out of more than two causes. The creations or becomings of the antecedent causes con-

---

[1] In Buddhism religion is understood as the practical application of the philosophical doctrine, making no reference to such ideas as God, creation and final judgment.

tinue in time-series—past, present and future—like a chain. This chain is divided into twelve divisions and is called the Twelve Divisioned Cycle of Causations and Becomings. Since these divisions are interdependent, the process is called Dependent Production or Chain of Causation. The formula of this theory is as follows : From the existence of *this, that* becomes ; from the happening of *this, that* happens. From the non-existence of *this, that* does not become ; from the non-happening of *this, that* does not happen.

There are several theories of causation which combine to give a complete explanation of things and events :

(a) CAUSATION BY ACTION-INFLUENCE [2]

There is law and order in the progress of cause and effect. This is the theory of Causal Sequence.

In the Twelve Divisioned Cycle of Causations and Becomings, it is impossible to point out which one is the first cause, because the twelve make a continuous circle which is called the Wheel of Life. It is customary to represent the Wheel of Life in the following manner : [See diagram opposite.]

The explanation of the principle of the Twelve Divisioned Cycle of Causations and Becomings is as follows :

People are accustomed to regard time as progressing in a straight line from the infinite past through present to infinite future. Buddhism, however, regards time as a circle with no beginning or end. Time is relative.

The death of a living being is not the end ; at once another life begins to go through a similar process of birth and death, and thus repeats the round of life over and over again. In this way a living being, when considered in relation to time, forms an endless continuum. It is impossible to define what a living being is, for it is always changing and progressing through the

---

[2] The Sanskrit original of 'action' is '*karma*,' but the term *karma* is avoided in this study because it is often confused with the idea of soul and thus leads to misunderstanding of the Buddhist doctrine. *Karma* simply means action and action means its influence. That influence determines the subsequent existence.

Divisions or Stages of Life. The whole series of stages must be taken in their entirety as representing the one individual being. Thus, a living being, when regarded in relation to space, forms a complex of five elements. The Wheel of Life is a clever representation of the Buddhist conception of a living being in relation to both space and time.

The Wheel of Life is a circle with no beginning, but it is customary to begin its exposition at Blindness (unconscious state). Blindness is only a continuation of Death. At death the body is abandoned, but Blindness remains as the crystallization of the effects of the actions performed during life. This Blindness is often termed Ignorance; but this Ignorance should not be thought of as the antonym of knowing; it must include in its meaning both knowing and not knowing—Blindness or blind mind, unconsciousness.

Blindness leads to blind activity. The 'energy' or the effect of this blind activity is the next stage, Motive, or Will to Live. This Will to Live is not the kind of will which is used in the term 'free will'; it is rather a blind motive toward life or the blind desire to live.

Blindness and Will to Live are called the Two Causes of the past. They are causes when regarded subjectively from the present ; but objectively regarded, the life in the past is a whole life just as much as is the life of the present.

In the life of the present the first stage is Subconscious Mind. This is the first stage of an individual existence which corresponds, in actual life, to the first moment of the conception of a child. There is no consciousness yet ; there is only the Subconscious Mind or the Blind Will toward life. When this Subconscious Mind advances one step and takes a form, it is the second stage of the present, Name-Form. The Name is the mind, because mind is something we know by name but cannot grasp. Name-Form is the stage of prenatal growth when the mind and body first come into combination.

In the third stage a more complex form is assumed and the six sense organs are recognized. They are the eyes, ears, nose, tongue, body (organ of touch) and mind.

The fourth stage corresponds to the first one or two years after the birth of the child. The six sense organs reach the state of activity, but the sense of touch predominates. The living being begins to come into contact with the outside world.

Now that the living being is able to manifest its consciousness, it begins to take in consciously the phenomena of the outside world. This is the fifth stage called Perception, representing the growth-scale of a child three to five years old. Here the individuality of the living being is definitely recognized ; in other words, the status of the present life has been formed.

The above five stages are called the Five Effects of the Past appearing in the Present. In those stages the individual is formed, but the individual is not entirely responsible for its own formation because the causes of the past have effectuated the development of these stages. From here on, the individual begins to create causes on his own responsibility, or, in other words, enters the proper sphere of self-creation.

The first of the Three Causes in the Present is Desire. Through Perception the individual experiences sorrow, pleasure, suffering, enjoyment, or neutral feeling. When the experience is sorrow, suffering, or neutral feeling, nothing much will happen.

But when it is pleasure or enjoyment, the individual will endeavor to make it his own. This effort is Desire ; it produces attachment. The first step of this attachment is the next stage, Cleaving, the effort to retain the object of Desire. The last state of this attachment is Formation of Being. The term Existence is often used for this stage, but as it is a link between the present and future, and the preliminary step for Birth, I believe that 'Formation of Being' is a more fitting term.

Desire, Cleaving and Formation of Being represent the three stages of the activities of an adult, and together constitute the Three Causes in the Present. While an individual is enjoying the effects of the past, he is forming the causes for the future. While the plum fruit is ripening on the tree, the core in the fruit is being formed. By the time the fruit is ripe and falls to the ground, the core too is ready to bring forth a new tree of its own to bear more fruits in the future.

As to the Future there are two stages—Birth and Old-age-Death, or, in short, Birth and Death. When viewed from the Three Causes in the Present, Birth and Death may be termed the effects. But when viewed in the light of the continuous Wheel of Life, we may regard the future as the time when the Causes in the Present open out and close. Also, the Effects of the Future contain in themselves causes for the life still further in the future.

The present is one whole life, and so is the future. Past, Present and Future are each a whole life. In this Wheel of Life, the present is explained particularly minutely with eight stages, but in truth Blindness and Will to Live of the past and Birth and Death of the future have the same constituent stages as those of the present.

Because we human beings are accustomed to make the present the starting point of consideration, naturally the future is regarded as effects of the present. Therefore the life in the future is given descriptively as Birth and Death. And because the past is regarded as the cause of the present, it is given as causal principles, Blindness and Will to Live.

It is quite possible to reconstruct the Wheel of Life in the following manner in which Birth and Death are to be regarded as merely an abbreviated description of a whole life and Blindness and Will to Live are to be regarded as an ideological description of a round of life. Past, Present and Future are relative terms.

It is clear that the Causation Theory of Buddhism is not like the theory of causality of classical physical science which is a fixed theory. In Buddhism every stage is a cause when viewed from its effect ; when viewed from the antecedent cause, it is an effect. It may be also said that there is a cause in the effect, and an effect in the cause. There is nothing fixed in this theory.

The Blindness which remains after the death of a living

thing is the crystallization of the actions (*karma*) which the living being performed during its life, or, in other words, the 'energy' or influence of the actions that remain. One's action (*karma*) is the dynamic manifestation of mental and physical energy. This latent energy may be called action-influence or potential energy. Action-influence remains after the action ceases, and this is what makes the Wheel of Life move. As long as there is energy, it has to work, and the Cycles of Causations and Becomings will inevitably—subconsciously or blindly—go on forever.

In other words, a living being determines its own nature and existence by its own actions. Therefore we may say the living being is self-created. The act of self-creation has continued in the past for thousands and millions of lives, and the living being has gone around the circle of the Twelve Divisioned Cycle of Causations and Becomings over and over again.

According to the nature of the preceding actions, the next Wheel of Life may be of a higher order or of a lower order. That is, a living being may assume any form of life—human form, or animal form, or even the form of a heavenly being (*deva*) according to the nature of the actions which caused its becoming. The repetition of the change from one form of life to another is called *saṅsāra* (undulation of life).

Often *saṅsāra* ('constant flow') is translated as 'transmigration of soul,' but that is a very misleading translation, for the idea is not that a soul lives after the death of the body and moves into another body. *Saṅsāra* means the creation of a new life by the influence of the actions of the former living being. In the first place, Buddhism denies the existence of the soul. Life is like the waves on water ; the vibration of one particle causes the vibration of the next particle and thus the waves are transmitted a long distance. One wave is one life, and the series of lives is *saṅsāra*. In Buddhism the series of lives do not go on infinitely as in a straight line. They turn in a circle and repeat the circle over and over again. The Wheel of Life is a small circle of one life, while the great circle (the series of the Wheel of Life) is *saṅsāra*.

Since this self-creation is regulated by the actions of the

individual being, it does not depend upon the authority of another—for instance, God.   Nor is there any confusion among the action-influence of different individuals. 'Self-acted, self-rewarded'; 'For a good cause, a good result ; for an evil cause, an evil result,'—these are the rules.

Sometimes action is divided into two kinds, 'drawing action' and 'fulfilling action.'   Drawing action causes a being to be born as a man, as a *deva*, or as a beast ; no other force can draw a living being into a particular form of life.   After the kind of life has been determined, the fulfilling action completes the formal quality of ·the living being so that it will be a thorough specimen of the kind.

There are two kinds of action-influence : individual action-influence and common action-influence.   Individual action-influence creates the individual being.   Common action-influence creates the universe itself.   This is the meaning of the words 'individual effect' and ' common effect' as used in Buddhism.

From another point of view action may be classified into three groups : good action, evil action and neutral action. Also, according to the way its retribution is received, action may be classified into four, as follows : action to receive retribution immediately, action to receive retribution in the present life, action to receive retribution in the life to come, and action to receive retribution in one of the lives following the next.

There are two ways of viewing the process of becoming. The order of cause and effect is usually regarded as arising in sequence in relation to time.   However, when all the factors of the Twelve Divisioned Cycle of Causation are considered as belonging to one being, we see that it possesses all at the same time.   (One does not abandon the Six Organs of Senses to gain Contact.)   Therefore we may regard all factors as mutually interdependent as if in a ring, developing simultaneously, none being purely a cause or purely an effect.

Buddhism regards all things in the universe as 'existence depending upon series of causes.'   Only when there are causes is there existence.   Without causes there can be no existence. No existence is permanent or conclusive.   In Buddhist terminology, such an existence is called 'conditional existence.' Such a way of regarding all things is called 'knowing and perceiving reality as such.' To regard all things in the universe as dynamic becoming is a characteristic doctrine of Buddhism.

Of the Twelve Stages of Causation, Blindness, Desire and Cleaving are called Delusions, while Will to Live and Formation of Being are called Effect-causing Actions. The rest of the cycle—the five effects in the Present and the two in the Future—are called Suffering or the effects which result in Suffering.

Delusion is the illness of the mind while Effect-causing Action is its physical manifestation, and the result is Suffering. For instance, one may be angry in mind and act accordingly, striking or killing, and later suffer retribution. From the suffering of retribution one will get into more delusions and act and suffer, thus repeating the same wandering again and again. Such is the Chain of Causation by Action-influence. Who or what is responsible for the progression of the Chain of Causation by Action-influence ? To explain this question clearly we pass on to a discussion of Causation by the Ideation-store.

(b) CAUSATION BY THE IDEATION-STORE (*Ālaya-vijñāna*)

Actions (*karma*) are divided into three groups, i.e., those by the body, those by speech and those by volition. When one makes up one's mind to do something, one is responsible for it and is liable to retribution, because volition is a mind-action even if it is not expressed in speech or manifested in physical action. But the mind being the inmost recess of all actions, the causation ought to be attributed to the mind-*store* or Ideation-*store*.

The Buddhist ideation theory divides the mind into eight faculties : the eye-sense, the ear-sense, the nose-sense, the tongue-sense, the body-sense, the co-ordinating sense-center (the 6th, *mano-vijñāna*), the individualizing thought-center of egotism (the 7th, *manas-vijñāna*), and the storing-center of ideation (the 8th, *ālaya-vijñāna*)—Ideation-store.

Of these eight faculties the seventh and the eighth require explanation. The seventh, the Individualizing Center of Egotism is the center where all the selfish ideas, egotistic opinions, arrogance, self-love, illusions and delusions arise. The eighth, the Storing Center of Ideation, is where the 'seeds' of all manifestations are deposited and later expressed in manifestations. Buddhism holds that the origin of all things and events is the effect of ideation. We shall return later to the subject when we come to the theory of cognition in the Idealistic School. Let it suffice at present to say that the Storing Center of Ideation is the 'seed bed' of all that exists. Every seed lies in the Storing Center and when it sprouts out into the object-world a reflection returns as a new seed. That is, the mind reaches out into the outer world and, perceiving objects, puts new ideas into the mind-store. Again, this new seed sprouts out to reflect back a still newer seed. Thus the seeds accumulate and all are stored there together. When they are latent, we call them seeds, but when active we call them manifestations. The old seeds, the manifestations and the new seeds are mutually dependent upon each other, forming a cycle which forever repeats the same process. This is called the Chain of Causations by Ideation.

That which makes the seed or subconscious thought sprout out into actual manifestation, that is, the motive force which makes the chain of causation move, is nothing but ideation. It is easy to see from this theory of Causation by Ideation that Delusion, Action and Suffering originate from mind-action, or ideation.

The Storing Center of Ideation is carried across rebirth to determine what the next form of life will be. This Storing Center might be regarded as similar to the soul in other forms of religion. According to the Buddhist doctrine, however, what is reborn is not the soul, but is the result of the actions performed in the preceding life. In Buddhism the existence of the soul is denied.

One may ask from where this Storing Center of Ideation comes. To explain this question we must study the third theory of Causation.

(c) CAUSATION BY THUSNESS (*Tathatā*)

Thusness, or suchness, is the only term which can be used to express the ultimate indefinable, the unnameable reality. It is otherwise called the Matrix of Thus-come. Thus-come is Buddha-nature hidden in ordinary human nature. 'Thus-come' is a designation of the Buddha employed by himself instead of 'I' or 'we,' but not without special meaning. After he had attained Enlightenment, he met the five ascetics with whom he had formerly shared his forest life. These five ascetics addressed him saying "Friend, Gotama." The Buddha admonished them, saying that they ought not treat the Thus-come (thus enlightened I come) as their friend and their equal, because he was now the Enlightened One, the Victorious, All-wise One. When he had 'thus come' in his present position as the instructor of all men and even of *devas,* they should treat him as the Blessed One and not as an old friend.

Again, when the Buddha went back to Kapilavastu, his former home, he did not go to the palace of his father, but lived in the banyan grove outside the town, and as usual went out to beg daily. Suddhodana, his king-father, could not bear the idea of his own son, the prince, begging on the streets of Kapilavastu. At once, the king visited the Buddha in the grove and entreated him to return to the palace. The Buddha answered him in the following words : "If I were still your heir, I should return to the palace to share the comfort with you, but my lineage has changed. I am now a successor to the Buddhas of the past, all of whom have 'thus gone' (*Tathāgata*) as I am doing at present, living in the woods and begging. So your Majesty must excuse me." The king understood the words perfectly and became a pupil of the Buddha at once.

Thus-come and Thus-gone have practically the same meaning. The Buddha used them both and usually in their plural forms. Sometimes the words were used for a sentient being who thus comes, i.e., comes in the ordinary way. Thus-come and Thus-gone can therefore be used in two senses : 'The one who is enlightened but comes in an ordinary way' or 'The one who comes in an ordinary way simply.' The phrase

'Son of man' in Christianity has somewhat the same meaning.

Now, Thusness or the Matrix of Thus-come or Thus-gone means the true state of all things in the universe, the source of an Enlightened One, *the basis of enlightenment*. When static, it is Enlightenment itself (with no relation to time or space); but, when dynamic, it is in human form assuming an ordinary way and feature of life. Thusness and the Matrix of Thus-come are practically one and the same—the ultimate truth. In Mahāyāna the ultimate truth is called Suchness or Thusness.[3]

We are now in a position to explain the Theory of Causation by Thusness. Thusness in its *static* sense is spaceless, timeless, all-equal, without beginning or end, formless, color-less, because the thing itself without its manifestation cannot be sensed or described. Thusness in its *dynamic* sense can assume any form ; when driven by a pure cause it takes a lofty form ; when driven by a tainted cause it takes a depraved form. Thusness, therefore, is of two states. The one is the Thusness itself ; the other is its manifestation, its state of life and death.

There are therefore three series of causations to be con-sidered : (a) Causation by Action-influence as depicted in the Wheel of Life ; (b) To explain the origin of action, Causation by Ideation-store ; (c) To explain the origin of the ideation-store, Causation by Thusness. The ideation-store of a human being is determined by his nature as a human being and this nature is a particular dynamic form of Thusness. One should not ask where Thusness or the Matrix of Thus-come originates, because it is the noumenon, the ultimate indescribable Thusness.

Next we must consider the wholesale causation of the universe, the universe being the dynamic manifestation of Thusness.

(d) CAUSATION BY THE UNIVERSAL PRINCIPLE (*Dharma-dhātu*)

We have now penetrated the depth of the origin of causa-

---

[3] For explanation see p. 41.

tion, but it is still necessary to consider the mutual relationship of the becomings of all things, and thus we pass on to the idea of universal causation.

The universe (all things) is the dynamic manifestation or expression of the static principle. All things are mutually dependent, mutually permeating without giving any hindrance to one another.

Dharma-dhātu means 'the elements of the principle' and has the two aspects of (1) the state of Thusness or noumenon and (2) the world of phenomenal manifestation. In this Causation Theory it is usually used in the latter sense, but in speaking of the ideal world as realized, the former sense is to be applied.

Buddhism holds that nothing was created singly or individually. All things in the universe—matter and mind—arose simultaneously, all things in it depending upon one another, the influence of each mutually permeating and thereby making a universal symphony of harmonious totality. If one item were lacking, the universe would not be complete ; without the rest, one item cannot be. When the whole cosmos arrives at a harmony of perfection, it is called the 'Universe One and True,' or the 'Lotus Store.' In this ideal universe all beings will be in perfect harmony, each finding no obstruction in the existence and activity of another.

Although the idea of the interdependence and simultaneous rise of all things is called the Theory of Universal Causation, the nature of the rise being universal, it is rather a philosophy of the totality of all existence than a philosophy of origination.

According to this theory, four states of the universe are to be distinguished : (1) the real, or the world of actual life—the factual world ; (2) the ideal, or the world of law or principle ; (3) the ideal realized, or the world in which the principle is applied in actual life, or the fact and the principle harmonized ; (4) the real harmonized, or the world in which actuality attains harmony in itself. The first, second and third states are easily understood, for those are the ideas often discussed by thinking men. But the fourth may be somewhat difficult to understand, because in these individualistic modern times it is usually thought that one individual is inevitably opposed to another, that classes in a society are opposed among themselves, that a business concern is in competition with another.

The idea of Universal Principle, on the other hand, demonstrates that all things in the real world ought to have harmony among themselves, and it advances the following reasons : (1) because of the simultaneous rise of all things ; (2) because of the mutual permeation of the influence of all things ; (3) because of the necessity of reciprocal identification between all beings (mutual self-negation to agree with each other) for the realization of harmony ; (4) because of the necessity of unity, or harmony, between the leaders and the followers for the attainment of a purpose ; (5) because all things have their origin in ideation—therefore a similar ideal ought to be expected of all ; (6) because all things are the result of causation and therefore are mutually dependent ; (7) because all things are indeterminate or indefinite in character but mutually complementary—therefore they are free to exist in harmony with all things ; (8) because of the fact that all beings have the nature of Buddha dormant in them ; (9) because of the fact that all beings, from the highest to the lowest, are parts of one and the same *Maṇḍala* (circle) ; (10) because of mutual reflection of all activities—as in a room surrounded by mirrors, the movement of one image causes the movement of the thousand reflections. Buddhist writers enumerate twenty reasons, but for our purpose the above ten will suffice.

(2) The Principle of Indeterminism and Indetermination

Determinism means the theory of being determined by Fate, Nature, God, or the like. Mechanism generally takes a similar attitude towards the question of free will of man. Some of the modern physicists have proposed the theory of indeterminism because it is experimentally impossible to determine the conditions for determinism ; the theory generalized is said to be that of 'uncertainty relation.' According to this idea, the nature of things or substances can in no way be determined by reason, experiment, or science. This theory can be called 'indeterminateness,' which is opposed to the old theory that everything can be determined by experiment. Generally speaking, Buddhism has no concern with either determinism or determinateness because it is a religion of self-creation : it holds the theory of free will (not absolute) within the sphere of human beings.

Buddhism, therefore, has nothing to do with fatalism, for it does not admit the existence of anything like destiny or the decree of fate. According to Buddhism all living beings have assumed the present life as the result of self-creation, and are, even at present, in the midst of creating themselves. In other words, every being is a stage of dynamic becoming. Although the grade and form of life vary in each birth, one should not think of the strict distinction of time as past or future. In truth there is present only. That is to say, we have a long continuity of existence, birth and death being simply the rise and fall of the waves in the ocean of life. Birth and death are not the predestined fate of a living being but a 'corollary of action (karma),' as it has been called by some. One who acts must sooner or later reap the effect ; while experiencing an effect, one is sowing seeds anew, thus causing the next wave of life to be high or low according to the nature of one's preceding actions.

Now, by way of contrast, let us examine other Eastern schools of thought. Confucianism is determinism in so far as it maintains that Heaven's decree is the basic principle of human life. The same is true of Taoism in that it holds Tao to be the source of all things. With Brahmanism of India, too, Brahman is made the creative principle or a personified god. Similar ideas of determinism can be found among many of the Western schools of thought.

Buddhism, on the other hand, has quite a different method of approach. While practically all the schools of thought begin with a static first principle, Buddhism begins with the actual, dynamic world, and the individual, by cultivating oneself, strives to realize the ideal in the end. *Saṅsāra* (the rise and fall of life) is not an onward flow, but a 'wavicle' circle, each wave being a cycle of life appearing on the great orbit of *Saṅsāra*. It has no beginning or end, just as one cannot point out the beginning of a circle.

There is, therefore, no room for the idea of a First Cause or Creation which might determine things. In the *Dhamma-pada* (Book of Religious Verse) the idea is described as follows : "All that we are is the result of what we have thought ; it is founded on our thoughts ; it is made up of our thoughts." We must remember, however, that though the will is free or undetermined in the human world, it may appear as abstract energy-instinct or animal desire which is not undetermined among the beasts and lower forms of life which are the lesser waves in the continuity of self-creation. The individual is self-creating and freely so, largely because he has no determinate nature or character.

The motion of the mind-action which defines the form of an individual life is like the motion of a corpuscle in the physical world. All things, matter and mind, have no substratum, no soul, no abiding self-reality, no such thing as absolute self or ego. What appears to be real is a temporary existence, an instant in a causal sequence, one ripple in the long line of waves, the effect of two or more causes combined.

If you do not insist on the existence of a central principle or absolute ego, you may define yourself in any way you please. When speaking roughly, it is quite correct to say that you exist and to describe yourself. But in minutely definite and exact language, it is impossible to define your own self or to describe yourself. However, there is no danger of losing yourself, for no one can extinguish the influence of your action, or latent energy. A particular manifestation of that energy in human form is yourself and the *whole* of you—for the present.

A substance may become energy and energy may become substance, but one must not think that the energy is preserved always in one and the same substance. By virtue of your own action you will get your next life and so on along the long line of lives. Having no permanent center, a living being changes itself as time goes on, sometimes for better, sometimes for worse. Your self does not exist apart from the changing manifestations, but the cycles of the changing manifestations as a whole constitute yourself. Therefore there is no possibility of the disappearance of your identity.

The idea of indetermination which has been seen as the basis of the idea of indeterminism is expressed by many terms : 'Having no special nature,' 'Having no definite nature,' 'All things are emptiness,' 'Having no special state,' 'All are of temporary existence,' 'All are existence by combination of causes.' 'No substance, no duration' is a root idea of Buddhism.

(3) THE PRINCIPLE OF RECIPROCAL IDENTIFICATION

Hīnayāna Buddhism is generally satisfied with analysis and is rarely inclined to synthesis. The Mahāyāna, on the other hand, is generally much inclined to the reciprocal identification of two conflicting ideas. If one party adheres to his own idea while the other party insists on his own, a separation will be the natural result. This is what happens in the Hīnayāna. The Mahāyāna teaches that one should put one's own idea aside for a moment and identify one's own position with that of the other party, thus mutually synthesizing the opposed positions. Then both parties will find themselves perfectly united. This is really a process of self-denial which is minutely taught in the dialectic method of the School of Negativism (Śūnyatā, Void).[4]

The word for 'reciprocal identification' is more literally 'mutual' and 'regarding,' that is, 'mutually viewing from each other's point,' 'mutual identification,' which is as much as to say an 'exchange of views.' It is indispensable to bring about a reconciliation of conflicting opinions or to effect a syncretism among opposing speculative systems. This trend of thought,

---

[4] To be discussed in detail later.

in fact, served greatly to restore the original idea of tolerance which was revealed in the Buddha's teaching but was almost entirely lost in the various Schools of Hīnayāna which resulted from differences of opinion.

Among the reasons which justify such identification of opposing views are the following : (1) Identity is assumed because two distinct factors are united into one as copper and zinc are mixed together to form one alloy, bronze. This identity in form is the explanation common to all Buddhist schools. (2) Identity is assumed because one's front and one's back may appear differently but in reality they are one. There are opposing views as are the front and back of the same house. In the same way, if life is looked at from an illusioned view, it is life, but, if it is looked at from an enlightened view, it is Nirvāna. The two views simply refer to one thing. Some Mahāyāna schools hold this explanation of identity in substance. (3) Identity is assumed because the whole entity is entirely one, as water and wave, the whole of water being manifested as wave.

These three aspects or connotations of identity may be summarized as : (1) Identity in form as two different elements combining to form unity. (2) Identity in substance although there may be opposing angles. (3) Identity in form and substance as water and wave (phenomenology).

Reciprocal identification by mutual self-negation, when realized, has a great practical value in smoothing out conflicting opinions or in creating sympathy among opposing parties. Through one or more of these methods diversity can be brought to union, and illusory existence is synthesized with the enlightened life. Such ideas as seeing noumenon in phenomenon, regarding motion as calm or calm as motion, identifying action and inaction, purity and impurity, perfection and imperfection, one and many, the particular and the general, permanence and impermanence, are all attainable by this theory. It is one of the most important ideas of Mahāyāna and is indispensable for a clear understanding of the Buddhist doctrine as taught in the Mahāyāna.

The most important application of this doctrine concerns

the identification of life and Nirvāṇa. Life itself is Nirvāṇa, just as water and wave are identical. Life is one thing and Nirvāṇa is another lifeless thing. If one attains Nirvāṇa while yet living, life becomes identified with Nirvāṇa but only in the sense of a state of mind because the body still exists. But perfect or complete Nirvāṇa is attained at death. The extinction of the body is the *sine qua non* of perfect Nirvāṇa, just as the cessation of the wave results in the perfect quiescence of the water.

(4) THE PRINCIPLE OF TRUE REALITY (THUSNESS)

Many of the problems concerning Thus-come, Thus-gone, Thusness, or Suchness have been studied in connection with the Causation theory. Thusness is the ultimate foundation of Buddhist thought concerning the real state of all that exists.

It is natural for people to seek first the innermost essence among the outward appearance of all things or to seek an unchanging fact among many changing things. Failing in this, people try to distinguish the unknowable from the knowable, the real from the apparent, or the thing-in-itself from the thing-for-us. This effort, too, will end in failure, for what they select as the real or the thing-in-itself is utterly beyond human knowledge. Such efforts may be called the search for the world-principle or for the life-principle. The method of search and the resulting theories are various. Some are monistic or pantheistic, while others are dualistic or pluralistic.

Against all these views Buddhism stands aloof by itself. Buddhism is atheistic—there is no doubt about it. When questioned about the First Cause or Principle, the Buddha always remained reticent. As to the life-principle, he denied the existence of an ego or soul or any kind of thing which one may call the real self, as we have discussed before. To see the true nature or the true state of all things is not to find one in many or one before many, nor is it to distinguish unity from diversity or the static from the dynamic. *The true state is the state without any special condition.* It is, in fact, 'the true reality without a reality,' i.e., without any specific character or nature. It is very difficult for the human mind to understand this idea of a reality in which there is no 'substance' at all.

The idea of an abiding substance with changing qualities is very deeply rooted in our habits of thought. Buddhist schools, no matter what they are, Hīnayāna or Mahāyāna, realistic or idealistic, are utterly free from such a habit of thought and all maintain the theory of pure change without substratum. When any Buddhist speaks of the true state of reality he means the state without a specific nature. According to the general views of the Hīnayāna, the state without any special condition is Nirvāṇa, because Nirvāṇa is perfect freedom from bondage. The Realistic School (the Sarvāstivāda), belonging to the Hīnayāna, goes a step further and assumes that selflessness, impermanence and Nirvāṇa (flamelessness) are the true state of all things. The Nihilistic School (the Satyasiddhi) holds that all things, matter and mind, are void or unreal and that nothing exists even in Nirvāṇa.

The Mahāyāna teaches, on the one hand, that the truth can be discovered only by negative views of becoming,[5] and, on the other hand, holds that true perfection can be realized negatively in the denial of the illusory and causal nature of existence.[6] The 'Wreath' School [7] of the Mahāyāna thinks that the ideal world, or the World One-and-True, is without any independent individual. The 'Lotus' School [8] identifies the manifested state as it is and the true entity immanent-in-nature.

On the whole, to see only the fact that a flower is falling is, after all, a one-sided view according to the theory of impermanence. We ought to see that immanent in the fact of a flower's falling there lies the fact of a flower's blooming, and also immanent in the blooming of the flower there is the fact of its falling. Thus the opposition of falling (extinction) and blooming (becoming) is synthesized and we form the view of

---

[5] Mādhyamika, the Negativistic School.
[6] Vijñāptimātra, the Idealistic School.
[7] Avataṁsaka, the Totalistic School.
[8] Puṇḍarīka, the Phenomenological School.

reciprocal identification which is an unbiased view of the mean, or Middle Path.

This amounts to saying that we see inaction in action and action in inaction, immotion in motion and motion in immotion, calm in wave and wave in calm. We thus arrive at the true state of all things, i.e., the Middle Path. And this is what is meant by Thusness or Suchness.

When the view is negatively expressed it indicates the true negation or Void, because any special state of things is denied altogether. Such is considered to be the ultimate idea of Buddhist philosophy. When the ultimate principle is considered from the universal point of view, it is called 'Dharma-dhātu' (the Realm of Principle), but when it is considered from the personal point of view, it is named 'Tathāgata-garbha' (the Matrix of Thus-come or Thus-gone). Other ways of expressing this same idea are : 'Buddha-tā' or 'Buddha-svabhāva' (the Buddha Nature), and 'Dharma-kāya' (the Spiritual- or Law-body). These are all practically synonymous.[9] Without knowing the principle of Thusness or Void in the highest sense of the word, one can in no way understand the Mahāyāna doctrine. The word 'void' in its highest sense does not mean 'nothingness,' but indicates 'devoid of special conditions,' 'unconditioned.'

(5) THE PRINCIPLE OF TOTALITY (Dharma-dhātu)

Concerning the principle of Totality much has been said already in connection with the discussion of the Principle of Universal Causation. We have seen that there were four kinds of universe to be considered, namely ; (1) the world of actual life, (2) the world of ideal principles, (3) the world of the ideal principles realized, (4) the world of actual life harmonized. The first, second and third can be easily understood, but the fourth is a rather uncommon idea. In the actual world

[9] Some of these will be encountered later in detail in studies of the special schools of Buddhism.

individualism is apt to predominate, and competition, conflict, dispute and struggle too often will disturb the harmony. To regard conflict as natural is the way of usual philosophies. Buddhism sets up a world in which actual life attains an ideal harmony.

The reasons brought forward to prove the possibility of such a world have already been shown.[10] According to this principle no one being will exist by itself and for itself, but the whole world will move and act in unison as if the whole were under general organization. Such an ideal world is called 'the World One-and-True' or 'the Lotus-store.'

The principle is based upon the universal causation of *Dharma-dhātu* (Realm of Principle) which we may regard as the self-creation of the universe itself. One should not forget that it is nothing but a causation by the common action-influence of all beings, and that the principle is also based on the theory of selflessness In the Buddhist terminology, the principle of totality is called 'the Avatansaka' ('Wreath'). This will be discussed in Chapter VIII.

(6) The Principle of Nirvana or Perfect Freedom

To understand Buddhism properly we must begin at the end of the Buddha's career. The year 486 B.C. or thereabouts saw the conclusion of the Buddha's activity as a teacher in India. The death of the Buddha is called, as is well known, 'Nirvāṇa'—'the state of a fire blown out.' When a fire is blown out, nothing remains to be seen. So the Buddha was considered to have entered into an invisible state which can in no way be depicted in word or in form.

Just prior to his attaining Nirvāṇa, in the Sāla grove of Kuśīnagara, he spoke to his disciples to the following effect : "Do not wail saying 'Our teacher has passed away. and we have no one to follow.' What I have taught, the *Dharma* (ideal) with the *vinaya* (disciplinary) rules, will be your teacher after

---

[10] See section I (d).

my departure. If you adhere to them and practice them uninterruptedly, is it not the same as if my *Dharma* body [11] (*Dharma-kāya*) remained here forever ?"

In spite of these thoughtful instructions some of his disciples were expressing a dissenting idea even before his funeral. It was natural, therefore, for the mindful elders to think of calling a council of elders in order to preserve the orthodox teaching of the Buddha.   They consulted King Ajātaśatru who at once ordered the eighteen monasteries around his capital to be repaired for housing the members of the coming Council of Rājagriha.

When the time arrived five hundred selected elders met together. Ānanda rehearsed the *Dharmas* (*Sūtras*) while Upāli explained the origin of each of the *Vinaya* rules.   There was no necessity of rehearsing the *Vinaya* rules themselves since they had been compiled during the Buddha's lifetime for the weekly convocation for confessions.   At the council a fine collection of the *Dharma* and the *Vinaya* was made, the number of *Sūtras* was decided, and the history of the disciplinary rules was compiled.

The result of the elders' activity was acknowledged as an authority by those who had a formalistic and realistic tendency. There were, however, some who differed from them in their opinion—Purana, for instance, who was skilled in preaching. Purana was in a bamboo grove near Rājagriha during the council, and, being asked by some layman, is said to have answered : "The council may produce a fine collection.   But I will keep to what I heard from my teacher myself."   So we may presume that there were some who had idealistic and free-thinking tendencies.

(a)   The Unwritten Sacred Literature

The whole collection of the sacred literature authorized by

---

[11] By '*dharma* body' the Buddha meant that his physical body would pass away but that his teaching would remain as his ideal 'body.' This is the interpretation by Hīnayānists.

the council was not written on paper or palm leaf during a period of about four hundred years. It is well known that Brahmanism has never written down its Vedic literature even to this day—especially those revealed texts called ' *śruti*' ('hearing'). We may imagine that Buddhism simply followed the example of the older religion, but there were other reasons as well. First, they dared not desecrate the sweet voice and kindly words of the Blessed One by putting them down in the profane letters of a foreign origin. The Buddha had once forbidden the translation of his words into the Vedic Sanskrit. How much less would it please him to write his words in the foreign Accadian alphabet, which was used only for commercial and popular purposes ? Secondly, the language they adopted in the council was, in all probability, a commingled one, something like the Pāli language, that is, the language of Pāṭaliputra. It was not advisable that their sacred language and literature should be open to the public, especially when there were some dissenting elders of a free-thinking tendency. Thirdly, to put the Buddha's holy words to letters might have seemed to them a sacrilege just as much as depicting his sacred image in painting or sculpture of which I shall speak immediately. At any rate, the whole literature was kept in memory and was not committed to writing until about four centuries later.

The Buddhist community, quite different from that of the Brahmans, was an assortment of all four castes coming from all quarters, and was not suitable for a serious recital of the holy words. The result was an imperfect transmission. Fearing the loss and distortion of the original teachings, King Vaṭṭagā-maṇī of Ceylon gave orders to commit the whole literature to writing in Sinhalese characters, about the year 80 B.C.

(b) The Unrepresented Sacred Image

None of the earlier sculptures of Sānchi and Bārhut represent the Buddha in human figure. It is remarkable to us that the principal events of the Buddha's life have been fully given in sculpture without a figure of the hero. How was that possible ? The Buddha at birth is represented by a full blooming lotus ; the Buddha in Enlightenment by the bodhi tree with a rail around it ; the Buddha in his first preaching by a wheel, above which a *tri-ratna* mark is sometimes added ; the Buddha in his begging round, or mendicancy, by a bowl ; and the like. If suggestion be a means of true art, the early Buddhist artists understood it perfectly and utilized the idea skilfully for practical purposes.

However, all this does not necessarily mean that the elders did not represent the Buddha at all during his lifetime, for there is a legend which tells of their making an image for the purpose of offering veneration during the Brother's (the Buddha's) absence. They were formalistic and realistic as mentioned above, and so if the Buddha was actually before them, they had a right to depict him in painting or sculpture. Now that he had passed into Nirvāṇa, however, it was improper to represent the one who no longer really lived. It was after a considerable development of the Gāndhāra art that the southern school of Buddhism began to have images of Buddha. This was, I believe, about the same time when the Buddha's teachings were committed to writing, i.e., 80 B.C.

The elders of idealistic and free-thinking tendencies, whom we might regard as the forerunners of the Mahāyāna, would not hold any meetings for the rehearsal of the Buddha's sermons, nor would they enlarge upon their *Vinaya* rules beyond what was. laid down by the Buddha himself. They would commit those sacred words to memory or to writing as they pleased. They did not hesitate in using their talents in painting or sculpture to depict the Buddha's image according to their own ideal of beauty and perfection, as they did in the Gāndhāra art.

The trend of the free-thinking mind can also be seen in the metaphysical treatises of the Vaibhāṣikas (Optionalists), in which several opinions about *dharmas* or *abhidharmas* (higher *dharma*) are gathered together and some optional ones have been selected and recommended for study. Though the Vaibhāṣika School belonged to the Hīnayāna, it already betrayed a tendency toward the free-thinking school. Such free-thinking people would be bold in exegesis, erudition, annotation, or in forming and expressing opinion. This, however, does not mean that they departed from the original teachings of the Buddha.

As to Nirvāṇa, the free-thinking group among the early Buddhists took the greatest liberty in interpretation, because the Buddha did not say much about it during his lifetime although it is sometimes touched upon and glorified in his poetic verses, as in the *Dhammapada*. Whenever he was asked by a questioner whether he was to live after death or what sort of world he was to enter after Nirvāṇa, he always remained silent. When the Buddha remained silent to a question requiring an answer of 'yes' or 'no,' his silence usually meant assent. But his silence on the question concerning Nirvāṇa was due to the fact that his listeners could not understand the profound philosophy involved.

One day a certain man said to the Buddha that he would join the band of his disciples if the Buddha would give clear answers to the questions : Would the Buddha ever die, and, if so, what would become of him after death ? What was the first cause of the universe, and what was the universe going to be like in the future ? Why do men live and what becomes of them after death ? The Buddha's answer was to the following effect : Suppose you were shot by a poison arrow and a physician came to draw the arrow from your body and to dress the wound, would you first ask him questions as to what the arrow was made of, what the composition of the poison was, and who shot the arrow, and, if the physician did not dress the wound, what was going to happen, and such blissful questions, and refuse the treatment until the physician answered all the questions to your satisfaction ? You would be dead before you obtained the answers.[12]

In this parable the Buddha advised the questioner to become his disciple without wasting his time on problems which were too profound to be understood by an ordinary man—probably after a long cultivation as a disciple of the Buddha he might come to understand.

[12] See *Majjhima-Nikāya*, 144.

After his departure most of the metaphysical discussions and speculations centered around the subject of Nirvāṇa. The *Mahāparinirvāṇa Sūtra,* the Sanskrit fragments of which were discovered recently—one in Central Asia and another in Kōyasan—indicates a vivid discussion on the questions as to what is 'Buddha-nature,' '*Dharma*-nature,' 'Thusness,' 'the Realm of Principle,' '*Dharma*-body' and the distinction between the Hīnayāna and Mahāyāna ideas. All of these topics relate to the problem of Nirvāṇa, and indicate the great amount of speculation undertaken on this most important question.

The main problem of Buddhism, either formalistic or idealistic, was concerning the extinction of human passion, because this distorted state of mind is considered to be the source of all the evils of human life. Human passion can be extinguished even during one's lifetime. Therefore liberation from such disorder of mind is the chief object of Buddhist culture. The extinction (Nirvāṇa) of passion, of desire, of sense, of mind and even of individual consciousness are often spoken of.

To the Buddhist mind Nirvāṇa did not contain any idea of deification of the Buddha. It simply meant the eternal continuation of his personality in the highest sense of the word. It meant returning to his original state of Buddha-nature, which is his *Dharma*-body [13] but not his scripture-body [14] as the formalists take it to be. *Dharma* means the 'ideal' itself which the Buddha conceived in his perfect Enlightenment. The idealists hold that the Buddha has *Dharma*-body—the body identical with that ideal. The ideal was expressed in the Buddha's preachings but these preachings were always restricted by the language and the occasion and the listeners. Therefore the idealists hold that the scripture is not the Buddha's ideal itself. This ideal 'body' without any restricting conditions whatever is Nirvāṇa.

The formalists, on the other hand, hold that the scripture

[13] In Mahāyāna, '*Dharma*-body' refers to the pure ideal conceived in his Enlightenment, not merely to his teachings, i.e., his ideal as expressed in words.

[14] 'Scripture-body' means, for the Hīnayānist, that the Buddha continues to live as scripture or teaching.

is the perfect representation of the ideal of the Buddha.   Hence
their opinion that the Buddha lives forever in the scripture-
body, Nirvāṇa being his entire annihilation and extinction
otherwise.

Now, let me further illustrate the principle of Nirvāṇa (the
state of a fire blown out) in the light of space and time.   It was
an illusion on the part of philosophers, especially some of the
Indian philosophers, to believe that space and time were
infinite.   Buddhism, however, has never treated space and time
as infinite, for Buddhism takes them to be physical matters.
Space is considered one of the five elements—earth, water, fire,
air and space—and it is sometimes represented to be of round
shape.

Time is treated as real in some schools while in other
schools it is treated as unreal.   But it is to be particularly
noted that time has never been considered to exist separately
from space.   That is to say, every being or thing has time of
its own.   Space and time are always correlative.   Men have
an average wave-length, or lifetime, of fifty years.   But a crane
is said to live for a thousand years, and a tortoise even ten
thousand years.   And with the heavenly beings, their one day
and night is said to be as long as the whole fifty years of the
earthly men.   A day-fly and a morning-glory, on the other hand,
live a short wave-length of only one day.

The theory that space is curved, set forth by modern physicists, has considerably facilitated the elucidation of the doctrine
of Nirvāṇa.   The universe, or the *Dharma-dhātu* (Realm of
Principle) as it is technically called, is the region which is
occupied by space and time and in which they control all the
waves of existence. So, in practice, the space-time world is the
ocean of the waves of life and death. It is the sphere of *saṅsāra*
(flowing cycles of life), the world of creation, of energy, of
action, of causation and ideation, of self-creation and of dynamic
becoming.   It is the sphere of desire, form (matter) and mind.

In opposition to such a world let us assume theoretically
that there must be a sphere that is spaceless and timeless, of
no creation, of no causation, and not disturbed by the waves of
life and death. There will be no *Dharma-dhātu* in the dynamic

sense of the word, i.e., the manifested world. But there will be the *Dharma-dhātu* in the static sense of the word, i.e., as it is in itself ; that is, Thusness or Suchness, the ultimate state of Nirvāṇa, the *Mahāparinirvāṇa,* or *Samyak-Sambuddha* (The Properly and Perfectly Enlightened One).

Dharma-dhātu in the sense of the phenomenal world is an encircled and restricted world which may be represented as follows :

The sphere of matter-mind.

The sphere of space-time.

Life–death, action, causation, creation, becoming.

Saṅsāra (life-flux).

The world of desire, form and mind.

Action–influence.

Nirvāṇa with life conditions remaining.

The realm of phenomena.

Aside from the *Dharma-dhātu* in this sense there is the unrestricted world to be described as follows :

Spaceless-timeless
Nirvāna without life-conditions.
Lifeless-deathless.
No creation, no causation, no becoming.
Perfect Enlightenment, perfect freedom.
Thusness, Suchness, the state of
Thus-come, Thus-gone.

Among the Buddhist texts which have come down to us we do not find passages expressly indicating these points. However, we have one text—though its Indian original has not as yet been discovered—which contains the idea much as I have expressed it here.

It says : "In the *dharma-dhātu* (phenomenal world), there are three worlds of desire, form and mind. All created things or beings, both noble and ignoble, both cause and effect, are within the *dharma-dhātu*. Only the Buddha is outside the *dharma-dhātu*." The idea in this text is practically identical with the diagram given above.

The Mahāyāna text of the *Mahāparinirvāna Sūtra*, not being satisfied with all the negative elucidations, explains Nirvāna in affirmative terms as permanency (against worldly impermanence), as bliss (against human suffering); as self (against the selfness of all beings) and as purity (against the pollution of human life). However, as they are all transcendental qualities of the Buddha, these terms ought not be taken in the ordinary senses of the words. For instance, one must not picture to himself a special location, a world of Nirvāna, where the Buddha lives in peace and joy, for the Buddha's Nirvāna is the 'Nirvāna of No Abode.'

An ordinary *arhat* (partially enlightened one) will cut off all the obstructions caused by passion or desire, thereby attaining his goal of annihilation. He finds satisfaction in the destruction of his intellectual life, because he thinks that the source of distinction, opposition or differentiation in things lies in consciousness. He thinks his state of annihilation is the ideal Nirvāna. But in truth he has returned to the original blindness (*avidyā*—ignorance) in leaving the obstruction of intellect.

He himself may be thinking that he has done away with blindness. But blindness is the basic principle of existence which cannot be simply cut off, just as darkness cannot be destroyed without a light. The only way to get rid of darkness is to bring a light into the room. By virtue of enlightenment the darkness that bars intellect will be removed.

As a technical term the extinction of human passion is called the 'Nirvāṇa with the condition of being still remaining' or, in a more literal expression, 'the Nirvāṇa with the *upādhi* remnant,' *upādhi* being the material and immaterial condition of being. Plainly, this means becoming a person without passion while yet alive.

Then the next question will be : What is the Nirvāṇa without the *upādhi* remnant ? It is the total extinction of the conditions of being as well as of passion. One may call it the annihilation of being. This is Nirvāṇa or 'Perfect Freedom,' the death of Śākyamuni the Buddha.

The formalistic view of Buddhism here comes to an end with the annihilation of being. But the speculative views of the idealistic standpoint have a fresh start with the passing of the visible Buddha into the invisible state. Even in his lifetime the Buddha had a perfect freedom in intellectual activity, and, while he was a person, he had been super-personally enlightened. How much more free must he be when he passed into the thoroughly unconditioned state of Nirvāṇa ? He had now returned to his 'ideal' body. It is called the Body of His Own Nature, 'Self-natured Body' in contradistinction to the 'Body Manifested for All Beings.' All the incarnation theories entertained in later years have their origin in this interpretation of Nirvāṇa.

The Buddha in Nirvāṇa has a perfect freedom to live anywhere he pleases ; he can act in whatever way he wishes and on that account he has no fixed abode and his Nirvāṇa is called the 'Nirvāṇa of No Abode.' The Blessed One may reappear in this world when he feels the necessity of saving all beings as the historical Śākyamuni did. Therefore, the Buddha, according to the idealistic view, does not live in the world of life and death as he is not bound by causation.

However, at the same time he does not rest at ease in Nirvāṇa because he is the sufferer of others' suffering.

IV. THE KUSHA SCHOOL
(THE ABHIDHARMA-KOŚA SCHOOL)[1]
(Sarvāstivāda, Abhidhārmika)

(Realism : *Ens* School)
[Hīnayānistic]

(1) PRELIMINARY

The Japanese name of the School, Kusha, is an abbreviation of *Abhidharma-kośa*[2] (*kośa=Kusha*) which is the title of Vasubandhu's[3] work on realism and may be translated 'The Story of the Higher Special *Dharma.*' To the text we shall return soon.

First of all let us consider what the word '*dharma*' means in Buddhism. It is derived from the verb *dhṛ* (to hold, or to bear), and its noun form, *dharma,* would mean 'that which is held to,' or 'the ideal' if we limit its meaning to mental affairs only. This ideal will be different in scope as conceived by different individuals. In the case of the Buddha it will be Perfect Enlightenment or Perfect Wisdom (*Bodhi*). Secondly, the ideal as expressed in words will be his Sermon, Dialogue, Teaching, Doctrine. Thirdly, the ideal as set forth for his pupils is the Rule, Discipline, Precept, Morality. Fourthly, the ideal to be realized will be the Principle, Theory, Truth, Reason, Nature, Law, Condition. Fifthly, the ideal as realized in a general sense will be Reality, Fact, Thing, Element (created and not created), Mind-and-Matter, Idea-and-Phenomenon. In the Realistic School of the Abhidharma teachers the word *dharma* is used mostly in the fifth and last meaning.

Now we are in a position to understand what *Abhidharma*

---

[1] Chü-shê.

[2] *Taishō,* No. 1558. French translation by L. de la Vallée Poussin : *L'abhidharmakośa de Vasubandhu,* 6 Volumes ; Paris, 1923-31.

[3] C. 420-500 A.D.

means. The prefix 'Abhi-' gives the sense of either 'further' or 'about.' Therefore, *Abhidharma* would mean 'The Higher or Special *Dharma*' or 'The Discourse of *Dharma*.' Both will do for our purpose. While the *Dharma* is the general teaching of the Buddha, the *Abhidharma* is a special metaphysical discourse brought forward by certain elders.

Most of the Abhidharma schools probably arose after the Council of Aśoka (c. 240 B.C.), because the Abhidharma literature, seven texts in all, was for the first time recognized as one of the Tripiṭaka (three baskets or collections) in this council.[4] At the time of the first and the second councils there were only two Piṭakas (*Sūtra* and *Vinaya*).[5] In this Aśoka Council *Abhidharma* was added to make the Tripiṭaka.

While the orthodox Elders' School (Theravāda) was flourishing in the south, chiefly in Ceylon, a more avowed Realistic School was getting a stronghold in the north, mostly in Kashmir and Gāndhāra.

The existence of this Sarvāstivāda School can be seen in Indian history from the time of the Buddhist Council held during King Aśoka's reign (240 B.C.) down to the time of I-tsing's[6] travel in India (671-695 A.D.).[7] In the *Kathāvatthu Controversy* compiled in the time of King Aśoka, Sarvāstivāda seems to have occupied a strong position among the disputing parties.[8] The principal seat of this school was in Kashmir where its doctrine was taught in its purity and it was finally developed into an elaborate system known as the Vaibhāṣika.

In time another branch of the Vaibhāṣikas was established in Gāndhāra and it seems to have differed from that of Kash-

---

[4] See my " On the Abhidharma Literature of the Sarvāstivādins," *Journal of the Pāli Text Society*, 1905.

[5] *Sūtra* : Discourses of the Buddha ; *Vinaya* : Disciplining rules enunciated by the Buddha.

[6] I-ching.

[7] See my translation of *A Record of the Buddhist Religion as Practised in India and the Malay Archipelago* (A.D. 671-695) by I-Tsing, Oxford, 1896.

[8] See C. A. F. Rhys Davids and S. Z. Aung's translation, *Points of Controversy*, Pāli Text Society Translation Series, Vol. V, Prefatory notes.

mir in its opinion to some extent, for both were often cited side by side in some texts in use.

The geographical extent of this school was much greater than that of any other school as it was found in all India, its northern frontier, Persia, Central Asia, and also to the south in Sumatra, Java, Cochin-China and all of China.

The Sarvāstivāda School was closely related to the ortho-dox Theravāda School, from which it was first separated pro-bably before the Council of Aśoka. The idea that all things exist may go back even to the time of the Buddha himself, for the word 'sabban atthi' (all things exist) is found already in the *Samyuttanikāya*.[9]

The principal *Abhidharma* text of this school was Kātyā-yanīputra's *Jñāna-prasthāna* (Source of Knowledge), otherwise called the *Aṣṭa-grantha* (Eight Books), probably compiled as early as 200 B.C. The subsequent works of the school seem to have been a special exegesis on the subject-matter contained in it. At least six *pādas* ('Legs'), as they are designated, have come down to us.

Then probably in the second century A.D.—whether before or after the Buddhist Council of King Kaniṣka's reign, we cannot tell—a great and minute commentary named *Vibhāṣā Śāstra* was compiled on Kātyāyanīputra's work. The word '*vibhāṣā*' means an extensive annotation or various opinions, and this title indicates that many opinions of the time were gathered and criticized in detail and that some optional ones were selected and recorded. The chief object of the *Vibhāṣā* commentary was to transmit the correct exposition of the Abhidharma School which has since then come to be called the Vaibhāṣika School.

Then there appeared a compendium of the Abhidharma doctrine called *Abhidharma-hṛdaya* ('heart of the Higher *Dharmas*,' translated into Chinese in 391 A.D.) by Dharmottara

---

[9] English translation by C. A. F. Rhys Davids and F. L. Woodward : *The Book of Kindred Sayings*, Pāli Text Society Translation Series, Vols. VII, X, XIII, XV, XVI, 1918-30. See Rhys Davids' Index to the *Samyutta*, p. 107.

who belonged to the Gāndhāra branch. A commentary on it
called *Samyukta-abhidharma-hṛdaya* was written by Dharmatrāta, a pupil of Dharmottara. This work became the fundamental text of the Gāndhāra branch and subsequently of the
Chinese Abhidharma School.

The Abhidharma Literature

I

Kātyāyanīputra's *Jñāna-prasthāna* (Source of Knowledge)
alias *Aṣṭa-grantha* (Eight Books)
Six *Pādas* (Legs)
on the above

1	2	3
Vasumitra's	Devaśarman's	Sariputra's
Prakaraña-	*Vijñāna-kāya*	*Dharma-*
pāda	(Consciousness-	*skandha*
(Category-leg)	body)	(Element-group)

4	5	6
Maudgalyāyana's	Purṇa's	Mahākausṭhila's
Prajñapti	*Dhātu-kāya*	*Saṅgīti-paryāya*
(World-	(Mental-	(Rehearsal-
system)	element-body)	reading)

Pārśva's *Mahāvibhāṣā* (Great Commentary)
200 Chinese volumes (*chüans* or parts)
Vibhāṣā (Abridged Commentary), 14 Chinese volumes

In Chinese we have thus two transmissions of the *Vibhāṣā*,
Large (200 parts) and Small (14 parts). Whether one was
an abridgement of the other we cannot tell for certain. But
from several points of view we can imagine that the larger one
belongs to the Kashmir School and the smaller to the Gāndhāra
School.

II

Compendium of the Abhidharma School
Dharmottara's *Abhidharma-hṛdaya*
(Transl. A.D. 391)
|
Dharmatrāta's *Samyukta-abhidharma-hṛdaya*
(Transl. A.D. 426. From this the Chinese
Abhidharma School called P'i-t'an was founded)
|
Vasubandhu's *Abhidharma-kośa*
|
Paramārtha's Chinese Translation
(A.D. 563-567)
From this the Chinese Kośa
School called Chü-shê was founded

Hiuen-tsang's (Hsüan-tsang, A.D. 596-664) Chinese Translation
(A.D. 651-654)
After this translation the Kośa School was
completed as a philosophical system chiefly
by Ki, (K'uei-chī, 632-682) pupil of Hiuen-tsang
|
Japanese Kośa School

The Realistic School

Sarvāstivādins
|
Gāndhāra- Abhidhārmikas	Kātyāyanīputra's	Kashmir- Abhidhārmikas
	Jñāna-prasthāna	
	Six *Pādas* on it	
	Vaibhāṣikas Parśva's *Mahāvibhāṣā*	

Neo-Vaibhāṣikas

Vasubandhu (c. 420-500 A.D.)   Samghabhadra
(Eclectic)   (Orthodox)
Texts   Texts
Abhidharma-kośa-kārikā (Verses)   *Nyāyānusāra*
and   and
Abhidharma-kośa Śāstra (Commentary) *Samaya-pradīpikā*

(2) HISTORICAL

The great philosopher Vasubandhu was born in Puruṣapura (Peshawar) in Gāndhāra and received his ordination in the Sarvāstivāda School. He went to Kashmir *incognito* to learn the Abhidharma philosophy. On his return home he wrote the *Abhidharma-kośa* which is preserved in sixty volumes (*chüans* or parts) of Chinese translation. The Sanskrit text is lost, but fortunately we have a commentary written by Yaśomitra called the *Abhidharma-kośa-vyākhyā* which has facilitated the restoration of the lost text undertaken by the late Professor L. de la Vallée Poussin of Belgium and completed by Rāhula Sānkrītyāyana of India.

According to the published text and the Chinese version, the contents of the *Abhidharma-kośa* are as follows :

1. On Elements
2. On Organs
3. On Worlds
4. On Actions
5. On Drowsiness (Passion)
6. On the Noble Personality and the Path
7. On Knowledge
8. On Meditation

The Chinese text has a ninth chapter on Refutation of the Idea of the Self.

In writing the *Abhidharma-kośa*, Vasubandhu seems to have followed the work of his predecessor, Dharmatrāta, called

Samyukta-abhidharma-hṛdaya, and this, again, is a commentary on Dharmottara's *Abhidharma-hṛdaya.* A careful comparison of the three works will indicate that Vasubandhu had before him his predecessor's works, or else such questions as discussed in these works must have been common topics of the school. The first eight chapters of the work explain special facts or elements of matter and mind, while the ninth and last chapter elucidates the general basic principle of selflessness that should be followed by all Buddhist schools. Especially the ninth chapter seems to originate from Vasubandhu's own idea, for there is no trace of this subject in the other books.

Though the *Kośa* thus resembles the *Hṛdaya* in subject-matter, there is no indication that the former is indebted to the latter in forming opinions, for Vasubandhu was very free and thorough in his thinking, and he did not hesitate to take the tenets of any school other than his own when he found excellent reasoning in them.

When Vasubandhu's *Abhidharma-kośa* was made public in Gāndhāra, it met with rigorous opposition from within and from without his school. Yet the final victory seems to have been on his side, for his work enjoyed popularity in India ; it was taught widely and several annotations of it were made in Nālandā, Valabhī and elsewhere. It was translated into Tibetan by Jinamitra and into Chinese first by Paramārtha of Valabhī during 563-567 A.D. and later by Hiuen-tsang who studied at Nālandā University during 651-654 A.D. In China especially serious studies were made, and at least seven elaborate commentaries, each amounting to more than twenty or thirty Chinese volumes, were written on it.

Before the translation of the *Abhidharma-kośa* there was in China a school called P'i-t'an Tsung which is the first one in the list of Chinese sects given above,[10] P'i-t'an being the Chinese abbreviation of *Abhidharma.* This Chinese school represents the Gāndhāra branch of Sarvāstivādins. The principal texts of this school with the *Vibhāṣā* commentary were translated into Chinese as early as 383-434 A.D. The

[10] See p. 6.

62   ESSENTIALS OF BUDDHIST PHILOSOPHY

larger *vibhāṣā* commentary belonging to the Kashmir branch
was also translated, but there appeared no Chinese school or
sect representing it.   When the *Kośa* text of Vasubandhu was
translated by Paramārtha during 563-567 A.D. and again by
Hiuen-tsang during 651-654 A.D., the Kośa School, or Chü-shê
Tsung, came into existence, was seriously studied, and was
made into an indispensable basis of all Buddhist studies.   The
P'i-t'an School came to be entirely replaced by the new Kośa
School.

The Kośa School, or the Kusha School as it is called in
Japan, is generally understood to have been brought into
Japan in 658 A.D. by Chitsū and Chitatsu, two Japanese priests
who studied some time under the famous Hiuen-tsang.   It was
brought in once again by Gembō (in 735 A.D.) who was a
pupil of Chih-chou, the third generation pupil of Ki, a direct
disciple of Hiuen-tsang.

In an official document of 793 A.D. the realistic Kusha
School was registered as a sect appended to the idealistic Hossō
School, no separate position being given to it, because it had
no adherents belonging exclusively to it.

(3) Philosophical

The Sāṅkhya philosophy (dualism), one of the oldest
philosophies of India, which has several tenets in common with
Buddhism, maintains that all things exist eternally though they
are constantly changing ; nothing new appears and nothing
disappears.

Buddhism, however, holds that everything exists only
instantaneously ; there is no abiding substance at all.[11]   Both
Buddhism and the Sāṅkhya philosophy deny the theory of
inherence.   Buddhism may be said to hold, therefore, the
theory of momentariness or instantaneous being.   All reality
may be split into separate elements which are instantaneous.

[11] Th. Stcherbatsky, *Buddhist Logic*, Vol. I, p. 109.   Substance is *substance, abiding essence*.

This form of pluralism stands in direct opposition to monism, especially that of the Upaniṣads.

The Kusha School further maintains the atomic theory and asserts the existence of three atoms : 1. The finest atom (*paramā-aṇu*) ; 2. The form atom (*aṇu*) ; 3. The fine dust atom (*rajas*). The finest atom is the finest divisible atom of all and cannot be further analyzed. It is conceived only by meditation.

Seven of these finest atoms constitute the form atom which is the finest substance. It is of cubic form. Seven of these form atoms constitute the fine dust atom which can be perceived by the eyes of a *Bodhisattva,* a future Buddha. Furthermore, the shortest of time measures is said to correspond to the transition of one atom to another, and thus space and time are always correlative. Though the atomic theory is set forth very minutely by the realistic Kusha School and also by the nihilistic Jōjitsu School,[12] I shall not dwell on it anymore, as I do not think it essential to these schools which hold the doctrine of momentariness of being.

All elements or *dharmas* which constitute momentary sense-data and thought-data were enumerated by the Realistic School, perhaps for the first time in the history of Indian philosophy. The idea that a thing has no 'sub-stance' goes along with the theory of change or impermanence—everything having no duration. According to this theory only the present exists. The past does not exist, because it is no more, and the future is not real, because it has not yet come into existence.

This theory has been faithfully held by such other Buddhist schools as the Mahāsaṅghika, the Mahisasaka and the Sautrāntika. The Sarvāstivāda School, however, because it has its origin in the orthodox Theravāda School, raises a rigorous objection and asserts that the past and the future are real, because the present has its root in the past and its consequence in the future. Besides, it holds that the three periods of time ought to exist separately, because the notions

[12] Satyasiddhi.

of past and future would not occur in us without separate
realities.

Judging from the discussions recorded in the *Mahāvibhāṣā*
literature, great importance seems to have been laid on the
separateness of the three periods of time and the reality of each.
The reality of the three periods of time, however, does not mean
that the three periods themselves are eternally extant, nor does
it mean that time is a real substance. It means that all things
or elements are real in the past and in the future as they are
in the present—but without enduring from one period to
another.

In connection with this theory four arguments are quoted
by Vasubandhu from the Exegetic Literature :

(1) Dharmatrāta's argument from the difference of kind
     or result—as a gold piece may be made into three
     different articles, yet each retains the real nature of
     gold.

(2) Ghoṣa's argument from the difference of mark or
     factor as the same service can be obtained from three
     different employees.

(3) Vasumitra's argument from the difference of function
     or position as in counting where the same numeral
     may be used to express three different values, for
     instance, the numeral one may be 1 or the index of
     10 or of 100.

(4) Buddhadeva's argument from the difference of view
     or relation—as a woman can at once be daughter,
     wife and mother according to the relation she holds
     to her mother, her husband and her child.

Vasubandhu prefers Vasumitra's opinion (3) as the best
of the four arguments though he was not entirely satisfied with
it. According to this argument it is possible to give different
values to each of the three periods of time—the future is the
stage which has not come to function, the present is the actually
functioning stage, and the past is the stage in which the function has come to an end. Owing to the differences in stage,
the three periods are distinctly separate, and all things or
elements in them are real entities. Hence the formula : "The

three periods (of time) are real and so is the entity of all elements at any instant." The tenet "Void of abiding self (but) reality of elements (*dharmas*)" indicates that selflessness is still the basic principle of the Sarvāstivāda School.

Nevertheless, the theory of Sarvāstivāda, according to Vasubandhu, is not found in the genuine discourses of the Buddha, but it is an innovation of the *Vibhāṣā* (Exegetic) Literature of the Abhidharma School. The opinion of the Abhidhārmikas is against the Sautrāntic School [13] which clings solely to the discourses (*Sūtrānta*) of the Buddha and maintains that only the present exists.[14] Accordingly Vasubandhu in his *Abhidharma-kośa* adopts the opinion of the Sautrāntic School, although professedly he follows the tenets of the Kashmiri Abhidhārmikas in general.

Although a strong realistic tendency is a deviation from the original teaching of momentariness or instantaneous being, it is not so conspicuous as it seems at first sight as long as the deviating party does not forsake the original formula : "No substance (*anātmā*), no duration (*anitya*) and no bliss (*duḥkha*) except Nirvāṇa." Consequently the real entity of the Sarvāstivāda School would mean a momentary existence or the continuity of separate momentary existences.

In Buddhism there is no actor apart from action, no percipient apart from perception ; therefore, no conscious subject behind consciousness. Mind is simply a transitory state of consciousness of an object. There is no permanent conscious subject, for no fabric of a body remains the same for two consecutive moments as the modern physicists say.[15] Buddhism contends that the same is true of the mind as well.

Seventy-five Elements or Dharmas of the Universe

All elements of the universe were minutely explained by Vasubandhu in his *Abhidharma-kośa*. The significant name

---

[13] See next chapter.
[14] Th. Stcherbatsky, *Buddhist Logic*, Vol. I, p. 111.
[15] *Compendium of Philosophy*, p. 8.

B.—5

of the School 'Sarva-asti-vāda' (all-things-exist-doctrine) affirms all existences, both material and mental, as well as that which is neither matter nor mind. This, however, does not mean to admit the existence of Self (Ātman), an individual ego or soul or the universal principle or First Cause. Whether or not he anticipated the danger of being involved in the admission of Self, Vasubandhu devoted the whole ninth chapter of his Abhidharma-kośa to the refutation of the Ātman theory.

The list of dharmas in the Abhidharma-kośa may well be compared with similar lists in the Pāli Compendium of Philosophy (Abhidhamma-saṅgaha) by Anuruddha of the eighth century A.D.,[16] the Essence of Metaphysics (Abhidharma-hṛdaya) by Dharmottara (transl. 391 A.D.) and by Dharmatrāta (transl. 426 A.D.) and possibly the Completion of Truth (Satyasiddhi) by Harivarman (c. 250-350).

In the Compendium of Philosophy all elements are divided into six classes and dharmas, whereas in the Essence of Metaphysics they are classified into five grades and dharmas. In the Abhidharma-kośa these are well arranged and systematized into five categories and dharmas. The Completion of Truth, which is a Sautrāntic and nihilistic text, enumerates eighty-four dharmas.

All these schools hold that all dharmas are to be classified into two categories, created and uncreated. The created, or conditioned, elements are again divided into four classes :

I. Form (11 dharmas) consisting of the five sense-organs, five sense-objects, and form-with-no-manifestations.

II. Consciousness (1 dharma) sometimes subdivided into five dharmas corresponding to the sense-organs.

III. The Concomitant Mental Functions (46 dharmas) are subdivided into six grades, i.e., general, good, foul, evil, minor foul and indeterminate functions.

IV. The Elements Independent of Consciousness : Neither Form nor Consciousness (14 dharmas).

[16] Translated by S. Z. Aung, revised and edited by C. A. F. Rhys Davids, Pāli Text Society Translations Series, Vol. II, 1910.

These (I-IV) are all created things (72 in number) and with uncreated things (3 in number) constitute the five categories and the seventy-five *dharmas*. Among these what all schools and texts treat with the utmost care is the group called 'Concomitant Mental Functions.' There are 52 elements in three grades in the *Compendium of Philosophy,* 58 elements in seven grades in the *Essence of Metaphysics* and 46 elements in six grades in the *Abhidharma-kośa.*

Compared roughly, they are found to contain more than 'mentals' in common, but the *Abhidharma-kośa* and the *Essence of Metaphysics* possess much closer affinities than the rest, the former being a systematized version of the latter.

The *dharmas* comprise the whole world of both matter and mind : positive and negative becomings, presentative and representative psychological elements or sense-data and thought-data. Vasubandhu's enumeration was of elements. The last four elements of the Indeterminate Functions—covetousness, hatred, pride and doubt—are treated by him separately and not definitely as Indeterminate Functions. The addition of these seems to have been finally established by Chinese authors, especially P'u-kuang.

The *dharmas* are generally arranged in a table, as in the attached chart.

Some Explanations of the Table

The table enumerates all the elements of what might be called the objective world. In fact those with which the realistic school of Buddhism is concerned are objects only. It does not recognize any subject in the ordinary sense of the word. Even mind itself is not a subjective thing, for there is no actor apart from action and no conscious subject apart from consciousness. There is only a transitory state of consciousness. All reality can be assumed to have only momentary existence.

According to the original principle of Buddhism, all things (matter and mind) are considered to be separate, momentary elements, equal in value. The arrangement of all the elements into a co-ordinated system, dividing matter into subjective and

objective groups or elements, and assuming the difference between the central elements of pure consciousness and the secondary elements of mental functions or moral forces, may seem,
as Prof. Stcherbatsky says, to be a great deviation by this school
from original Buddhism (the doctrine of no substance). But
as long as we do not lose sight of momentariness of being,
we cannot regard it as an entire deviation.

The conditioned elements (*sarva-sanskāra* or *sanskṛta-
dharmas*) constitute the first grand division in our table. Their
specific character is impermanence.

Sanskṛta-dharmas : (I) Forms (*Rūpa,* 11 *dharmas*).
This group comprises practically all that we call matter. Of
the eleven, the first five are sense-organs and the next five are
sense-objects. The four gross elements—earth, water, fire,
air—are represented by the sense-objects. In addition to these,
there is a peculiar one. That is the 'form-element not manifested' outwardly (*avijñapti-rūpa*). When we will to act, the
mental function itself is called will (*cetanā*). In Buddhism
it is called will-action. This is usually expressed in words or
in body, and is called word-action or body-action respectively.
These two actions manifested outwardly, whether they are good
or bad, present a corresponding and similar action in mind,
and form an abiding impression or image. They are then called
unmanifested action (*avijñapti-karma*). These actions being
taken as form-elements are considered to be sense-objects
though not manifested (*avijñapti-rūpa*).

II. Consciousness or Mind (*Citta,* one *dharma*). This is
consciousness itself. Though one, it naturally functions in five
ways corresponding to the five sense-organs.

III. The Concomitant Mental Functions (*Citta-sampra-
yukta-sanskāra* or *Caitasika,* 46 *dharmas*). This category of
mental faculties is the division given most attention by this
school and on that account it seems quite reasonable to
designate the school a psychological school of Buddhism. The
mental elements, in all, are again grouped into six classes :
(1) 'General functions' or 'universals' (*Mahābhūmika,* 10
dharmas). *Mahābhūmika* means 'of the universal ground,'
the 'ground' meaning the mind. Whenever the mind functions,

the universals such as perception, idea, will, etc., always appear concomitantly (*sarva-dharma-sādharaṇa*). (2) 'General functions of good' or 'moral universals' (*Kuśala-mahābhūmika*, 10 *dharmas*) which accompany all good mental functions. (3) 'General Foul Functions' (*Kleśa-mahābhūmika*, 6 *dharmas*) are those tainted with earthly desire or passion (*kleśa*). (4) 'General Functions of Evil' (*Akuśala-mahābhūmika*, 2 *dharmas*), which are concomitant with all evil thoughts. (5) 'Minor Foul Functions' (*Upakleśa-bhūmika*, 10 *dharmas*) are those of ordinary passionate character. They always accompany evil mind and also the 'neutral mind which hinders the Noble Path' (*nivṛtta-avyākṛta*), and they are to be eliminated gradually by the way of self-culture (*bhāvanā-mārga*), not abruptly by the way of insight (*darśana-mārga*). (6) 'Indeterminate Functions' (*Aniyata-bhūmika*, 8 *dharmas*) are those which cannot be classified as belonging to any of the five functions.

IV. Among the created, or conditioned, elements there are those which have no connection with form or mind (*Citta-viprayukta-saṅskāra*, 14 *dharmas*). They are neither matter nor mind. (1) Acquisition (*prāpti*) is the power that binds an acquired object to the one who acquires it. (2) Non-acquisition (*aprāpti*) is the power that separates an object from the possessor. (3) Communionship (*sabhāga*) is the power that causes a species or a class to have similar forms of life. As to (4), (5) and (6), all of them are thoughtless and conditionless effects attained by meditation. (7) Life, or vital power, (*jīvita-indriya*) is the power that gives longevity. The next four elements, (8), (9), (10) and (11), imply the life and death of being, i.e., the waves of becoming. The last three elements, (12), (13) and (14), are the groups (*kāya*) of names, sentences and letters, all related to speech (*vāk*).

Now we come to the second of the two grand divisions, i.e., the uncreated, or unconditioned, elements (*Asaṅskṛta-dharma*, 3 *dharmas*). (1) Space (*ākāśa*) is that which gives no hindrance and itself penetrates through any hindrance freely and manifests no change. The second element is an extinction attained by an intellectual power, (*pratisaṅkhyā-nirodha*) such as

Nirvāṇa, and (3) is an extinction caused by the absence of a productive cause (apratisaṅkhyā-nirodha).

So much for the exposition of the elements of reality as enumerated in the seventy-five dharmas.

Some Peculiar Doctrines of the Kusha School

Several tenets peculiar to the Sarvāstivāda School which were finally established by Vasubandhu are to be noticed.

First of all, such distinctions as those between created (sanskṛta) and uncreated (asanskṛta), manifested (vijñapti) and unmanifested (avijñapti), determinate (niyata) and indeterminate (aniyata), and concomitant with mind (citta-samprayukta) and non-concomitant with mind (citta-viprayukta), ought to be carefully studied.

These seventy-five elements, though separate from one another, are found linked together in the actual world. This phenomenon is explained by the theory of causal relation or combination, sometimes called the Doctrine of the Ten Causes, in which six Chief Causes (Hetu) and four Sub-causes (Pratyaya) are assumed.

The six Chief Causes are :

(1) The Active Cause (Karaṇa-hetu) as the leading factor in the production of an effect ; (2) the Co-existent Cause (Sahabhūhetu)—more than two factors always working together ; (3) the Similar-species Cause (Sabhāga-hetu), a cause helping other causes of its kind ; (4) the Concomitant Cause, (Samprayukta-hetu), appearing at any time, from any motive, with regard to any fact, on any occasion and in any environment ; (5) the Universally Prevalent Cause (Sarva-traga-hetu), a cause always connected with wrong views, doubts or ignorance which produces all the errors of men ; (6) the Cause Ripening in a Different Life (Vipāka-hetu), a cause which produces its effect in a different life, as when retributions are obtained in the life after death.

The four Sub-causes are as follows :

(1) The Cause-Sub-cause which acts as Chief Cause (*Hetu-pratyaya*), there being no distinction between the Chief Cause and the secondary cause ; e.g., the water and the wind cause a wave ; (2) the Immediate Sub-cause (*Samanantara-pratyaya*), occurring in order, one after another—consequences coming immediately and equally after antecedents, as waves following one after another ; (3) the Objective Sub-cause (*Ālambana-pratyaya*), which has an object or environment as a concurring cause, as waves are conditioned by a basin, a pond, a river, the sea, or a boat ; (4) the Upheaving Sub-cause (*Adhipati-pratyaya*) which is the most powerful one to bring all the abiding causes to a culmination, as the last wave that upsets a boat in a storm.

Of the above, the first, the Cause-Sub-cause, which acts as chief cause, and the fourth, the Upheaving Sub-cause, are most important, and, in order to elucidate these two, the six Chief Causes have been taught. To speak more plainly, the Active Cause is itself the Upheaving Sub-cause while the other five causes are identical with the Cause-Sub-cause. We must understand from this that the terms Cause and Sub-cause are not strictly defined ones. They concur either as chief or secondary cause as the occasion requires.

These four Causes roughly correspond to the Aristotelian four causes : (1) the Cause-Sub-cause as the 'efficient cause' ; (2) the Immediate Sub-cause, the 'material cause' ; (3) the Objective or Referent Sub-cause, the 'formal cause' ; and (4) the Upheaving Sub-cause, the 'final cause.' A difference between the two groups of causes is that the Sub-cause in the Kusha School refers only to mental activities in which a similar function occurs immediately after another function has passed.

(4) RÉSUMÉ

Buddhism assumes no substance, no abiding individual self, no soul, no Creator, no root principle of the universe. But this by no means implies that all beings and things do not exist. They do not exist with a substratum or a permanent essence in them, as people often think, but they do exist as causal relatives or combinations. All becomings, either personal or universal, originate from the principle of causation, and exist in causal combinations. The center of causation is one's own action, and the action will leave its latent energy which decides the ensuing existence. Accordingly, our past forms our present, and the present forms the future. This is the theory of self-creation.

We are, therefore, always creating and always changing. Men are ever floating on the waves of dynamic becoming called 'saṅsāra,' the stream of life. Creating and changing ourselves as a whole, we go on. There should be no fear of the loss of identity, for our present self as a whole is an effect of the cause which we may call our past self ; similarly in the future it is impossible that our self will be lost since we are necessarily self-creating beings. It is unreasonable to seek an unchanging essence in an all-changing being.

The seed-elements are assumed to be four—earth (hardness), water (wetness), fire (warmth) and air (motion)—and all matters or forms are one or another combination of these four.

The formation of a personality and that of the universe are similar, both consisting of matter and mind, the difference being that in a personality mind is prevalent while in the universe matter is prevalent. Personality consists of five groups (*skandhas*)—Form (body), Perception, Conception, Volition and Consciousness (mind). The Form or body, again, consists of earth, water, fire and air. Man is therefore to be considered as one who has a form, perceives, conceives, wills and thinks. These are his actions (*karma*) which altogether form his personal existence which has no other reality. A man is a temporary entity, and is only living in the contiguity of momentariness. In order to change his personality for better, the cultivation of his knowledge and wisdom is necessary, because the perfection of wisdom is the perfection of personality—Enlightenment.

The Kusha School, though it states that all things exist, is quite different from general naïve materialism, because, according to its theory, all things are *dharmas* (elements) which include mind as well as matter, all on an equal footing. It asserts the reality of all *dharmas* and yet it admits the theory of no substance, no duration and no bliss except Nirvāṇa.

V. THE JŌJITSU SCHOOL
(THE SATYASIDDHI SCHOOL)[1]
(Sarvaśūnyavāda, Sautrāntika)

(Nihilism : Non-*ens* School)
[Hīnayānistic]

(1) PRELIMINARY

The Jōjitsu School is opposed to the Kusha School in that
it asserts that nothing (matter or mind) exists at all. It is a
Hīnayānistic Negativism or Nihilism and is called Jōjitsu in
Japanese (Satyasiddhi—Completion of Truth) after the title
of the work by Harivarman who lived in India (c. 250-350 A.D.)
about a century before Vasubandhu.[2] The author says in his
introductory note that he intended to elucidate the true purport
of the sacred literature. From this we can infer that the title,
'Completion of Truth,' means the complete establishment of
the truth propounded in the discourses of the Buddha himself.

Of the eighteen schools of Buddhism in India the Jōjitsu
belongs to the Sautrāntika [3] School which adheres to the original
sacred scripture against the realistic Sarvāstivāda School, some
tenets of which are regarded by Vasubandhu as innovations of
the Vaibhāṣikas or those who adhere to the *Abhidharma*
doctrine. If the realistic doctrine can be called a deviation from
original Buddhism, this Nihilistic doctrine should be considered
as a reversion to it. This Jōjitsu School, in a way, can be
considered to be an orthodox school of Buddhism, especially
because it is much nearer than the Realistic School to the
original teaching of the Buddha : "No substance (*anātmā*),
no duration (*anitya*), and no bliss (*duḥkha*) except Nirvāṇa.

---

[1] Ch'êng-shih.   [2] 420-500 A.D.
[3] The word *Sautrāntika* is derived from *Sutrānta* (Scripture).

(2) HISTORICAL

We know little or nothing of the history of this school from the Indian side. Perhaps there never was a separate school called Satyasiddhi in India. If there was a mother school to which Satyasiddhi belonged, it must have been one which adhered to the original discourse of the *sūtras*. The Sūtra-vādin, or Sautrāntikavādin School, is mentioned as the latest offshoot among the eighteen schools of Buddhism.[4] Though Harivarman's connection with that school is not known, several points of the doctrine set forth by him can be traced to that school. It seems to have had an influential position in India, for it is referred to directly or indirectly by Vasubandhu, who adopted, in fact, the tenets of the school in some of the important points of contention, e.g., the problem of time.

The text, *Satyasiddhi*,[5] was translated into Chinese as early as 411-412 A.D. by Kumārajīva who ordered some of his pupils to lecture on it. One of them, Sêng-jui by name, while discoursing on it discovered that the author, Harivarman, had refuted the tenets of the Abhidharma School on several occasions—more than seven times. Hence we can assume that the two schools (Realistic and Nihilistic) used to hold antagonistic positions at or before the author's time.

Among the pupils of Kumārajīva there were two or three lines of transmission of this school between 411 and 498 A.D., and several important commentaries—twelve in all—were compiled. Many hundred lectures were delivered on the text all over China, each repeated twenty, thirty, forty, or even ninety times in one and the same place.

At first the text was taken by some authorities to be Mahāyānistic, as by the three noted savants of the Liang dynasty (502-557), namely, Fa-yun,[6] Chih-tsang[7] and Sêng-min. By other authorities such as Chih-i,[8] Chi-tsang[9] and

---

[4] C.A.F. Rhys Davids, *Kathā-vatthu*, pp. 3, 5. Vasily Pavlovich Vasil'ev, *History of Buddhism, Second Supplement*, p. 222.
[5] *Taishō*, No. 1464.   [6] 476-529.   [7] 458-522.
[8] Chih-kai, 531-597.   [9] 549-623.

Ching-ying it was taken to be Hīnayānistic. It was Tao-hsüan,[10] a famous pupil of Hiuen-tsang,[11] who finally settled the question by pronouncing that it was Hīnayānistic and Sautrāntic, because the Jōjitsu School had not gone beyond the level and influence of the Vaibhāṣika School. However, he recognized that it had a certain tendency toward the Mahāyāna doctrine.

The Jōjitsu School was introduced into Japan by Ekwan, a learned priest of Kaoli, a state in Korea, who arrived at Hōryūji Temple in 625 A.D., and was appointed the first Buddhist prelate. Ever since that time the school has been studied in all Buddhist colleges and universities, but it was never recognized as an independent sect in Japan, always being treated as a subdivision of the Sanron School (The Three-Treatise School, Mahāyānistic (Negativism) which will be explained in Chapter VII.

(3) PHILOSOPHICAL

The doctrine of the Satyasiddhi or Jōjitsu School is generally understood to be the void of self (*pudgala-śūnyatā*) and of elements (*sarva-dharma-śūnyatā*). It is, therefore, the twofold void in contrast to the doctrine of the Realistic School (Kusha) which is the void of self (*pudgala-śūnyatā*) but the reality of elements (*dharma-tā*). Personality which is made up of five groups (Form, Perception, Conception, Volition and Consciousness) has no substratum and no individual self, just as an empty jar has no water or inner essence. Again, the universe consists of eighty-four elements, but all of them have no abiding reality at all, just as a jar itself has no permanent reality. Each of the five groups or the four great elements (earth, water, fire and air) of which the universe is composed has no permanent, changeless substance. They are only temporary names.

According to Harivarman, all beings should ultimately

596-667.   [11] Hsüan-tsang, 596-664.

come to the truth of extinction (*nirodha-satya*), i.e., Nirvāṇa, which is the final extinction. Thus voidness alone is the ultimate truth. This does not mean that this school denies the common-sense or phenomenal temporary existence of all beings, for it admits the five categories of all elements which are subdivided into eighty-four *dharmas*—instead of the seventy-five *dharmas* of the Kusha School. We see from the following table that its contents are not very different from those of the table of the Realists :

The Eighty-four *Dharmas* [12] of the Jōjitsu School

Created *Dharmas*			Non-created *Dharmas* (3) 1-3 k
Forms (14)	**Mind (1)**	**Mental Functions (49)**	**Elements Neither Substantial Nor Mental (17)**
1-10 k		General, 1-10 k	1-2 k
11 earth		Good, 1-10 k	3 (k3, 7) life
12 water		Foul, 1-6 k	4-6 k
13 fire		Evil, 1-2 k	7 (k8) birth
14 wind		Minor Foul, 1-10 k	8 old age
		Indeterminate	9-11 k
		1-8 k	12 death
		9 dislike	13-15 (k12-14)
		10 pleasure	16 mediocrity
		11 sleep	17 things with no manifestation (k1, 11)

The Satyasiddhi list of all the *dharmas* was certainly made after the model of the Realistic School. It is taught only in

---

[12] The letter 'k' indicates that the same items are also in the list of *Dharmas* given by the Sarvāstivāda or Realistic School in the previous chapter.

accordance with the worldly or common-sense or ordinary truth, for in the supreme truth there will be no *dharmas* at all. Of these, the five objects of sense (form, sound, smell, taste and touch) are regarded relatively while the four elements (earth, water, fire and air) and the five sense organs are considered more transitory.

Analyzing those five objects the school reduces them to molecules, and further reduces them to even finer atoms, and by thus repeating the process the school finally attains the finest element which has an entirely different nature from the first objects. Going one step further, the school attains the Void. Thus the nihilism of this school is a 'destructed' or abstracted Void. In other words, the non-entity asserted in this school is simply an abstraction from entity, or merely an antithetic Void as against existence. And this is not the synthetic Void or transcendental Void advanced by the Sanron School.[13] We may call it the doctrine of nothingness or non-*ens*, for it denies the existence of individual self and of all elements, matter and mind. To speak more clearly, mind (*citta*) is not abiding and mental functions (*caitasika*) have no independence ; those *dharmas* or elements which are neither matter nor mind (*citta-viprayukta*) are all temporary ; the uncreated elements (*asaṅskṛta*) are also unreal. The doctrine of Void is here complete and it can be taken as total nihilism (*sarva-śūnyatā*) if we follow the supreme truth. It is only from the point of view of worldly truth that they admit the existence of all things.

The doctrine of Void does not disavow the theory of the Chain of Causation, for our worldly existence is of causal combination, nor does it reject the principle of the stream of life (*saṅsāra*), for it is necessary to explain the state of dynamic becoming.

We have seen already that the Realistic School assumes that the three worlds of time are real and so are all *dharmas* at any instant. Against this assertion, the nihilistic Jōjitsu School contends that the present only is real while the past and the future have no entity. The school asserts, as all the other Mahāyānistic schools do, the Void of all elements (*sarvadharma-śūnyatā*) as well as the Void of self (*pudgala-śūnyatā*). In addition, it recognizes the two-fold truth—the supreme truth and worldly truth. These are chiefly the reasons for which this school had long been treated as Mahāyāna in China.

To realize Total-Voidness, one must do away with the three attachments—attachment to the temporary name, attachment to all elements and attachment to the Void itself. All beings and things, since they exist as the combination of causations, are given temporary names, because there is no way to designate their changing existence except by name. One must realize that it is useless to be attached to a self which is in truth only an appellation. One must first get rid of this attachment to one's temporary name. The elements are the basis on which the temporary name arises. To be rid of the attachment to the elements is to realize their voidness. When, as above, we have realized the voidness of both the individual self and of the elements, we may seem to have attained Total-Voidness, but in truth there still remains the consciousness of the Void, and we are liable to be attached to the idea of the Void as much as if it were something existent. This Void-consciousness can be removed when one enters into the Meditation of Extinction (*nirodha-samāpatti*) or into Perfect Nirvāṇa. The former is, as in an *arhat*, a state in which all passions have been done away with, and the latter is,[14] as in the case of the Buddha, the state in which all conditions of life, matter and mind, have been extinguished by virtue of Enlightenment as darkness is extinguished by light, because the Buddha had attained the state of perfect Nirvāṇa which is in itself devoid of any distinguishing qualities and he had transcended the 'four arguments.'

In India it is thought that there are only four arguments on any problem—'Yes,' 'No,' 'Either Yes or No according to the circumstance' and 'Neither Yes nor No, meaning out of the question.' The state in which the Buddha is said to have

[14] This is true especially in Mahāyāna.

transcended the four arguments is called the Buddha's True Body, and the body of the Buddha which appeared in this world is called his Transformed Body. This Transformed Body possessed all the attributes of a man in its forms, and followed all the ways of a human being, but he was a man of perfect knowledge and wisdom. In the elucidation of this point the Jōjitsu School relies upon the Mahāyāna *sūtras* such as the *Prajñā-pāramitā*, the *Saddharma-puṇḍarīka*, or the *Parinirvāṇa*. This was another reason why this school had long been thought to belong to Mahāyāna.

The way by which one attains the final state constitutes, as usual, the objects of learning—Precept (*śīla*), Meditation (*dhyāna*), and Wisdom (*prajñā*). The latter two are especially recommended to be seriously pursued.

VI. THE HOSSŌ SCHOOL
(THE MERE-IDEATION SCHOOL)[1]
(Vijñaptimātratā, Yogācāra)

(Idealism : Both *Ens* and Non-*ens* School)
[Quasi-Mahāyānistic]

(1) PRELIMINARY

Hossō (*Dharma-lakṣaṇa*) means 'Characteristics of *Dharma*,' *Dharma* here denoting things substantial and mental (matter and minds), for the chief object of this school is to investigate the nature and qualities of all existences. The first founder of the school was Asaṅga[2]—an elder brother of Vasubandhu[3]—who was the author of the text *Yogācāra-bhūmi.*[4] In India the school was formerly called the Yogācāra, which means the practice of self-concentration.

Vasubandhu, when he was converted to Mahāyāna by his brother and succeeded in systematizing the philosophical views of the Yogācāra School, designated the tenet of the school as Vijñaptimātra (Mere Ideation), attributing the existence of all the outer world to inner ideation—in short, holding that nothing but ideation exists. As to ontology this school stands between the realistic and nihilistic schools, given above. It adheres neither to the doctrine that all things exist, because it takes the view that nothing outside the mind (mental activity) exists, nor to the doctrine that nothing exists, because it asserts that ideations do exist. It firmly adheres to the doctrine of the mean, neither going to the extreme of the theory of existence (*ens*) nor to that of non-existence (non-*ens*). This school can, therefore, be called the 'Ideal-realism' or

---

[1] Fa-hsiang   [2] c. 410-500 A.D.
[3] c. 420-500 A.D.   [4] *Taishō*, No. 1579.

B.—6

'Ideation Theory.' The academic name of this school is Yuishiki (Wei-shih, Mere Ideation), or Vijñaptimātra (Ideation only), Shōzō-gaku, a Study of the Nature (*Svabhāva*) and Characteristics (*Lakṣaṇa*) of *dharmas* or elements.

The Middle Path which the Buddha himself taught against the two extremes of the hedonistic worldly life and the pessimistic ascetic life has now been promoted to the middle path between the two ontological views of the Hīnayāna schools.

For several reasons this school is considered to be still within the range of the formalistic, realistic Hīnayāna. It aims at an analysis of the phenomenal world, and is called Quasi-Mahāyāna. This we shall see later.

(2) HISTORICAL

The Shê-lun (Samparigraha) School, the forerunner of Fa-hsiang (Dharma-Lakṣaṇa or Hossō) School :

A representative work of Mahāyāna idealism named the *Mahāyāna-samparigraha* (Acceptance of the Great Vehicle) [5] was written by Asaṅga in the fifth century, annotated by Vasubandhu (420-500), and translated into Chinese in 531 by Buddhaśānta, in 563 by Paramārtha, and again by Hiuen-tsang during 648-649. Of these, the second, Paramārtha's translation, laid the foundation of the Shê-lun School in China.

Paramārtha,[6] a native of Ujjayinī, probably connected with Valabhī University, a center of Buddhist learning, came to China in 548, and between that time and 557 translated thirty-two texts. He is also said to have written more than forty works—altogether amounting to two hundred Chinese volumes. His chief object was to propagate the doctrine of the *Abhidharma-kośa* and the *Mahāyāna-samparigraha*. His literary and religious activity seems to have greatly influenced the Chinese mind of the time as is testified by the fact that he had many able pupils under him.

Paramārtha founded the realistic Kośa School, as we have

---

[5] *Taishō*, Nos. 1592-1597.   [6] 499-569.

seen before, and the Saṃparigraha (Shê-lun) School. His
activities can be compared only with Kumārajīva [7] who came
before him and Hiuen-tsang [8] who came after him.

In studying the Shê-lun School we should know first the
contents of the text, *Mahāyāna-saṃparigraha*. This text, with
the commentary on it by Vasubandhu, is the first and the
foremost comprehensive work which sets forth the doctrine of
Mere Ideation and is a representative compendium of the
Idealistic school. The text dwells chiefly on the ten special
characteristics of Mahāyāna.

The contents are : 1. The store-consciousness (*Ālaya-
vijñāna*), from which all elements are manifested ; 2. The
theory of mere ideation—all elements have either the nature
of interdependence, or that of imagination, or that of real
truth ; 3. The attainment of the insight of mere ideation ;
4. The six perfections (*pāramitā*) ; 5. The ten stages (*bhūmi*)
of the holy personages ; 6. Moral precepts (*śīla*) ; 7. Meditation (*samādhi*) ; 8. Perfect wisdom (*prajñā*) ; 9. The higher
knowledge without discrimination ; 10. The threefold body
of the Buddha.

When all things are reflected on our mind, our discriminating or imaginating power is already at work. This is called
our consciousness (*vijñāna*). Since the consciousness co-ordinating all reflected elements stores them, it is called the store-
consciousness or ideation-store—I prefer to use the term
ideation-store. The ideation-store itself is an existence of
causal combination, and in it the pure and the tainted elements
are causally combined or intermingled. When the ideation-
store begins to move and descend to the everyday world, then
we have the manifold existence that is only an imagined world.
The ideation-store, which is the seed-consciousness, is the
conscious center and the world manifested by ideation is its
environment. It is only from the Buddha's Perfect Enlightenment that pure ideation flashes out.

This pure ideation can purify the tainted portion of the
ideation-store and further develop its power of understanding.

[7] 344-413.   [8] Hsüan-tsang. 596-664.

The world of imagination and the world of interdependence will be brought to the real truth (*parinispanna*). This having been attained, the seed-store, as consciousness, will disappear altogether and ultimately will reach the state where there is no distinction between subject and object. The knowledge so gained has no discrimination (*avikalpa-jñāna*). This ultimate state is the Nirvāṇa of No Abode (*apratiṣṭhita-nirvāṇa*), that is to say, the attainment of perfect freedom—not being bound to one place.

According to this text the Buddha has a threefold body :

1. The *Dharma-* or Ideal-body whose nature is Principle and Wisdom ; 2. The *Saṃbhoga-*, Enjoyment- or Reward-body which appears only for the *Bodhisattva* ; 3. The Nirvāṇa- or Transformation-body which manifests itself for ordinary persons for their worship.

The *Ālaya* (store) is the consciousness in which the true and the false unite—practically the same as in the theory set forth in the *Awakening of Faith* [9] of Aśvaghoṣa. The Shê-lun School regards the *Ālaya*-store that has become pure and taintless as Thusness (*Tathatā*) and gives it a special name *Amala-vijñāna* (Taintless Consciousness). It is designated as the Ninth Consciousness. Accordingly the conscious organs recognized in this school founded by Paramārtha are as follows :

The Ninefold Consciousness :

The First Five Consciousnesses :

Visual consciousness
Auditory consciousness
Odor consciousness

[9] *Taishō*, No. 1666. English translation by Timothy Richard and Yang Wen-hwui : *The Awakening of Faith in the Mahāyāna Doctrine*, 1894 ; and by D. T. Suzuki : *Aśvaghoṣa's Discourse on the Awakening of Faith in the Mahāyāna*, Chicago, 1900.

Taste consciousness
Touch consciousness

The Four Central Consciousnesses :

Sixth, Sense-center Consciousness
Seventh, Thought-center Consciousness
Eighth, Ideation-store Consciousness
Ninth, Taintless Consciousness

The Shê-lun School in this state was replaced by the new Fa-hsiang (Hossō) School which was taught by Hiuen-tsang and founded by his pupil Ki (Kuei-chi), 632-682 A.D.

The Fa-hsiang (Dharma-lakṣaṇa, Hossō) School :

In India there seem to have been three lines of transmission of Yogācāra Idealism after the death of Vasubandhu. The first was the line of Dignāga [10] (fifth century), Agotra, and Dharmapāla [11] whose center of transmission was Nālandā University. Śīlabhadra of Nālandā and his Chinese pupil Hiuen-tsang belong to this line. The second was the line of Guṇamati and Sthiramati whose seat of transmission seems to have been Valabhī University ; Paramārtha the founder of the Shê-lun School in China belongs to it. The third was the line of Nanda, whose tenet was followed by Paramārtha, and Jayasena, who instructed Hiuen-tsang on certain questions. This last line of transmission did not flourish much in India and seems to have soon disappeared.

Hiuen-tsang, while still at home in China, heard lectures on the *Samparigraha* doctrine from more than seven different teachers. He was actually an earnest student of the Idealistic School. However, the opinions of his teachers varied greatly and, since he could not see which was the best to follow, he decided to go to India where he hoped to find an able instructor. In 629 he started from Ch'angan for India. In 629 he was

---

[10] Diṅnāga.   [11] 439-507.

still in Karakobjo in Sinkiang. In 632 or later he arrived in Nālandā near Rājagṛha, where Śīlabhadra, 106 years of age, was the head of the university.

Hiuen-tsang studied under Śīlabhadra the important doctrines of Buddhism—first the reformed idealism of Vasu-bandhu in his *Vijñaptimātratā* and then the realism of the same author in his *Abhidharma-kośa*. After a seventeen-year sojourn in India, he came home in 645 and translated Dharma-pāla's *Vijñapti-mātratā-siddhi* (Completion of Mere Idea-tion) [12] in addition to seventy-four other texts.

Hiuen-tsang's able pupil Ki seems to have monopolized the transmission of the idealistic doctrine. The Fa-hsiang (Hossō) School was actually systematized and founded chiefly by Ki. Ki's two important works, *Fa-yüan-i-lin-chang* [13] and *Wei-shih-shu-chi*,[14] are the fundamental texts of this school.

Dōshō (628-700), a Japanese priest, was sent to China in 653. He studied under Hiuen-tsang for more than ten years, living in the same room with Ki. The teacher specially instructed him in Meditation (Zen) and recommended that he propagate its practice to the East. On the eve of his departure he received from the teacher several sūtras, treatises and com-mentaries on the works on Idealism. On his return home, Dōshō at once set out to transmit the Hossō doctrine in the monastery of Gwangōji. His first pupil was Gyōgi (667-748).

This first transmission was called that of the Southern Monastery. The second transmission was by Chitsū and Chitatsu who were sent to China in 654 and who also received an earnest training from Hiuen-tsang and Ki. The third transmission was by Chihō, a Korean priest from Simla, together with his friends Chiran and Chiō who were in China for a while and studied under Hiuen-tsang. They arrived in Japan in 703 and transmitted the idealistic doctrine to Giyen,[15] a pupil of Gyōgi. The fourth transmission was by the learned Gembō who was sent to China in 616 and was instructed by

---

[12] *Taishō*, No. 1585. French translation by L. de la Vallée Poussin : *La Siddhi de Hiuen-tsang*, 2 Vols., Paris, 1928.
[13] *Taishō*. No. 1861.   [14] *Taishō*, No. 1830.   [15] d. 724.

Chih-chou,[16] a pupil of Ki. He stayed abroad for nearly twenty years and in 735 came home and taught the doctrine in the monastery called Kōfukuji. He transmitted the teaching to Genjū [17] who devoted himself to its propagation. This is called the transmission of the Northern Monastery, and is generally accepted as the orthodox line.

Thus Japan has received the orthodox teaching sacrosanct from first-hand authorities of the Indian and Chinese idealistic school, and with the Japanese even now it is the chief subject of Buddhist learning.

(3) PHILOSOPHICAL

The idealistic school of Vasubandhu is a reformed Yogā-cāra system and its fundamental text is Vasubandhu's *Vijñapti-mātratā-trimśikā*,[18] a versified text on the theory of mere idea-tion in thirty stanzas, of which the first twenty-four are devoted to the special character (*svalakṣaṇa*) of all *dharmas*, the next to the nature (*svabhāva*) of all *dharmas*, and the last four to the stages of the noble personages.

The Hossō School, though idealistic, is different from the She-lun School, which was representative idealism and was later replaced by the Fa-hsiang (Hossō) School in China. The Hossō idealists profess to have transmitted the orthodox system of Vasubandhu, but in reality this is rather uncertain. Vasu-bandhu's *Trimśikā* was annotated by ten authorities of whom Hiuen-tsang and his pupil Ki followed chiefly the opinions of Dharmapāla of Nālandā. The result was summed up in thirty Chinese volumes (*chüans*) of the *Vijñapti-mātratā-siddhi* which is the fundamental treatise of the school. Thus the Hossō idealists of China accepted Vasubandhu's opinions through Dharmapāla's interpretation which may or may not be exactly in accordance with the original author's purports.

[16] 688-723.   [17] 723-797.

[18] French translation by S. Lévi: *Matériaux pour L'étude du système Vijñāptimātra*, Paris, 1932.

Dharmapāla recognized the distinction between the specific character (*lakṣaṇa*) of *dharma* and the nature (*svabhāva*) of *dharma*, i.e., Thusness (*Tathatā*). His point of view was that of what is called the 'worldly truth' (*laukika-satya*) and not the 'highest truth' (*paramārtha-satya*). The worldly truth assumes that fact and principle always go 'parallel' and can never be synthetically identified. Such a view is not quite Mahāyānistic but is half Hīnayānistic, and on that account this school is generally classified as quasi-Mahāyānistic.

The doctrine of the Hossō School concerns itself chiefly with the facts or specific characters (*lakṣaṇa*) of all elements on which the theory of idealism was built in order to elucidate that no element is separate from ideation. Although it is usually expressed by the saying that all *dharmas* are mere ideation or that there is nothing but ideation, the real sense is quite different. It is idealistic because all elements are in some way or other always connected with ideation.

As to the Ideation Theory of the school, an argument should be in accordance with the Sacred Word and also with dialectic reason. The Ideation Theory that the three worlds exist only in ideation can be proved from the Word of the Buddha in the *Avataṅsaka Sūtra*.[19]

But how can this be proved logically? The outer world does not exist but the internal ideation presents appearance as if it were an outer world. We know this from the fact that we can nowhere discover any self or element that is real. What we consider real is not real but only an outward manifestation of ideation. The whole world is therefore of either illusory or causal nature and no permanent reality can be found. But, one may ask, if everything is produced from ideation, how can anything be produced definitely in one place and at one time and not everywhere and at any time according as one ideates? Why, again, can all beings perceive one and the same thing and their enjoyment of it have similar effects?

The customary answer brought forward by this school is very simple : even in a dream which has no actuality one sees

---

[19] *Taishō*, Nos. 278 and 279.

a definite place at a certain time with all its surroundings. In it one may even have the bodily effect of sweating, crying, or dancing. Various men, again, see similar definite objects, just as several departed spirits have before their eyes one and the same river which changes itself to filth the moment they attempt to drink from it. This is because they have had similar past actions (*karma*).

In this way all sorts of arguments and refutations are given in the Idealistic treatises, but I do not think it necessary to go into detail here.[20]

From the table of all *dharmas* given below,[21] one will notice that they are divided into five categories : 1. Mind or Consciousness (*Vijñāna*, 8 *dharmas*); 2. Mental functions (*Caitasika*, 51 *dharmas*); 3. Form (*Rūpa*, 11 *dharmas*); 4. Things not associated with mind (*Citta-viprayukta*, 24 *dharmas*) ; 5. Non-created elements (*Asaṅskṛta*, 6 *dharmas*). Altogether they amount to one hundred *dharmas*.

Among them, 'form' is an outward manifestation of consciousness ; 'things not associated with mind' is a name given to a partial process of the conscious manifestation ; and the 'non-created' is the static nature of consciousness. All of these have some relation to the mind. There is nothing separate from ideation.

The eight consciousnesses (mind) are all separate. The first five constitute sense-consciousness (*Vijñāna*), the sixth is the sense-center (*Mano-vijñāna*), the seventh is the thought-center or self-consciousness (*Manas*), and the eighth is the store-consciousness (*Citta*). By nature all of these consciousnesses are dependent on something else, i.e., cause (*paratantra-lakṣaṇa*), but they are not of mere imagination (*parikalpita-lakṣaṇa*). The assumption of the separate reality of the eight consciousnesses is Dharmapāla's special tenet and nowhere else in Buddhism can it be seen, not even in Hīnayāna.

---

[20] See Vasubandhu's *Viṁsatika, Taishō,* No. 1590. English translation by Clarence H. Hamilton, *Wei Shih Er Shih Lun or The Treatise in Twenty Stanzas on Representation-only,* New Haven, 1938.

[21] Facing page 96.

Each of the consciousnesses has four functional divisions of interdependent nature : 1. the objective or the seen portion (*lakṣaṇa-bhāga*), 2. the subjective or the seeing portion (*darśana-bhāga*), 3. the self-witness or the self-assuring portion (*sakṣātkāri-bhāga*), 4. the rewitnessing of self-witness or the reassuring portion. The objective is a shadow image of an outer object reflected on the mind-face, and the subjective illumines, sees and experiences it. Now, who will know that the subject has seen the object or the shadow-image ? It is the mind itself that will see and acknowledge the subjective function. This function of cognition is called the Self-witness, without which no knowledge can be obtained. The Rewitnessing of Self-witness completes the mental faculty. These are the four mental functions.

For instance, a sheet of paper presented in mind is the objective, i.e., the shadow-image of it. The subjective is a measuring instrument to see its length and width. The self-witnessing function cognizes how long and how wide it is, according to that measure. The rewitnessing function recognizes the accuracy of that measurement. Because there is this mutual recognition, no other function is needed.

Among the Indian Yogācārins, Dignāga and Agotra do not admit the fourth rewitnessing function in addition to the other three functions. Dharmapāla and his successor, Śīlabhadra of Nālandā, hold the theory of four functional divisions, yet they think that either the three or the four will do, because the fourfold analysis is only a more minute division of three. Sthiramati, though he allows the existence of three functions, admits in fact only the one function of self-witness which is the function of the consciousness itself. According to him the subjective and the objective are by nature a false imagination arising from the consciousness itself, while the self-witness, i.e., the consciousness itself, is a causal existence and has reality. Nanda assumes the existence of only two functions, the subjective and the objective. The former is the main function and the latter originates from it, thus completing the theory of mere ideation.

The Hossō School regards both the three and the four

functions as orthodox. The objective portion of mental faculty is simply a shadow-image of the outer world and belongs to the subjective domain in the ordinary sense of the word. The original substance from which the shadow issues is quite separate from sense-data and thought-data.

The objects of the outer world (*viṣaya*) which throw shadows on the mind-face are of three species : 1. The object-domain of nature or immediate perception, i.e., the object that has the original substance and presents it as it is, just as the five objects of the senses—form, sound, smell, taste and touch —are perceived as they are. The first five sense-consciousnesses and the eighth, the store-consciousness, perceive the object in this way. 2. The object-domain of mere shadow or illusion. The shadow-image appears simply from one's own imagination and has no real existence. Of course, it has no original substance as a ghost which does not exist at all. Only the sixth, the sense-center, functions on it and imagines it to be. 3. The object-domain with the original substance. The object has an original substance and yet is not perceived as it is. When the seventh, the thought-center, looks at the subjective function of the eighth, the store-center, it considers that it is self or ego. The subjective function of the eighth, the store-center, has its original substance (entity) but it is not seen as it is by the seventh consciousness and is regarded to be self or an abiding ego, which is in reality an illusion since it is not self at all.

The theory of three species of the object-domain may have originated from Nālandā but the four-line memorial verse current in the school is probably of Chinese origin. It runs as follows :

1. The object of nature does not follow the mind (=subjective) . . . The subject may be good or evil but the object is always neutral.

2. The mere shadow only follows the seeing (=subjective) . . . The object is as the subject imagines.

3. The object with the original substance.

4. The character, seed, etc. are various as occasions require . . . The object has an original substance, but the subject does not see it as it is.

This four-line verse explains how the three species of the object-domain are related to the subjective function and the outer original substance. One may be puzzled in understanding how an idealism can have the so-called original substance. We should not forget that though it is an outer substance it is after all a thing manifested out of ideation.

The eighth, the *Ālaya*-consciousness itself, is not an unchangeable fixed substance (*dravya*) but is itself ever changing instantaneously (*kṣaṇika*) and repeatedly ; and, being 'perfumed' or having impressions made upon it by cognition and action, it becomes habituated and efficient in manifestation. It is like a torrent of water which never stops at one place for two consecutive moments. It is only with reference to the continuity of the stream that we can speak of a river.

That efficiency or energy to produce a result is called a 'seed' as it is stored in a seed-bed and sprouts in time when a cause occasions it. From the stored seeds come the object-world corresponding to the manifestation of former cognition and action. Hence the stock saying :

> A seed (*bīja*) produces a manifestation (*samudācāra*) ;
> A manifestation perfumes a seed ;
> The three elements (seed, manifestation and perfume)
>   turning on and on ;
> The cause and the effect at one and the same time.

And another saying :

> A seed produces a seed ;
> The cause and the effect differing in time.

Thus the world of life and the world of 'vessel to live in' are instantaneously issued from the *Ālaya*-store and restored to it at once ; this constitutes our daily life of error and illusion.

The old seeds latent in the eighth, the store-consciousness, exist from time immemorial. These are called the original seeds. The new seeds are perfumed afresh from time to time. These are called the newly perfumed seeds. The old and new seeds together produce all manifestations of an error-stricken existence of life. Therefore, the eighth, the store-consciousness, may seem to be a false-natured or unreal one. However, it contains a taintless seed which is attached to it. As it grows up by self-culture, etc., it gradually subjugates the false nature of the eighth consciousness and as the result of this subjugation the life of error becomes a refined one until the highest stage of enlightenment is attained.

The Hossō School takes the nature (*svabhāva*) of *dharma* to be quite distinct from the specific character (*lakṣaṇa*) of *dharma*. Thus the principle is quite different from the fact, that is to say, the nature stands 'parallel' to the specific character, and so does the principle with facts. The parallel lines will never meet. The specific character or the fact, or, in other words, the manifestations of all elements, are the chief concern of this school. Hence the name *Dharma-lakṣaṇa* (*Hossō*). It is distinguished clearly from the schools which treat mainly the nature of *dharma* or the principle, i.e., the *Dharma-svabhāva* (*Hosshō*).

The Hossō School, therefore, does not admit that all beings have the Buddha-nature. The five species of men are all separate and distinct. There is a species of men who can never become a Buddha (*icchāntika*). Therefore, according to this school, the three vehicles (*Śrāvaka-yāna*—Teaching for Buddha's direct disciple, *Pratyeka-Buddha-yāna*—Teaching for Buddha-for-himself, *Bodhisattva-yāna*—Teaching for the would-be Buddha) are real, because they belong to the actual world, i.e., they correspond to the conditions of the actual world of men. The *Ekayāna* (One Vehicle leading to Buddhahood) is for 'convenience' and is temporary. Exactly the opposite holds good in other schools. Further, they do not recognize the identification of the nature with the specific character of *dharmas*. So, Thusness (*Tathatā*) as the nature of all *dharmas* is in no way connected with the specific character of *dharmas*. The thing as in itself is separate forever from the thing for us. Thusness or Suchness will never be perfumed or influenced by the actual life. Noumenon has no relation at all with phenomenon. This school rejects the theory that Thusness receives any perfume or influence and that it manifests itself as a causal consequence.   It firmly holds that Thusness lies ever in a static congelation and will never become dynamic in the sphere of *dharmas*.

The schools which lay importance on the nature (*svabhāva*) are attacked mercilessly by this Hossō School. Such a doctrine as set forth in the *Awakening of Faith* that Thusness manifests itself according to a cause either pure or tainted is the main object of their rigorous attack.   But this is only the passive side of the argument as to the purport of Thusness.   We will study the positive side of the argument toward the end of the chapter.

The Shê-lun School takes a somewhat different attitude on this point.[22]   In the *Awakening of Faith* the author who is said to be Aśvaghoṣa starts from Thusness which is somehow tainted by ignorance and takes the store-consciousness to be of a mixed nature, true and false, while the Hossō School starts from the world of phenomena that originates from the ideation-store, the eighth consciousness being of an unreal, false nature.   The store-consciousness may in some way have a taintless seed attached to it and eventually develop it to enlightenment.   The Shê-lun School, siding with the author of the *Awakening of Faith*, goes a step further and admits the existence of a ninth taintless consciousness (*amala-vijñāna*).   Thus all seem to assume the existence of two elements, true and false, in the store-consciousness.   But still the Hossō School differs from the rest in treating Thusness as the nature and the store-consciousness as the characteristic of *dharmas*.   Thusness is the ultimate entity (*pariniṣpanna*) while the store-consciousness is of the quality dependent on another, i.e., cause (*paratantra*).

Pariniṣpanna, paratantra and *parikalpita* are all called *lakṣaṇa* in Sanskrit, but in the case of *pariniṣpanna* it is not *lakṣaṇa* but is *alakṣaṇa*—'Bereft of specific character,' i.e., *Svabhāva*.

[22] See above, section (2), Historical.

THE ONE HUNDRED ELEMENTS IN FIVE CATEGORIES

The Hossō School, though idealistic, takes the model of the analytical method used in the Realistic and Nihilistic Schools, and classifies the world of becoming into five categories which are subdivided into one hundred *dharmas*. This list, facing p. 96, is much more minute than the other tables.

A special point in the table is that mind is divided into eight consciousnesses, each being a separate reality. No other school of Buddhism has such a doctrine. In addition to the first five mental faculties (eye-, ear-, nose-, tongue-, skin-senses or consciousnesses) there are the sixth, the sense-center, a general perceiving organ or conscious mind, the seventh, the thought-center or the self-conscious mind, and the eighth, the store-center or store-consciousness. The last two are called *Manas* (thought) and *Ālaya* (store-consciousness).

Among these eight consciousnesses the former six constitute the sense-consciousness (*Vijñāna*), the seventh is thought (*Manas*) and the eighth is mind (*Citta*). To put it more plainly, the first five consciousnesses are simply the senses ; the sixth, the sense-center, forms conceptions out of the perceptions obtained from the outside ; the seventh, the thought-center, thinks, wills and reasons on a self-centered basis ; the eighth, the store-center, stores seeds, i.e., keeps efficiency or energy for all manifestations. The sixth, the seventh and the eighth always act on one another, for the sixth is the general center of perception and cognition inwardly which acts outwardly on the basis of the thought-center which in turn acts on the basis of the all-storing center. The *Manas* is responsible for self-consciousness, self-interest, or selfish motives. The subjective function of the eighth is seen and regarded by the seventh as self (*ātman*) though in reality there is no such thing as self. This false idea pollutes all thoughts and gives rise to an idea of individual or personal ego or soul.

According to the Buddhist idea, all things are 'born from mind' (*manoja*) and 'consist of mind' (*manomaya*), and especially in the idealistic theory what we generally call existence proceeds from consciousness. Accordingly, everything that

exists is classified as to the nature of its origin into three
species :

First, those of false existence which are at the same time
bereft of an original substance (*adravya*), just like a ghost
that exists merely in one's imagination but not in reality.

Second, those of temporary or transitory existence, having
no permanent character (*asvabhāva*), like a house that is built
by timbers, stones, tiles, etc. It exists only by a combination
of causes, and is not self-existent. It has no permanent reality.

Third, those of true existence, that is to say, non-existent
in the highest sense of the word, bereft of all false and temporary nature (*alakṣaṇa*). This is, in truth, not non-existence
but transcendental existence.

Technically these three are called (1) character of sole
imagination (*parikalpita-lakṣaṇa*), (2) character of dependence
upon others (*paratantra-lakṣaṇa*), (3) character of ultimate
reality (*pariniṣpanna-lakṣaṇa*).

Of these the first exists in mere imagination, the second
only in causal combination, and the third as the substratum
(so to speak) of all and can be known only by a person of
supreme knowledge. This third aspect of reality must not be
interpreted too positively—it represents merely the remainder
after the elimination of the first two.

This classification of all *dharmas* is in accordance with the
viewpoint of *ens* (being), but when viewed from the point of
view of non-*ens* (non-being), these three species will be the
three of non-specific reality (*abhāva*). The first is non-
existent as regards the characteristics (*lakṣaṇa*)—no substance,
no quality at all. The second is non-existent as regards the
origination (*jāti*)—no birth, no self-existent nature, no existence though it looks like an existence. The third is non-
existent in the highest sense (*paramārtha*)—it is the true non-
reality, far transcending all specific characters and conditions
of life. This is Thusness, the true noumenon, and the true
nature of *dharmas*.

According to the Hossō School it is untainted knowledge
to realize that all the phenomenal world with all beings is but
a temporary and illusory existence manifested by ideation on

the ultimate perfect 'reality' (*pariniṣpanna*). The Middle
Path, the Golden Mean (*Madhyama-pratipād*) of the Buddha,
is now identified with Thusness which is the ultimate reality
just mentioned. How the meaning of the Middle is established
is explained by the mutual relation of the three species of
elements. The first species of imagination does not exist, and
therefore is void. The second species of causal combination does
exist, and therefore is temporarily real. The Middle Path is,
therefore, neither real nor void. Thus the ultimate 'reality'
of the third transcends voidness and reality.

Thusness transcends all the ideas of *ens* or non-*ens*. We
can say 'It exists,' but it is not a phenomenal existence. Or we
can say 'It does not exist,' but it is not a phenomenal non-
existence. In contradistinction to phenomenal existence we
call it non-*ens*, and to avoid a confusion with phenomenal
nothingness we call it *ens*. Consequently we are obliged to
designate it the ' *true* non-*ens*' and the ' *true ens*.' The true
non-*ens* is *śūnyatā* (absence of speciality) in the highest sense
and the true *ens* is *pariniṣpannatva* (ultimate reality). All this
is beyond the reach of human knowledge.

When one's knowledge and wisdom have been perfected
by self-culture, the eight consciousnesses will turn into perfect
wisdom as follows :

The first five consciousnesses will become the wisdom that
accomplishes all that should be performed.

The sixth, the sense-center (*Mano-vijñāna*), will become
the wisdom of good observation.

The seventh, the thought-center (*Manas*), will become the
wisdom of equanimity.

The eighth, the ideation-store, will become the 'wisdom of
magnificent mirror.' These constitute the fourfold wisdom of
the Buddha.

As we have seen before, the Kusha School had the theory
of 'causation through action-influence.' The Hossō School has
replaced it with the theory of 'causation through mere ideation.
This indicates a development of the causation theory, because

action is nothing but a result of ideation and the causation of an idealistic school ought to be built on the assumption of mind-action as the origin of all *dharmas.*

Thus Hossō idealism is seen to be an elucidation of the causation theory of ideation.

VII. THE SANRON SCHOOL
(THE THREE-TREATISE SCHOOL)[1]
(Sarvaśūnyavāda, Mādhyamika)

(Negativism : *Neither* Ens *nor Non*-ens *School*)
[Quasi-Mahāyānistic]

(1) PRELIMINARY

The Indian name of the Mahāyānistic Negativism is
Mādhyamika, the 'doctrine of the Middle Path,' or Śūnyatāvāda,
the 'Theory of Negativity' or 'Relativity.' In China and Japan
this school is known by the appellation of San-lun or Sanron,
the 'Three Treatises.'   There are three fundamental texts which
are devoted to the Doctrine of the Middle Path by seriously
refuting the wrong views of Brahmanism, Hīnayāna, and Mahāyāna schools other than the Sanron School.   Of these, the first
text is the *Mādhyamika Śāstra*,[2] by Nāgārjuna.[3]   Fortunately
the Sanskrit text of it has been preserved.[4]   It was translated
into Chinese by Kumārajīva.[5]   In a treatise of 400 verses
Nāgārjuna refutes certain wrong views of Hīnayāna or of
general philosophers thereby rejecting all realistic and pluralistic
ideas and indirectly establishing his monistic doctrine.

The second text is the *Dvādaśa-dvāra*, the 'Twelve Gates,'[6]
of Nāgārjuna, which is not known in Sanskrit but is preserved
in a Chinese translation.   It has twelve parts or chapters in

---

[1] San-lun.

[2] *Taishō*, No. 1564.   German translation by Max Walleser : *Die Mittlere Lehre des Nāgārjuna*, Heidelberg, 1912, English translation of chapters
1 and 25 with Candrakīrti's commentary by Th. Stcherbatsky : *The Conception of Buddhist Nirvāṇa*.   See also Walleser's *Die Mittlere Lehre, nach
der tibetischen version*, Heidelberg, 1911.

[3] 100-200 A.D.

[4] See Th. Stcherbatsky, *The Conception of Buddhist Nirvāṇa*, Leningrad, 1927, p. 65.

[5] 409 A.D.   [6] *Taishō*, No. 1568.

all, and is devoted chiefly to correcting the errors of the Mahāyānists themselves. The third text is the *Sata Śāstra*, the *'One Hundred Verse Treatise'*[7] of Āryadeva, a pupil of Nāgārjuna. This treatise of Āryadeva is mainly a refutation of the heretical views of Brahmanism.

As the Sanron School is much inclined to be negativistic idealism, there arose the more positive Shiron School (Shih-lun, Four-Treatise School) which adds a fourth text by Nāgārjuna, namely, the *Prajñāpāramitā Śāstra*[8] in which we see that he establishes his monistic view much more affirmatively than in any other text. But, all being from Nāgārjuna's hand, the general trend of metaphysical argument is much the same. As the Mādhyamika system in India had become a pure negative ontology, the Yogācāra system of Asaṅga[9] and Vasubandhu[10] came forward to restore Buddhism to the original more positive idealism. Yogācāra idealism, however, ended in a causation theory of the ideation-store, and was ontologically very passive.

In China many renowned scholars appeared and made great strides in the idealistic philosophy ; they were by no means inferior to their contemporary Indian authors. As the Sanron School carried the day, the Shiron School gave way to it and soon disappeared from the arena of *Śūnyatā* controversy.

The efforts of the Sanron School are centered on the refutation of all positive and affiirmative views of other schools which have no foundation of dialectical negation. The refutation is directed first against the wrong views of heretics, secondly against the one-sided views of Hīnayāna, and thirdly against the dogmatic views positively set forth by the Mahāyānistic authors. The ideal of the Sanron School seems to have been *Niṣprapañca,* the 'inexplicable in speech and unrealizable in thought.' The basis of all arguments is what we call the 'Four Points of Argumentation' : 1. *ens (sat)*, 2. non-

---

[7] *Taishō*, No. 1569. English translation by Giuseppe Tucci : *Pre-Diṅnāga Buddhist Texts on Logic from Chinese Sources,* Gaekwad's Oriental Series, No. XLIX, Baroda, Oriental Institute, 1929, pp. 1-89.
[8] *Taishō*, No. 1509.   [9] c. 410-500 A.D.   [10] c. 420-500 A.D.

ens (*asat*), 3. either *ens* or non-*ens*, 4. neither *ens* nor non-*ens*. If we are to answer a question put to us, we have no other way to answer than by one or more of these Four Points of Argumentation. If we express our answer it must be : 1. Yes; or 2. No; or 3. Either yes or no according to circumstances ; or 4. Neither yes nor no, i.e., having nothing to do with the question or no use answering.

Without understanding the above fundamental ideal underlying their arguments, it is by no means easy to follow the negativistic trend of this Sanron School.

(2) HISTORICAL

Prof. Stcherbatsky has indicated the following periods in the development of the Mahāyāna philosophy with special reference to Mādhyamika :

1. First Century A.D. The rise of Mahāyāna *Ālaya-vijñāna* (Store-consciousness) and *Tathatā* (Thusness), both admitted by Aśvaghoṣa.

2. Second Century A.D. The theory of universal relativity (*Śūnyatā*) formulated by Nāgārjuna and Āryadeva.

3. Third and Fourth Centuries. A gap.

4. Fifth Century. The idealistic interpretation of Asaṅga and Vasubandhu.

5. Sixth Century. A split between the idealistic and relativistic schools. Sthiramati and Dignāga representing the former, and Buddhapālita and Bhāvāviveka the latter.

6. Seventh Century. Final establishment of the Mādhyamika system in its extreme form by Candrakīrti.

The above is Prof. Stcherbatsky's list, but the gap of the third and the fourth centuries may be filled by bringing in Sāramati and Maitreya. Maitreya is a direct or indirect teacher of Asaṅga and his historicity cannot be doubted, although, because of mysterious legends surrounding him, some scholars are inclined to regard him as an imaginary person. We must reserve this problem for future studies. In any case the Indian Śūnyavāda with its idealistic reaction, Vijñānavāda,

exhibited a great flourishing of Buddhist philosophy and the
memory of its intellectual activity is forever preserved in the
history of Indian philosophy.[11]

The history of the Sanron School begins in China with the
advent of the famous Kumārajīva of Kucca ; [12] the line of
transmission is said to have been as follows :

1. Fifth Century A.D. Nāgārjuna's *Mādhyamika Śāstra*
was translated and expounded by Kumārajīva and handed
down to his pupils Tao-shêng, T'an-chi and Sêng-lang.
Sêng-lang, a distinguished successor, finally separated the
Sanron School clearly from the Jōjitsu School,[13] the Hīnayānistic Nihilism, which we have studied before. The Sanron
School owes its real foundation to Sêng-lang's work.

2. Sixth Century. Fa-lang [14] was a great leader who
had twenty-five pupils under him. Chi-tsang [15] was the out-
standing member of this group. His father had entered the
order and often took him to hear lectures by Paramārtha, the
then flourishing Indian teacher in China. Chi-tsang himself
joined the order under Fa-lang and received a special training
from him. When nineteen years of age, he lectured and
recapitulated his teacher's lectures without any mistakes, to the
great astonishment of the listeners. He lived in the Chia-
hsiang monastery and is known by the name Chia-hsiang
Tashih (great master of Chia-hsiang).

Chi-tsang wrote a commentary on the three Treatises,
a compendium of the Sanron system, a work on Mahāyāna,
and a short treatise on the twofold truth. Further, he compiled seven different works on the 'Lotus' text, two works each
on the *Mahāprajñā-pāramitā* and the *Mahāparinirvāna* and
altogether one hundred and twenty Chinese volumes (*chüans*)
of commentaries on the *Avataṅsaka* (Wreath), the *Śrīmalā*,
the *Vimala-kīrti*, the larger *Sukhāvatī*, the *Amitayur-dhyāna*,
the *Vajracchedikā*, the *Suvarṇaprabhāsa*, the *Maitreya-Sūtra*,
the *Book on Benevolent King*, etc. His literary activity,

indicating his wide reading and exhaustive references, is un-paralleled in his age or before, and it is remarkable that all was done in a period of continuous warfare between the Ch'ên and the Sui dynasties.

3. Seventh Century. Chi-tsang's Korean pupil, Ekwan (Hui-kuan) from Kauli, a state in Korea, came to Japan in 625 and taught the Sanron doctrine at the monastery Gwangōji in Nara. This is the first transmission of the school to Japan. The second transmission was by Chizō, a pupil of Ekwan. The third transmission was by Dōji, a pupil of Yüan-k'ang,[16] the author of a commentary on the three *Treatises*.

In China the Sanron School did not flourish after the rise of the Hossō School of the famous Hiuen-tsang [17] and his pupil Ki.[18] However, an Indian teacher, Sūryaprabhāsa, came to China in 679 and taught the Sanron to Hsien-shou, the author of a work on the *Twelve Gates* of Nāgārjuna. His line of transmission is called the New Sanron School to distinguish it from the Old Sanron School, a name given to that system from Kumārajīva to Chi-tsang during 409-623 A.D.

In Japan the school was never an independent institution, but the study of its doctrine has been ardently continued even to the present time because it is indispensable for a student of Buddhism as one of the chief objects of Buddhist learning and a strong weapon of dialectic argument, as well as the theoretical basis underlying many of the more positive and active schools of Buddhism in Japan today.

(3) PHILOSOPHICAL

The teaching of the Sanron School has three aspects : 1. the refutation of erroneous views and the elucidation of right views ; 2. the distinction between worldly truth and the higher truth ; 3. the Middle Path (*Madhyama-pratipād*) of the Eightfold Negation.

What the school aims at is the absolute *Sūnyatā*, i.e.,

[16] c. 649 A.D.   [17] Hsüan-tsang. 596-664.   [18] K'uei-chi, 632-682.

nothing 'acquirable' (*aprāptavya-śūnyatā*), i.e., the right view of 'non-acquisition' (*aprāpti-tva*). Generally speaking, when one error is rejected by refutation, another view is grasped and held as right and as a natural outcome of it. In the case of this school, however, a selection is also an attachment to or an acquisition of one view and is therefore to be rejected. The refutation itself of a wrong view ought to be, at the same time, the elucidation of a right view. That is to say, refutation is identical with elucidation, for there is to be nothing acquired. This is one of the peculiarities of the school.

However, the two terms are retained separately for practical purposes, since refutation is necessary to save all beings who are drowned in the sea of attachment while elucidation is also important in order to propagate the teaching of the Buddha.

Such refutation is to be complete. First, views based on acquisition are all refuted. Also, views such as the *ātman* (self) theory of the Brahmanic philosophers, the pluralistic doctrines of the Buddhist Abhidharma schools (Vaibhāṣika, Kośa, etc.) and the dogmatic principles of Mahāyāna teachers are never passed without a detailed refutation. The Realistic ('All exists') and the Nihilistic ('Nothing exists') are equally condemned.

Among the Chinese Buddhistic views, Hui-kuan's view that divides the teachings of the Buddha into two teachings and five periods, Chi-tsang's view of unity of the two truths, worldly and higher, and Sêng-chao's [19] as well as Fa-yün's [20] view of diversity of the two truths are all to be mercilessly attacked if they are too much adhered to. On the positive side, however, this school accepts the right man and the right teaching. Nāgārjuna is regarded as the right personage because of the Buddha's prophesy concerning his appearance.[21] The right teaching is the Middle Path devoid of name and character where no speech or thought can reach. It transcends all the points of dispute such as 'the four forms of argument and the

[19] 384-414.   [20] 467-529.
[21] In the *Laṅkāvatāra Sūtra*.

hundred negations,' thus even going further than Yājñavalkya's famous theory of 'neti, neti' (not this ! not this !) in the Upaniṣads.[22]

The truth can be attained only by negation or refutation of wrong views within and without Buddhism and of errors of both the Great and Small Vehicles. When retaining wrong views or error, one will be blind to reason. How can a blind man get a right view without which the two extremes can never be avoided ? The end of verbal refutation is the dawn of the Middle Path. Refutation—and refutation only—can lead to the ultimate truth.

The Middle Path, which is devoid of name and character, cannot be named and characterized, yet we are forced to designate it somehow for the sake of distinction. Therefore it is called 'the right (as) elucidated.'

Two aspects of right can be assumed : right in substance and right in function. The right in substance is the transcendental truth which is beyond both the higher and the worldly truths, while the right in function is the twofold truth, the higher and the worldly. In the *Mādhyamika Śāstra* it is said that the Buddhas of the past proclaimed their teachings to the people by means of the twofold truth. It was by the worldly truth (*saṃvṛti-satya*) that the Buddha preached that all elements have come into being through causation ; but it is by the higher truth (*paramārtha-satya*) that all elements are of universal relativity (*sarva-śūnyatā*) or Void. After all, the twofold truth is proclaimed in order to lead people to a right way.

For those who are attached to Nihilism the theory of existence is taught in the way of the worldly truth, and for those who are attached to Realism the doctrine of non-existence is proclaimed in the way of the higher truth in order to teach them the nameless and characterless state which is 'right in substance.'

Though we may speak of existence, it is temporary and not fixed. Even non-existence (Void) is temporary and not

[22] *Bṛhadāraṇyaka Upaniṣad*, II, 3, 6; III, 9, 26; IV, 4, 22; IV, 6, 15.

fixed. So there is neither a real existence nor a real Void.
Being or non-being is only an outcome of causal relation and,
therefore, unreal. Thus the ideal of the two extremes of being
and non-being is removed. Therefore, when we deal with the
worldly truth, the phenomenal world can be assumed without
disturbing the noumenal state. When we deal with the higher
truth, the noumenal state can be attained without stirring the
world of mere name. Non-existence is at the same time existence, and existence in turn is non-existence. Form or matter is
at the same time the Void, and the Void is at the same time
form or matter.

Thus the noumenon of all *dharmas* is without specific
character.

It may be seen, therefore, that the twofold truth is taught
only for the sake of convenience in instruction. The present
Sanron School regards the theory of twofold truth to be word-
teaching, i.e., teaching for an explicatory purpose, while other
Mahāyānists take it to be the principle-teaching, i.e., the twofold truth itself is the principle which the Buddha has taught.
The question of differences is : whether the truth is the means
or the object. The Sanron School takes it to be the means.
This is another peculiarity of the school.

The theory of the eightfold negation is of similar purport.
It is set forth by Nāgārjuna in his dedicatory verse of the
Mādhyamika Śāstra, which runs as follows :

> "The perfect Buddha,
> The foremost of all teachers I salute,
> He has proclaimed
> The principle of (universal) relativity.
> 'Tis like Blissful (Nirvāṇa),
> Quiescence of plurality.
> There nothing disappears,
> Nor anything appears,
> Nothing has an end,
> Nor is there anything eternal,
> Nothing is identical (with itself),
> Nor is there anything differentiated,

Nothing moves,
Neither hither nor thither." [23]

This eightfold negation is formulated in Chinese as follows :

> No production
> No extinction
> No annihilation
> No permanence
> No unity
> No diversity
> No coming
> No departure

Thus all specific features of becoming are denied. The fact that there are just eight negations has no special purport ; this is meant to be a wholesale negation. It may be taken as a crosswise sweeping away of all eight errors attached to the world of becoming, or a reciprocal rejection of the four pairs of one-sided views, or a lengthwise general thrusting aside of the errors one after the other—for instance, refuting the idea of appearing (birth) by the idea of disappearance ; the idea of disappearance by the idea of motion hither ; this idea of motion hither by the idea of motion thither ; this last idea by the idea of permanence ; permanence by destruction (end) ; destruction by unity ; unity by diversity ; diversity by appearance ; and so on.

In this way all discriminations of oneself and another or this and that are done away with. Therefore a refutation of a wrong or one-sided view is at the same time an elucidation of a right view. When right is opposed to wrong, it is an antithetic right, i.e., right as opposed to wrong. When wrong is utterly refuted, there will be the right devoid of antithesis, i.e., transcendental right. When the idea of right or wrong is altogether thrown aside, there will be the absolute right, i.e., the truth.

[23] Th. Stcherbatsky, *The Conception of Buddhist Nirvāṇa*, p. 69

Right is the middle. The middle versus two extremes is antithetic middle or relative middle. The middle, after the two extremes have been totally refuted, is the middle devoid of extremes. When the idea of two extremes is removed altogether, it is the absolute middle. Thus the absolute right is the absolute middle.

When the absolute middle condescends to lead people at large, it becomes a temporary middle or truth. We have thus the fourfold Middle Path.

Out of a practical necessity to guide people another gradation theory is adopted. This gradation theory will be explained in four stages below :

1. When the theory of being is opposed to the theory of non-being, the former is regarded as the worldly truth and the latter the higher truth.

2. When the theories of being and non-being are opposed to those of neither being nor non-being, the former are regarded as the worldly truth and the latter the higher truth.

3. If the four opposed theories just mentioned together become the worldly truth, the yet higher views denying them all will be regarded as the higher truth.

4. If the theories expressed in the last stage become the worldly truth, the denial of them all will be the higher truth.

Thus, however high we proceed, if we adhere to one view or a group of views, we shall meet their denial again and again. Negation alone can lead us to the door of the absolute truth. In short, what we are driving at is the Principle of Non-acquisition (*aprāptitva*) which is attained by the doctrine of universal negation expounded crosswise by the *eightfold nega-tion* and lengthwise by the *four stages of the twofold truth*. It is in fact an infinite negation until the tinge of worldly truth is utterly washed off. Therefore, the ultimate truth thus arrived at by dialectical method is called either the Middle Path of the Eightfold Negation or the Middle Path of the Two-fold Truth.

Further, the Middle Path of the Twofold Truth is ex-

pounded in several complicated ways. If one maintains the
theory of the real production and the real extinction of the phenomenal world, it is called the one-sided worldly truth. If, on
the other hand, one adheres to the theory of the non-production
and non-extinction of the phenomenal world, it is called the
one-sided higher truth. If one sees that there is a temporary
production and a temporary extinction of phenomenon, it is
the middle path of worldly truth. If one sees that there is
neither temporary production nor temporary extinction, it is
the middle path of the higher truth. If one considers that
there is neither production-and-extinction nor non-production-
and-non-extinction, it is the middle path elucidated by the
union of both popular and higher truths.

The above are called *the five terms and the three middle
paths*. It is the 'true state of Middle Path.'

The Sanron School divides the sacred teaching into two
Piṭakas—Śrāvaka and Bodhisattva, i.e., smaller and larger
vehicles (Hīnayāna and Mahāyāna). The sacred teaching is
also divided into three *dharma-cakra* (the wheels of the law) :
1. the root wheel is the *Avataṅsaka* (Wreath) ; 2. the branch
wheel is all Hīnayāna and Mahāyāna texts ; 3. the wheel that
contracts all the branches so as to bring them back to the root,
i.e., the 'Lotus.'

The root wheel was first preached for *Bodhisattvas* soon
after the Buddha's Enlightenment. It was the truth gained by
the Buddha in his Enlightenment, but this Buddha-*yāna* was
too profound for people to understand. Then the Buddha
began to propound the three *yānas* (*śrāvaka, pratyekabuddha*
and *bodhisattva*) to lead up to the Buddha-*yāna*.

'*Sūnya*' negatively means 'Void,' but positively 'relative,'
i.e., 'devoid of independent reality' or 'devoid of specific
character.' Thus *Śūnyatā* is non-entity and at the same time
'relativity,' i.e., the entity only as in causal relation. The idea
of relativity seems to be strongly presented in the Indian
Mādhyamika School. In the Chinese San-lun School, too, we
have the term 'causal union' as a synonym of the Middle Path,
absence of nature (*svabhāva-abhāva*), *Dharma* nature
(*Dharma-svabhāva*) and Void. These words doubtless con-

vey a similar idea, for it is well known that the causal origination is called *Śūnyatā*, but I cannot definitely state whether
the Chinese San-lun teachers went so far as to treat casual
relation (*pratitya-samutpāda*) as an exact synonym of
Śūnyatā or not. However, it is certain that the Chinese did
not make much of the idea of relativity, because the Chinese
equivalent of *Śūnyatā, K'ung*, connotes all the necessary phases
of meaning : first, Void in the sense of antithesis of being,
second, the state of being devoid of specific character (*svabhāva
śūnyatā, svalakṣana-abhāva*) ; third, Void in the highest sense,
or transcendental Void, i.e., all oppositions synthesized,
(*paramārtha-śūnyatā*) ; fourth, the absolute Void (*atyanta-
śūnyatā*) ; and several others.

The word 'Void' is not entirely fitting and is often misleading, yet, if we look for another word, there will be none better.
It is, after all, an idea dialectically established. It is nameless
(*akhyāti*) and characterless (*alakṣana*). It is simply the negation of an independent reality or the negation of specific
character. Besides the negation there is nothing else. The
Sanron system is on that account a negativism, the theory of
negation. All things are devoid of independent reality, that
is, they are only of relative existence, or relativity in the sense
of what is ultimately unreal but phenomenally real. ٠

(4) RÉSUMÉ

The object of negativism is the realization of perfect
wisdom. Wisdom here is opposed to all partial knowledge,
or rather is inclusive of all partial knowledge. Thus, by not
clinging to the knowledge of special things, one can attain perfect
wisdom ; and by not adhering to one thing or another, one can
attain perfect freedom. Perfect emptiness or Void compre-
hends all things. Emptiness is different from space, for space
is what anything can occupy. The doctrine of Void of this
school is in reality Non-Void, i.e., not one-sided, abstracted
Void, because it can comprehend anything whatever.

Denial or refutation is only the method of obtaining the

white-paper state instead of the colored-paper state which we generally possess, cling to and cannot get rid of. Again, there is the principle of non-acquisition.

In fine, the training by negation means having no partial knowledge, dwelling in no special view, holding on to no abstracted Void, adhering to no special attainment, assuming no special characteristics and expecting no special interest or any special merit.

VIII. THE KEGON SCHOOL
(AVATAŃSAKA, THE 'WREATH' SCHOOL)[1]

(Totalism)
[Mahāyānistic]

(1) PRELIMINARY

Kegon means 'flower-ornament' and is considered a translation of the Sanskrit term '*Avatańsaka*' denoting a wreath or garland. It is the name of a *Sūtra* in which the mystic doctrine of the Buddha Mahāvairocana[2] is minutely described. The scripture is said to have been preached by the Buddha soon after his Enlightenment, but none of those listening to him could understand a word of it as if they were deaf and dumb. Therefore he began anew to preach the easy four Āgamas (discourses) and other doctrines.

What he preached first was what he had realized in his Enlightenment. The truth he had conceived was proclaimed exactly as it was. An advanced personage such as a *Bodhisattva* (saintly person) might have understood him, but an ordinary person could not grasp his ideas at all.

The *Avatańsaka Sūtra*[3] is represented in Chinese by three recensions, in eighty, sixty, and forty Chinese volumes. Of the first two we do not possess their Sanskrit original. For the last, the forty-volume text, we have its original which is called *Gaṇḍa-vyūha*, now published in Japan.[4]

In the text, a pilgrimage undertaken by the youth Sudhana to visit fifty-three worthies, religious and secular, is described. The object of the pilgrimage was to realize the principle of *Dharma-dhātu* (Realm of Principle or Elements).

In India the Avatańsaka School, as an independent school,

---

[1] Hua-yen.   [2] To be described in Chapter X.
[3] *Taishō*, Nos. 278, 279 and 293.
[4] By H. Izumi of the Ōtani University, Kyoto.

is unknown. However, the story of Sudhana's pilgrimage is minutely told in the *Divya-avadāna*, and his journey is depicted in detailed sculptures in Java.

In the *Sūtra* it is stated that the Bodhisattva Mañjuśrī is living on the Ch'ingliang Mountain in China, and is proclaiming the law at all times. This Ch'ingliang Mountain is identified with the Wut'ai Mountain of China. The name Wut'ai (five heights) itself seems to indicate Pañca-śikha (five top-knots), a name of Mañjuśrī. The great Avataṅsaka Monastery of that mountain is the shrine sacred to that Bodhisattva. Such a belief in India as well as in China seems to go back to the fifth century A.D. or still earlier.

In 477 A.D. an Imperial prince went up that mountain and burned himself to death as a sign of his ardent desire to meet the Bodhisattva. Later, in 735 A.D., an Indian priest, Bodhisena, with a Malay-Indian musician named Fa-triet, came to China and went up there to see Mañjuśrī. They passed on to Japan in search of that saint when they were told that he was not on the mountain then but was sojourning in the Far East. At their arrival in Ōsaka they were received by Gyōgi Bosatsu (= *Bodhisattva*), a learned Japanese priest who is generally called Bosatsu because Bodhisena and Fa-triet took him to be Mañjuśrī himself. The two men were given some Imperial grants and were happily settled in Nara. Bodhisena, as the officiating priest, performed the dedication ceremony of the Grand Buddha of Nara and shared the honot of becoming one of the founders of the Tōdaiji Monastery.[5] He taught the 'Wreath' doctrine while in the Daianji Monastery, Nara.

The name 'Manch'u' of the last dynasty of China is said to have been an abbreviation of Mañjuśrī. In the letters from Nepal to the Chinese court the Chinese emperors are addressed 'Śrī, Śrī, Śrī Mañjuśrī.' The official name of the dynasty was Ch'ing which itself is said to have been taken from the designation of Ch'ingliang Mountain. Even now Wut'ai

___

[5] There were four among the founders ; see section 2.

B.—8

Mountain is one of the most sacred spots of all the places connected with Buddhism in China.

(2) HISTORICAL

Prior to the Kegon School there was in China a school named Ti-lun which was founded on Vasubandhu's commen- tary on the *Daśa-bhūmi Sūtra*. The text was translated into Chinese in 508-512 A.D. by Bodhiruci,[6] Ratnamati[7] and Buddhaśānta,[8] all from India.

There appeared in time a split in the Ti-lun School. Tao-ch'ung, a pupil of Bodhiruci, lived in the north district of Lo-yang and exercised a great influence on the people, while Hui-kuang,[9] a pupil of Ratnamati, lived in the south district of the capital and was equally influential in his religious activities. The line of the former was called 'the Branch of the Northern Path,' and that of the latter 'the Branch of the Southern Path.'

As the *Daśa-bhūmi Sūtra* was annotated by Vasubandhu,[10] the *Ālaya* (store) Consciousness as well as the first six sense-consciousnesses were expounded in it. The relation between these consciousnesses and their connection with Thusness (*Tathatā*) or the so-called 'Matrix of Tathāgata' (Thuscome) were not expressly taught. On this account the two Indian teachers differed from each other in their opinions, and the two lines went so far as to take a separate way.

The Ti-lun (Daśa-bhūmi) School

Northern Path	Southern Path
Tao-ch'ung, a pupil of Bodhiruci.	Hui-kuang, a pupil of Ratnamati.
Ālaya-consciousness is un-real (false) and separate from Thusness.	*Ālaya*-consciousness is real (true) and identical with Thusness.

Kegon School

---

[6] 508-515.   [7] 508.   [8] 520-539.   [9] 468-537.   [10] 420-500 A.D.

At the outset the Northern Path seemed to have flourished, as the founder Tao-ch'ung is said to have had more than ten thousand pupils, he himself having been honored as one of the six Great Virtuous Men of the Ch'ên dynasty and later as one of the ten Great Virtuous Men of the Sui dynasty. But for some reason his successors did not succeed so well.

In the Southern Path, Hui-kuang seemed to have been more a scholar than a propagandist. He was well versed in Sanskrit, having studied under Buddhabhadra and Ratnamati, and understood the points of dispute as to the *Dasa-bhūmi* text. He had ten able pupils among whom Fa-shang (495-580) was the most prominent. The literary activity of his pupils also was worthy of admiration. However, when Tu-shun, the nominal founder of the Kegon School, made his appearance on the scene, the best workers of this line were all attracted around him. Or, we can say at best the Ti-lun School was finally united with the new rising school of the Hua-yen (Kegon, Avataṅsaka, ' Wreath ') philosophy.

The Kegon School, having absorbed the Ti-lun School, opened a flourishing period of Chinese Buddhism. The foundation-stone of the Kegon doctrine was laid once and for all by the famous Tu-shun. His priestly name was Fa-shun, but as his family name was Tu, people generally called him Tu-shun. He was famous as a miracle-worker, and Emperor T'ai-tsung of T'ang invited him to his palace and gave him the title of 'the Venerable Imperial Heart.' He was believed to be an incarnation of Mañjuśrī.

His able pupil, Chih-yen (602-668), the succeeding patriarch of the school, received from him all the culture of contemplation. He wrote several important works on the basis of his teacher's instructions. One of his pupils, I-hsiang (625-702) from Simla, a state of Korea, returned home in 668 and founded the first Kegon School in Korea. But the third patriarch, Fa-tsang (643-712), was the real founder of this school, for he was responsible for the final systematization of the philosophy. His activity was not only in literary work but also in translations and lectures. When in 680 Divākara (613-687) brought the *Gaṇḍa-vyūha* (forty-volume text) to China, Fa-tsang went to him, made several inquiries about the doctrine and requested him to translate the section on the pilgrimage of the youth Sudhana which was wanting in the hitherto translated sixty-volume text. When Śikṣānanda (652-670) of Khotan brought the eighty-volume text, Fa-tsang assisted him in his translation. He further helped I-ching (635-713), that famous traveler in India, and Devaprajñā (who was in China during 689-691) in the work of translation. In 704 he lectured on the Kegon School for the Usurper Queen Wu-hou. The subject-matter of his lecture then was the 'tenfold profundity' and 'sixfold special nature,' to which we shall return soon. His profound lectures were often accompanied by witty examples. His works in commentaries and dictionaries are of eighteen kinds in more than one hundred Chinese volumes. His last commentary on the eighty-volume text is said to have been left in an unfinished state. His posthumous or honorary titles are Hsien-Shou (Head of the Wise) and Kuo-i (One in the State).

One of Fa-tsang's pupils, Shên-hsiang of Simla, came to Japan in the twelfth year of the Tempyō Era (A.D. 740) and lectured on the school for the first time. Ch'êng-kuan (760-820), another pupil, was honored as the fourth patriarch for his earnest effort in refuting the heresy of Hui-yüan, also a pupil of Fa-tsang, and restoring their teacher's doctrine to its original purity.

Another pupil, Tao-hsüan, came to Japan in 730 and taught the doctrine. Bodhisena from Central India arrived in Nara at the same time or earlier (probably 726) and taught the Avataṅsaka doctrine.

Emperor Shōmu (724-748) intended to govern Japan by the totalistic principle of the Kegon School. He built the Tōdaiji, or the Eastern Great Monastery, and in it he installed the gigantic bronze statue of Mahāvairocana (the Great Sun Buddha). This monastery was to be the Sanctuary for Permanently Preaching the Avataṅsaka Doctrine. Four founders of the monastery are recognized, namely, Shōmu the Emperor, Bodhisena the Brahman prelate, Gyōgi the *Bodhisattva*, and Rōben the abbot.

In spite of these memorable monumental works of the

Nara period, people of the time were soon aware of the fact that the religious institution and the political government should not be confounded. At present the Tōdaiji is the only prominent monastery which belongs to the Kegon School. In the Kamakura period Myōe, a learned priest of Toganoo, Kyoto, endeavoured to establish a new school of the Avataṅsaka, and later in the Tokugawa period Hōtan, a scholar of the Kegon doctrine, made an effort to have a special institute. But neither of them succeeded. However, the study of the Avataṅsaka doctrine is actively pursued in all the centers of Buddhist learning in Japan even today.

The Kegon School

China		Japan
Hua-yen School		Kegon School
1. Tu-shun (557-640)	= =	Tojun
2. Chih-yen (602-668)	= =	Chigen
3. Fa-tsang (643-712)	= =	Hōzō
4. Ch'êng-kuan (c. 760-820)	= =	Chōkwan
	5. Shinshō (Chên-hsiang)	
	(to Japan in 736)	
	6. Rōben (689-772)	

(3) PHILOSOPHICAL

The Totalistic principle of the Kegon School was developed chiefly in China. It is indeed a glory of the learned achievements of Chinese Buddhism. The Kegon School stands, as other schools do, on the basis of the theory of causation by mere ideation, but as held in the Kegon School the theory has a peculiarity. It is designated 'the theory of universal causation of *Dharma-dhātu*' (Realm of Principle or Element of the Elements). The term '*Dharma-dhātu*' is sometimes used as a synonym of the ultimate truth. Therefore, the translation ' the Element of the Elements ' is quite fitting. But at other times it means the universe, 'the Realm of All Elements.'

The double meaning, the universe and the universal principle, must always be borne in mind whenever we use the term. Either meaning will serve as the name of the causation theory.

The theory of causation by *Dharma-dhātu* is the climax of all the causation theories ; it is actually the conclusion of the theory of causal origination, as it is the universal causation and is already within the theory of universal immanence, pansophism, cosmotheism, or whatever it may be called. The causation theory, as we have seen before, was explained first by action-influence, but as action originates in ideation, we had, secondly, the theory of causation by ideation-store. Since the ideation-store as the repository of seed-energy must originate from something else, we had, thirdly, the causation theory explained by the expression 'Matrix of the Thus-come' (*Tathāgata-garbha*) or Thusness. This curious term means that which conceals the Buddha. Because of concealment it has an impure side, but because of Buddhahood it has a pure side as well. It is a synonym of Thusness (*Tathātva* or *Tathatā*, not Thisness or Thatness=*tattva*) which has in its broadest sense both pure and impure nature. Through the energy of pure and impure causes it manifests the specific character of becoming as birth and death, or as good and evil. Thusness pervades all beings, or better, all beings are in the state of Thusness. Here, as the fourth stage, the causation theory by *Dharma-dhātu* (universe) is set forth. It is the causation by all beings themselves and is the creation of the universe itself, or we can call it the causation by the common action-influence of all beings. Intensively considered the universe will be a manifestation of Thusness or the Matrix of *Tathāgata* (Thus-come). But extensively considered it is the causation of the universe by the universe itself and nothing more.

Dharma-dhātu—in its double meaning as Realm of Principle and Element of all Elements—is synonymous with Matrix of the Thus-come (*Tathāgata-garbha*) and also with the universe or the actual world, i.e., the realm of all elements. This causation can be taken in the double sense accordingly. The causal origination (*pratitya-samutpāda*) of *Dharma-dhātu* is thus the theory that the universe is universally co-relative, generally interdependent and mutually originating, having no single being existing independently. In the Twelve-Divisioned Cycle of Causation 'dependence on antecedent' was taught and, therefore, it was a dependence in time sequence. In this universal causation, on the other hand, it is a dependence of all upon one another and, therefore, it is meant in a spatial sense.

According to the critical classification of the Buddhist teaching set forth by this school, there are five aspects of teaching subdivided further into ten doctrines. During the early flourishing periods of Chinese Buddhism many critical divisions of Buddhism were proposed, but, as they are confusing, I have not given any of them. Here for the first time we shall have a clear exhaustive classification, and I consider it worthwhile to review it in considerable detail.

Critical Classification of Buddhism

1. The Doctrine of the Small Vehicle (Hīnayāna).

This refers to the teaching of the four Āgamas.[11] Although they deny the existence of the personal self (*pudgala-śūnyatā*), they are realistic and admit the existence of all separate elements (*dharma*). They hold that Nirvāṇa is total extinction, and yet they do not understand much of the unreality of all elements (*dharma-śūnyatā*), e.g., the Kusha (Realistic) School. As to the causation theory, they attribute it to action-influence. They can be designated the small vehicle for the foolish.

2. The Elementary Doctrine of the Great Vehicle (Mahāyāna).

Two grades are distinguished in it. First, the elementary doctrine based on the specific character of all elements (*dharma-lakṣaṇa*), e.g., Hossō (Idealistic) School ; second, the elementary doctrine based on negation of all elements (*dharma-*

---

[11] In Pāli there are 5 *Nikāyas* or divisions : 1. *Digha*, 2. *Majjhima*. 3. *Anguttara*, 4. *Samyutta*, 5. *Khuddaka*. Chinese *Āgamas* (Discourses) have only the first four.

śūnyatā), e.g., Sanron (Negativistic) School. Since neither admits the existence of the Buddha-nature (*Buddha-svabhāva*) in all beings, both are considered to be elementary.

The former (Hossō) sets forth the theory of causation by ideation-store (*Ālaya-vijñāna*) on the basis of phenomenal characteristics (*lakṣaṇa*) and does not recognize the unity of fact and principle. Also, since it maintains the basic distinction of five species of men, it does not admit that all men can attain Buddhahood. The latter (Sanron), on the other hand, holds the one-sided view of Void on the basis of 'own nature' (*svabhāva-alakṣaṇa*) or no abiding nature. But admitting the unity of being and non-being, it affirms that men of the three vehicles (*yāna*), and the five species (*gotra*), are all able to attain Buddhahood. In making this point the Sanron (Mādhyamika) School is treading one step within the final doctrine of Mahāyāna which is as follows :

3. The Final Doctrine of the Great Vehicle (Mahāyāna).

This is the teaching of Thusness of all elements (*dharmatathatā*), asserting that all living beings have Buddha-nature and can attain Buddhahood, according to the teaching found in the *Laṅkāvatāra* text, the *Mahāparinirvāṇa* text and the *Awakening of Faith.*[12]   (The Tendai School adheres to this doctrine).

By this teaching the Ultimate Truth of Mahāyāna is expounded. Therefore, it is called the Doctrine of Maturity. As it agrees with reality, it is also called the True Doctrine. In the elementary doctrine fact and principle were always separate, while in this final doctrine fact is always identified with principle, nay, the two are one. The causation theory by Matrix of the Thuscome is special to this doctrine. It is also called the theory of causation by Thusness (*Tathatā*).

4. The Abrupt Doctrine of the Great Vehicle.

This means the training without word or order, directly appealing to one's own insight, by virtue of which one can

---

[12] *Taishō*, No. 670. English translation by D. T. Suzuki : *Laṅkāvatāra Sūtra*, London, 1932 ; *Taishō*, No. 1527 ; See footnote on p. 84.

attain perfect enlightenment all at once. All words and speech will stop at once. Reason will present itself in its purity and action will always comply with wisdom and knowledge—if thought ceases to arise in his mind, the man is a Buddha. Such an attainment may be gained through silence as shown by Vimalakīrti, a saintly layman of Vaisāli, or through meditation (Zen) as in the case of Bodhidharma, an Indian priest and the founder of the Chinese Zen School. It teaches no special causation theory because it has no method of teaching of its own.

5. The Round Doctrine of the Great Vehicle.

Two grades of the round or perfect doctrine are set forth.

A. One Vehicle (Ekayāna) of the 'Identical Doctrine' in which the One Vehicle is taught in an identical or similar method with the other three Vehicles. The three Vehicles recognized by the Kegon School are different from the ordinary three. They are : 1. the Small (Hīnayāna). 2. the Gradua (a. the elementary ; b. the final Mahāyāna). 3. the Abrupt (e.g., Zen practice of Mahāyāna).

The One Vehicle of the Kegon is inclusive of all Vehicles. For convenience the three Vehicles are taught to prepare the aspirants. The three flow out of the One Vehicle and are taught in the identical method as the one. In the Identical Doctrine the two aspects are distinguished : one within the meditation and the other outside of meditation. The meditation into which the Buddha entered before he preached the Avataṅsaka doctrine was the *Samādhi* of Sea-impression (*Sāgaramudrā*) in which all the doctrines that were to be preached during his lifetime and all beings that were to be converted during fifty years of his career were all at once reflected, just as all images are reflected in a quiet sea. The other doctrines were preached when he was out of that meditation.

The Avataṅsaka doctrine is the representation of the Buddha's Enlightenment as it was conceived and experienced by him. The other discourses were preached to suit the occasion. The Kegon School is thus to be taken as the most fundamental of all.

B. One Vehicle of the 'Distinct Doctrine' in which the

One Vehicle is set forth entirely distinct or independent from the other Vehicles, as in the case of the teaching of the Kegon School in which the doctrine of the world of totalistic harmony mutually relating and penetrating is set forth. The One Vehicle is higher than the other three. The One Vehicle is real while the three are considered as temporary.

Thus analyzing the whole teaching of the Buddha, the Kegon School was founded and systematized. The object of its teaching is the establishment of a harmonious whole of all beings having the perfectly enlightened Buddha at the center. The totalistic principle of the Avataṅsaka is further based on the theory of selflessness (*anātman*), on the causation theory by pure ideation, and on the belief in the existence of Buddha-nature dormant in every being.

Further, ten tenets are enumerated as the subdivisions of the five doctrines. They are :

1. The existence of both *ātman* (self) and *dharma* (element), as admitted by the unusual—almost non-Buddhistic —Vātsiputrīya School.

2. The existence of *dharma* and the non-existence of *ātman*, the reality of the three time-periods (past, present and future), and the reality of all *dharmas*. This tenet is admitted by the Sarvāstivāda School.

3. All *dharmas* devoid of motion hither and thither, the reality of present and unreality of past and future, as admitted by the Mahāsaṅghika School.

4. The present possessed of both unreality and reality. In the reality of the present the five *skandhas* (aggregates)—form. perception, conception, volition and consciousness—are real, but the twelve *ayātanas* (six senses and six sense-organs) and the eighteen *dhātus* (six sense-organs, six sense-objects and six senses) are temporary or unreal, as admitted by the Prajñaptivāda School.

5. The popular truth (*laukika* or *saṃvṛti-satya*) as false but the higher truth (*lokottara* or *paramārtha-satya*) as real as admitted by the Lokottaravāda School.

6. All *dharmas* as nominal or mere names (*ākhyāti mātra* or *nāma mātra*). All elements are simply names and

of no reality, as admitted by the Ekottiya School.

7. All *dharmas* as void, or devoid of specific character (*sarva dharma śūnyatā* or *sarva śūnyatā*), as taught by the *Prajñāpāramitā* text or as admitted by the Sanron (Mādhyamika) School. This is the teaching of the Mahāyāna denying specific character (*lakṣaṇa abhāva*) with the two elementary doctrines.

8. The attribute of Thusness not empty or 'void.' Thusness, though it is without any determinate character, is possessed of innumerable potentialities from which all determinate or differentiated *dharmas* are manifested. This tenet is admitted in the final doctrine of Mahāyāna (the Tendai School) and in the *Awakening of Faith*.

9. The stage in which the distinction between subjective ideation and objective reality is entirely removed, the coalescence of subject and object, the state without specific character and without sense and thought. All the ' Abrupt Doctrines ' belong to it, especially the Zen School.

10. The 'round and bright doctrine' in which all attributes exist in a harmonious whole, as in the Round Doctrine of the Kegon School.

A critical division of the interpretation of the Buddha's teaching was proposed first by Ki (K'uei-chi, 632-682), a pupil of Hiuen-tsang (Hsüan-tsang, 596-664). It was a classification into eight doctrines. The present division into ten tenets is a modification of it. Of these ten, one to six are Hīnayāna, but five and six can be said to be semi-Mahāyāna, and seven to ten are the true Mahāyāna doctrines.

The fourfold universe peculiar to the Kegon School roughly corresponds to the five critical divisions of the Buddha's teaching. The universe is fourfold as follows :

1. The world of reality, the factual, practical world. It represents the Realistic Doctrine (Hīnayāna).

2. The world of principle or theoretical world. It is represented by the Sanron and Hossō Schools which teach that principle is separate from facts.

3. The world of principle and reality united, or the ideal world realized. It represents the doctrine of the *Awakening of*

Faith and the Tendai doctrine which teach the identity of fact and principle.

4. The world of all realities or practical facts interwoven or identified in perfect harmony. It is represented by the Kegon School which teaches that all distinct facts or realities will, and ought to, form a harmonious whole by mutual penetration and mutual identification so as to realize the ideal world of One-true.

Generally speaking it should not be difficult to make practice adapted to theory, but such being the evil of men, some make too much of theory while others make too much of practice. So a rational solution becomes necessary. Moreover, in the world of realities (fact) practice often goes against practice, fact against fact, business against business, individual against individual, class against class, nation against nation. Such is the feature of the world of individualism and thus the whole world goes to pieces. Mere collectivism or solidarity will not prevent the evil of life. To harmonize such a state of being and to make all things go smoothly, the world of mutual reliance or interdependence ought to be created. Such an ideal world is called 'the fact and fact world perfectly harmonized.'

To elucidate the possibility of such an ideal world, the 'Ten Profound Theories' are set forth :

1. The theory of co-relation, in which all things have co-existence and simultaneous rise. All are co-existent not only in relation to space but also in relation to time. There is no distinction of past, present and future, each of them being inclusive of the other. Distinct as they are and separated as they seem to be in time, all beings are united to make one entity—from the universal point of view.

2. The theory of perfect freedom in which all beings 'broad and narrow' commune with each other without any obstacle. The power of all beings as to intension and extension is equally limitless. One action, however small, includes all actions. One and all are commutable freely and uninterruptedly.

3. The theory of mutual penetration of dissimilar things. All dissimilar existences have something in common. Many

in one, one in many, and all in unity.

4. The theory of freedom—i.e., freedom from ultimate distinctions—in which all elements are mutually identified. It is a universal identification of all beings. Mutual identification is, in fact, self-negation. Identifying oneself with another, one can synthesize with another. Negating oneself and identifying oneself with another constitute synthetical identification. This is a peculiar theory or practice of Mahāyāna. It is applied to any theory or practice. Two opposed theories or incompatible facts are often identified. Often a happy solution of a question is arrived at by the use of this method. As the result of mutual penetration and mutual identification, we have the concept, One in All, All in One, One behind All, All behind One, the great and small, or the high and low, moving harmoniously together. Even the humblest partaking of the work in peace, no one stands separately or idependently alone. It is the world of perfect harmony.

5. The theory of complementarity by which the hidden and the manifested will make the whole by mutual supply. It one is inside, the other will be outside, or vice versa. Both complementing each other will complete one entity.

6. The theory of construction by mutual penetration of minute and abstruse matters. Generally speaking, the more minute or abstruse a thing is, the more difficult it is to be conceived. Things minute or abstruse beyond a man's comprehension must also be realizing the theory of one-in-many and many-in-one as in No. 3.

7. The theory of inter-reflection, as in the region surrounded by the Indra net (a net decorated with a bright stone on each knot of the mesh) where the jewels reflect brilliance upon each other, according to which the real facts of the world are mutually permeating and reflecting.

8. The theory of elucidating the truth by factual illustrations. Truth is manifested in fact and fact is the source of enlightening.

9. The theory of 'variously completing ten time-periods creating one entity.' Each of past, present and future contains three periods, thus making up nine periods which altogether

form one period—nine and one, ten periods in all. The ten periods, all distinct yet mutually penetrating, will complete the one-in-all principle. All other theories are concerned chiefly with the mutual penetration in 'horizontal plane,' but this theory is concerned with the 'vertical connection,' or time, meaning that all beings separated along the nine periods, each complete in itself, are, after all, interconnected in one period— the one period formed by the nine.

10. The theory of completion of virtues by which the chief and the retinue work together harmoniously and brightly. If one is the chief, all others will work as his retinue, i.e., according to the one-in-all and all-in-one principle, they really form one complete whole, permeating one another.

The above are called the ' New Profound Theories.' The 'Old Theories' coming down from Tu-shun to Chih-yen were afterward reformed by Fa-tsang (643-712), and this reformed version, called the New Profound Theories, is now used by the school as the authoritative theories. They are somewhat complicated, but the theories of co-relation (1), mutual penetration (3), mutual identification (4), and the completion of common virtue (10) are to be studied with special care as illustrating the one-in-all and all-in-one principle of this school.

Next we have the 'Sixfold Specific Nature of all *Dharmas*.' They are as follows :

1. Universality ; 2. Speciality as to character itself ; 3. Similarity ; 4. Diversity as to the relation of beings ; 5. Integration ; 6. Differentiation as to the state of becoming.

For example, the human being. All human beings, in common, are entities.

    (1) *Universality* : consisting of five aggregates.

    (2) *Speciality* : (But) the organs of different human beings have ' speciality ' in the sense of unique character or power.
        All have eyes but not all eyes have the same power.

    (3) *Similarity* : All organs are similar as organs, or in the sense of co-relation in one organism.

    (4) *Diversity* : (But) each organ also possesses

'diversity' since it has a special relation to the whole.

(5) *Integration* : All organs work together to complete the whole unitary being.

(6) *Differentiation* : (But) each organ, being in its own special position, performs its own differentiating function.

Universality is the total of special parts, while Speciality is the special parts constituting the whole. Similarity means that all Specialities have the capacity of being equally harmonious in constituting the whole. Diversity means that Specialities, in spite of their being mutually harmonious, keep their special features. Integration means that Specialities, though they are special, make up Universality by uniting themselves. Differentiation means that Specialities, though they make up Universality, do not lose their own special features. For example, as to a building, Universality is the whole house ; the one includes many special constituents. Speciality is the constituents themselves ; the many are not one, but are not separate from one. Similarity means that the constituents do not conflict with one another and that they all, together, constitute the whole house. Diversity means that all the constituents of the house keep their own Specialities. Integration is the perfect union of all parts, an interdependent causation of the one and the many. Differentiation means that all constituents, each staying in its proper position, keep their Specialities.

The Sixfold Nature indicates that no elements (*dharma*) have single and independent existence, each possessing the Sixfold Nature immanent in itself. The theory of the Sixfold Nature is thus necessary for the proper understanding of the Ten Profound Theories.

Of the six characteristics 1, 3 and 5 are of the nature of equalization and unification while 2, 4 and 6 are of the nature of discrimination and distribution. Every *dharma* has a sixfold specific nature, and the one-in-all and all-in-one principles are expounded by the Ten Profound Theories.

The ground on which the Ten Theories are established is

further explained.   The ground is based on the general Buddhistic ideas.   It is tenfold :

1.   Because all beings as well as all things are manifested
from ideation, the source is one.

2.   Because all beings as well as all things have no determinate nature, all move freely, selflessness being the ultimate
truth.

3.   Because the causation theory means interdependence
or interrelation, all are co-related.

4.   Because the *dharma*-nature (*dharmatā*) or the Buddha-
nature (*Buddha svabhāva*) is possessed in common by all,
they have similar liability.

5.   Because the phenomenal world is said to be as a dream
or illusion, the world of One-Truth can be molded in any way
without restraint.

6.   Because the phenomenal world is said to be as shadow
or image, the world of One-Truth can be molded in any way.

7.   Since, in the Enlightenment of the Buddha, the causes
of production are known to be boundless; the effects are
manifold or limitless, but they do not hinder each other ; rather
they cooperate to form a harmonious whole.

8.   Because the Buddha's Enlightenment is ultimate and
absolute, the transformation of the world is at his will.

9.   Because of the function of the Buddha's profound
meditation the transformation of the world is at his will.

10.   Because of the supernatural power originating from
deliverance, the transformation of the world is free.

Of the above, 1 to 4 are most important and are easily
realized.   The principle 'one-in-all and all-in-one' (mutual
penetration) is based on function, action, energy or efficiency,
while the principle 'one-is-all and all-is-one' (mutual identification) is expounded according to beings or things themselves
or according to their own characteristics (*svalakṣaṇa*) .

The ten theories interdependently cause the manifestation
of the ideal world, and such a causation theory is called the
'Causation by Ten Theories.' The theory of causation is
otherwise called, as we have seen above, the Causation by
Dharma-dhātu (Element of the Elements).   These causations

are, after all, the causation of mere mind, that is, pure idealism. The causation theories peculiar to this school mean general interdependence, universal relativity, causes and effects being interwoven everywhere. Thus it makes from the beginning one perfect whole without any single independent thing—all-comprehensive *maṇḍala* (circle) and the Cycle of Permanent Wave illumined throughout by the great compassionate Sun-Buddha (Vairocana).

This is in fact the world of dynamic becoming on the basis of selflessness (*anātmatā*). The ideal world in perfection is called the 'Lotus-store' or the Universe of One-Truth, or the World of Illumination by the Buddha, the Perfectly Enlightened.

The Ten Stages of the *Bodhisattva*, originally found in the *Daśa-bhūmi Sūtra* of this school, are simply namesakes for ordinary persons who have no experience in the Path of No Learning (*aśaikṣa-mārga*). These Mahāyānistic Stages are said to have been propounded in order to distinguish the position of the *bodhisattva* from those of the Hīnayānistic *śrāvaka* (direct disciple) and *pratyeka-buddha* (Buddha for himself).

The first is the Stage of Joy (*pramuditā*) in which one attains the holy nature for the first time and reaches the highest pleasure, having been removed from all errors of Life-View (*darśana-mārga*) and having fully realized the twofold *śūnyatā* (*pudgala* and *dharma*).

The second is the Stage of Purity (*vimala*) in which one reaches the perfection of discipline (*śīla*) and becomes utterly taintless with regard to morality.

The third is the Stage of Illumination (*prabhā-karī*) in which one gets the perfection of forbearance (*kṣānti*) and becomes free from the errors of Life-Culture (*bhāvanā-mārga*), having attained the deepest introspective insight.

The fourth is the Stage of Flaming Insight in which one attains the perfection of bravery or effort (*vīrya*), thereby increasing the power of insight more and more.

The fifth is the Stage of Utmost Invincibility (*sudūrjayā*) in which one gets the perfection of meditative concentration (*samādhi*), thereby completing, in the mental activity, the correspondence of the twofold truth (worldly truth and higher truth).

The sixth is the Stage of Mental Presence (*abhimukhi*) in which one attains the perfection of wisdom or insight (*prajñā*) and ever retains equanimity as to purity and impurity.

The seventh is the Stage of Far-Going (*dūran-gama*) which is the position farthest removed from the selfish state of the two Vehicles. Here one completes the perfection of expediency (*upāya*) and begins to exercise great mercy to all beings.

The eighth is the Stage of Immovability (*acala*) in which one completes the perfection of vow (*praṇidhāna*) and, abiding in the View of No Characteristic (*alakṣaṇa*), wanders freely according to any opportunity.

The ninth is the Stage of Good Wisdom (*sādhumati*) in which one attains the ten holy powers, having completed the perfection of power (*bala*), and preaches everywhere discriminating between those who are to be saved and those who are not.

The last is the Stage of Ideal Cloud (*dharma-megha*) in which one is able to preach the Ideal to all the world equally, just as the rainclouds pour down heavy rains during drought. This is practically the Stage of the Buddha who is represented by such a *Bodhisattva*.

These Ten Stages are given in the 'Wreath' text (*Daśa-bhūmi Sūtra*)'and are special to the Mahāyāna. Although they are an enumeration of the ascending Stages of the *Bodhisattva*, they can be used for practical purposes by any aspirant who is studying or practicing meditation in order to proceed to the holy stages in the future.

Besides these there are other different enumerations in the Hīnayāna as well as in the Mahāyāna, but the above is representative of the Ten *Bodhisattva* Stages.

IX. THE TENDAI SCHOOL
(THE LOTUS SCHOOL)
(Saddharma-Puṇḍarīka)

(Phenomenology)
[Mahāyānistic]

(1) PRELIMINARY

'Tendai' (T'ien-t'ai) is the name of a mountain in T'aichou, South China. A great philosopher, Chih-i (Chih-kai 531-597) lived on the mountain and taught his disciples during the Ch'ên and Sui dynasties. The school founded by him was generally called the T'ien-t'ai after the mountain but was properly named the 'Fa-hua' (Japanese, Hokke) after the title. of the text *Saddharma-puṇḍarīka*[1] from which the doctrine of the school is derived—'Fa-hua' being a translation of this title. We often designate it the '*Lotus*' text or school as the '*Lotus of the Good Law*' is the full translation of the title.

Prior to the establishment of the school a study of the *Lotus* text was commenced as early as 300 A.D. and lectures were delivered everywhere. A commentary (in 4 vols.) was completed by Chu Fa-tsung but research into the subject matter of the *Lotus* was started after Kumārajīva's translation of the text in 406 A.D.

By noticing the many commentaries compiled in the fifth century by his pupils and successors, we can well understand and appreciate to what an extent and how seriously the study of the *Lotus* was undertaken. During this time eight complete commentaries were written and many special studies of particular aspects of the doctrine were made.

Although the study was commenced in the North and the

---

[1] English translation by H. Kern : *The Saddharma-puṇḍarīka, or the Lotus of the True Law*, Sacred Books of the East, Vol. XXI, London, 1884 and by W. E. Soothill : *The Lotus of the Wonderful Law*, London, 1930.

work on the *Lotus*, i.e., the translations and commentaries, was begun in the North, the school of learning flourished particularly in the South, a fact which eventually gave rise to the foundation of the Tendai School.

The *Lotus* text, we should bear in mind, was originally translated by Kumārajīva into seven volumes of twenty-seven chapters. Fa-hsien, in quest of another chapter (28th), started for India in 475 A.D. When he reached Khotan, he found the chapter on Devadatta, a treacherously acting cousin of the Buddha. He returned and requested Fa-i, an Indian, to translate it. This translation was later added to the earlier text. Thus, there are twenty-eight chapters in the present *Lotus*.

The doctrine of the *Nirvāṇa* text was another fascinating subject of learning at that period. Tao-shêng, already conspicuous in the study of the *Lotus*, was also a leader in the exposition of the ideal of Nirvāṇa. On reading the old *Nirvāṇa* text, which was in six Chinese volumes, he set forth the theory that the *icchāntika* (a class of men who were bereft of Buddha-nature and destined to be unable to evolve to the Buddha stage) could attain Buddhahood. Soon afterwards, a Sanskrit text of the *Mahāparinirvāṇa Sūtra* [2] was introduced and translated. The theory that the *icchāntika* could attain Buddhahood was found in the text. People marveled at his deep insight, and he himself was satisfied. He compiled a commentary on the *Nirvāṇa* soon thereafter. His other theory of an abrupt attainment of Buddhahood is equally famous.

Although the study of the *Nirvāṇa* text continued in the South and in the North, the Nirvāṇa School was founded in the South where most of the able scholars lived. When the T'ien-t'ai School appeared, the southern branch of the Nirvāṇa School was absorbed into it.

Nirvāṇa is not a natural death according to both Hīnayāna and Mahāyāna. Even in Pāli Buddhism, Nirvāṇa is held to have happened at the free will of the Buddha. Mahāyāna goes one step further and asserts that the birth and death of his physical body were simply manifestations but his 'spiritual'

[2] *Taishō*, No. 1527.

body exists permanently. The term 'spiritual body' is
'dharma-kāya' in Sanskrit. The Buddha said, "Grieve you
not, O Brethren, saying 'Our master has past!' What I have
taught, (Dharma, ideal, and Vinaya, disciplinary rules) will
be your masters after my death. If you keep to my teachings
and practice them, is it not the same as if my Dharma-body[3]
remained here forever?"[4] The Dharma-kāya here means that
his body remains as 'dharma' (scripture) after the death of
his physical body. According to the development of the idea
of Dharma, the intensive meaning of Dharma-kāya will also
be changed. The body is conceived as scripture, element,
principle, cosmical, spiritual and ideal. The Mahāyāna takes
it to be a spiritual body or a cosmic body that remains forever.
This is the fundamental idea of the Nirvāṇa School.

The pansophistic idea developed out of the cosmical body
of the Buddha does not admit the existence of the icchantika
who are destined never to attain Buddhahood. Further study
disclosed the theory that all beings without exception have the
Buddha-nature. Even the attribute of the cosmical body which
is bereft of attribute is described as permanence, bliss, self and
purity, the first three being contrary to the fundamental ideas
of Buddhism ; i.e., impermanence, suffering, and selflessness
(anitya, duḥkha, anātman). Nirvāṇa for this school is liberation (from human desire, mokṣa), perfect wisdom (prajñā)
and the Dharma-kāya (cosmical body). On the whole, the
Nirvāṇa School of the South held the doctrine of permanency
of Nirvāṇa while the Nirvāṇa scholars of the North regarded
the Nirvāṇa doctrine as subordinate to the Avataṅsaka
(Wreath) doctrine. Although the Nirvāṇa School was not very
influential, its tenets of Dharma-kāya (cosmical body) and
Buddha-svabhāva (Buddha-nature) have had immense influence over all Mahāyānistic schools of China.

In the end, this school lost its independence and was
absorbed into the T'ien-t'ai School, just as the Ti-lun School
was united with the Avataṅsaka School, as we have seen before.

Cf. pp. 44-5.   [4] The Nirvāṇa Sūtra.

(2) HISTORICAL

The founder of the T'ien-t'ai School is Hui-wen (550-577) who seems to have been a great scholar and a leader of many hundreds of students. When he discovered a verse on the Middle Path in the *Mādhyamika Śāstra* and an annotation concerning the word 'insight' in the *Mahāprajñāpāramitā Śāstra* both by Nāgārjuna, he at once awoke to the truth. The verse runs as follows :

"What is produced by causes,
   That, I say, is identical with Void.
   It is also identical with mere name.
   It is again the purport of the Middle Path." [5]

This would make the causal origination (*pratītya-samut-pāda*) a synonym of 'Void' (*Śūnyatā*) and the temporary name of the Middle Path. The triple truth of the T'ien-t'ai School originates here.

Hui-wen further found in the *Mahāprajñāpāramitā* a sentence concerning the knowledge of the species of the path or teaching, the knowledge of all that exists, and the knowledge of the species of all that exists. By the knowledge of the species of the path, the knowledge of all that exists is obtained. By this, the knowledge of the species of all that exists is attained. By this last, the residue of human desire is cut off.

In annotating the above passage, Nāgārjuna says : "All the aspects of knowledge now in question are obtained at the same time. But in order to promote the understanding of the perfection of wisdom (*prajñāpāramitā*), they are propounded distinctly one after another." Reading this annotation, Hui-wen at once understood the meaning. The knowledge of the species of the path is the knowledge of the path or teaching that illumines the world of distinction and mere name. The knowledge of all that exists is that of non-existence (*śūnyatā*) and reveals the world of non-distinction and equality, while

[5] Ch. XXIV, verse 18.

the knowledge of the species of all that exists is the knowledge of the middle view that illumines the Middle Path which inclines neither to existence nor to non-existence and neither to distinction nor to non-distinction. Thus the threefold knowledge of this school is obtained.

Therefore, objectively, we have the triple truth, and, subjectively, we have the triple knowledge. Of the triple truth the Void is at the same time the temporary, the temporary is at the same time the middle, which is at the same time the Void.

The triple identity is the fundamental theory of this school.

The second patriarch, Hui-ssu (514-577), received careful training from his teacher, Hui-wen. When he became ill, he realized that illness originates from action which, in turn, originates from the mind and has no objective reality. If we trace it to its source in the mind, action cannot be seized and our body is like the shadow of cloud which has specific character but no reality. He thus acquired purity of his mind. In 554, he retired to Mount Tasu in Kuang-chou, where he taught many hundred pupils.

The third patriarch, Chih-i (Chih-kai 531-597), came to him at this time and received special instruction in the meditation of the *Lotus*. Later Chih-i, at the age of thirty-eight, went to T'ien-t'ai with his pupil Hui-pien and some twenty others. Here he found an old scholar, Ting-kuang who had come there forty years ago. He welcomed Chih-i and gave instructions in all branches of Buddhist learning.

Chih-i lived on the mountain for nine years and built the great monastery called Kuo-ch'ing. He was generally honored by the name 'Great Master of T'ien-t'ai.' The Emperor Yang-ti of Sui, who was then the Governor-General of Yangchou, gave him the title of 'Chih-chê,' a Man of Great Wisdom. As regards the superiority of his personal character and the depth of his learning, he stands high above all the rest of the Buddhist scholars of China. In his power of organization of Buddhist doctrine and of training of Buddhist students, no one will ever measure up to him. The final completion of the T'ien-t'ai School is due to him, and, therefore, he is honored as the first patriarch of the school, though he was actually the third patriarch in the lineage of learning of the T'ien-t'ai doctrine.

The second patriarch of the school was his able pupil Kuan-ting (561-632). The three great works of Chih-i are all compilations of Kuan-ting.

The sixth patriarch, Chan-jan (717-782), was a great scholar and the reviver of the school which was somewhat declining in later years. One of his pupils, Tao-sui, was the next patriarch and the teacher of Saichō, or Dengyō Daishi, founder of the school in Japan. Saichō, when twenty years old, went to Nara and studied the T'ien-t'ai doctrine under some scholars who came to Japan with the *vinaya* master Kanjin, and read the three great works of Chih-i. When he was half-way through in his second perusal of those works, he received an Imperial order to go to China for Buddhist study. He received the T'ien-t'ai doctrine and the *bodhisattva* ordination from Tao-sui, the mystic doctrines (*mantra*) from Shun-chiao and the Zen meditation from Hsiu-jan. On his return after one year's sojourn in China, he founded the Tendai School and taught the '*Lotus*' doctrine, the Shingon mysticism, the Zen meditation and Vinaya practices. The educational head-quarters on the Mount Hiei was established by Saichō and became the greatest center of Buddhist learning in Japan. Once there were some 3,000 monasteries to house the students thronging there from all branches of Buddhism, exoteric and esoteric. At present there are three branches of the Tendai School ; namely, Sammon, Jimon and Shinsei, the last being an Amita-pietism.[6] The monasteries belonging to the three branches number more than 4,000 at the present time.

(3) PHILOSOPHICAL

The critical classification of the Buddha's teaching by the Tendai School is 'Five Periods and Eight Doctrines.' The first

[6] See Chapter XII.

period was the Time of Wreath (Kegon). The doctrine taught in this period was what the Buddha had conceived in his Enlightenment, i.e., the elucidation of his Enlightenment itself. His disciples could not understand him at all and they stood as if they were 'deaf and dumb.'

The second period was the Time of the 'Deer Park' where he preached the early Āgamas to suit the people of inferior capacity. His disciples were now able to follow his teaching and practiced accordingly in order to attain the fruition of *arhat* (saintly position). This period is also called the Time of Inducement, or a period in which the people were attracted to the higher doctrine.

The third period was the Time of Development. It was the time when the Hīnayānistic people were converted to the Mahāyāna doctrine and for that purpose the Buddha preached what we call *Vaipulya* (developed) texts. As the Buddha often rebuked the *arhats* for their wrong or short-sighted views, this period is called the Time of Rebuke. The Hīnayānists, after the Buddha's reasoning, became aware of their short-sightedness and learned to appreciate Mahāyāna.

The fourth period was the Time of Wisdom (*prajñā*), when the *Prajñāpāramitā* was preached and all the ideas of distinction and acquisition were mercilessly rejected. It is, therefore, called the Time of Selection. During this period, the doctrine of 'Void' was taught but the Void itself was again negated. In the end everything reverts to the ultimate Void. So the time of *prajñā* was also called the Time of Exploring and Uniting of the *Dharmas,* denying all analysis and unifying them all in one.

The fifth period was the Time of the *Lotus* and *Nirvāṇo Sūtras.* Here the exploring or analyzing and the uniting of the doctrines are taught. The view that the three Vehicles (those of disciples, self-enlightened ones and would-be Buddhas) can obtain saintly fruition was only a temporary teaching (exploring), but the three finally were united into one Vehicle (uniting). Thus the fifth period is specially called the Time of Opening and Meeting. The object of the Buddha's advent on earth was to save all beings and that object can be accom-

plished only by the *Lotus*.   Therefore, the *Lotus* is the ultimate
doctrine among all the Buddha's teachings and is the king
of all the *sūtras*.   The *Nirvāṇa* text was taught at the same
time, but it is a résumé of all that he had expounded before.

The division into five periods shows that the Buddha's
teaching is here arranged chronologically.   But the Buddha,
while teaching, would utilize all five at once when occasions
required.   Therefore, in order to know the nature of the Buddha's teachings we must arrange them properly.   This division
into eight doctrines is proposed to meet this purpose.   First
the four doctrines as to the method of teaching :

1. *Abrupt Doctrine*. In it the Buddha preaches what he
   had conceived without using any expediency ; this is
   the time of the *Wreath*.
2. *Gradual Doctrine*. In it the Buddha induces people
   gradually into deeper thinking, using all sorts of
   measures ; this is the time of the Deer Park, of Development and of Wisdom.
3. *Mystic Doctrine*. It is in reality a mystical indeterminate doctrine.   It is indeterminate and varied
   because many a listener is concealed from another by
   the Buddha's supernatural power and each thinks that
   the Buddha is teaching him alone.   Thus, all hear
   separately and variously.   Such indeterminacy exists
   from the time of the *Wreath* to the time of Wisdom.
4. *Indeterminate Doctrine*. It is a non-mystical indeterminate doctrine.   All listeners know that all are hearing
   together and yet they hear differently and understand
   variously.

These four methodological doctrines are to cultivate the
learners' capacity, and are, therefore, applied only prior to the
preaching of the *Lotus*.   Such methodology is useless in the
Lotus because the teaching of the *Lotus* is neither abrupt, nor
gradual, nor mystical, nor indeterminate.   That is, the time
of the *Wreath* will include the abrupt, mystic, and indeterminate doctrines while the times of the Deer Park, Development

and Wisdom include the gradual, mystic and indeterminate.

Next, the four doctrines as to the nature of the teaching itself :

1. *The Doctrine of Piṭakas* (Scripture). Āgamas (traditions or discourses) and all Hīnayāna doctrines, such as those found in the *Vaibhāṣika* literature.

2. *The Doctrine Common to All.* It is common to the three Vehicles and is the elementary doctrine of Mahāyāna. While an inferior *bodhisattva* follows the same practices as the people of the three Vehicles, a superior *bodhisattva* will penetrate into the state of the following two steps or doctrines.

3. *Distinct Doctrine.* It is purely Mahāyāna and is special to *bodhisattvas.* The first and second doctrines teach the simple one-sided Void while this doctrine teaches the Middle Path, and, therefore, is distinct and separate.

4. *Round Doctrine.* 'Round' means perfection, all-pervading, all-fulfilling, all-permeating. The Distinct Doctrine teaches an independent and separate Middle Path and is a simple-separate mean, while the Round Doctrine teaches the Middle Path of perfect permeation and mutual identification. Therefore, it is not a separate, one-sided Middle Path, but the Middle Path as noumenon, perfectly harmonious, theoretically and practically. Thus, 'round' means that one element contains all elements, i.e., the principle of "One is all and all is one."

Now if we examine these five periods of teaching in relation to the four doctrines as to the nature of the teaching, we have the following result :

1. The Time of the *Wreath* is not yet pure 'round' because it includes the Distinct Doctrine.

2. The Time of the Deer Park is only one-sided as it teaches only Hīnayānistic views.

3. The Time of Development teaches all four doctrines together and therefore is still relative.

4. The Time of Wisdom mainly teaches the Round Doctrine and yet is linked with the Common and Distinct Doctrines. Therefore, it is not quite perfect or complete.

5. The Time of the *Lotus* alone is purely 'round' and superlatively excellent, wherein the purpose of the Buddha's advent on earth is fully and completely expressed.

The supplementary *Nirvāṇa Sūtra* summarizes what the Buddha had preached during his whole life, i.e., the three Vehicles and the four doctrines were dismissed by converting the three Vehicles to the One Vehicle and combining the four doctrines with the one ultimate Round Doctrine. Thus, all teachings of the Buddha are absorbed finally into the *Lotus* which is considered by Tendai to be the Supreme Doctrine of all Buddhism.

The school admits the existence of only One Vehicle (Ekayāna) to convey all beings across the ocean of life, though it also admits the temporary existence of the three Vehicles (Triyāna), i.e., *śrāvaka* (hearers, disciples), *pratyeka-buddha* (self-enlightened, enlightened for himself), and *bodhisattva* (would-be Buddha).

For expediency, these three Vehicles are taught, but ultimately they are all brought back to the one true *Buddha-yāna*.

In Nāgārjuna's commentary on the *Mahāprajñāpāramitā* there is an annotation of the fundamental principles : All conditioned things are impermanent (*sarva-saṅskāra-anityam*) ; all elements are selfless (*sarva-dharma-anātman*) ; and Nirvāṇa is quiescence (*nirvāṇa-śāntam*), in which it is said that these 'three law-seals' (signs of Buddhism) can be extended to four by adding another, all is suffering (*sarva-duḥkham*), or can be abridged to one 'true state' seal. The 'true state' may be translated as 'noumenon.'[7] This school interprets the 'true state'

---

[7] This 'true state' or noumenon must not be interpreted as separate from, or above, or beyond phenomena. The word 'noumenon' is only a partially accurate term.

as 'no state' or no truth,' but it does not mean that it is false ;
' no truth ' or ' no state ' here means that it is not a truth or
a state established by argument or conceived by thought but
that it transcends all speech and thought. Again, Tendai
interprets it as ' one truth ' (*eka-satya*), but ' one ' here is not
a numerical ' one ' ; it means ' absolute '. The principle of
the Tendai doctrine centers on this true state of all elements.

The true state or noumenon can be realized only through
phenomena. In the second chapter of the *Lotus* it is said :
"What the Buddha has accomplished is the *dharma* foremost,
rare and inconceivable. Only the Buddhas can realize the
true state of all *dharmas* ; that is to say, all *dharmas* are thus-
formed, thus-natured, thus-substantiated, thus-caused, thus-
forced, thus-activated, thus-circumstanced, thus-effected, thus-
remunerated and thus-beginning-ending-completing."

Through these manifestations of Thusness or phenomena
we can see the true state. Nay, these manifestations *are* the
true state. There is no noumenon besides phenomenon ;
phenomenon itself is noumenon.

One should not think, as is ordinarily done, that there
exists an abiding motionless substance at the center, around
which its qualities exist, moving and changing. If you suppose
noumenon to be such an abiding substance, you will be misled
altogether. Even the Mahāyānistic people who maintain the
doctrine of two truths—the worldly or popular truth and the
higher truth—are often mistaken by a dichotomic idea of
argument. The Tendai School, therefore, sets forth the threefold truth ; i.e., the truth of void, the truth of temporariness
and the truth of mean. All things have no reality and, therefore, are void. But they have temporary existence. They are
at the same time mean or middle, that is, true state, Thusness.[8]

According to this school the three truths are three in one,
one in three. The principle is one but the method of explanation is threefold. Each one of the three has the value of all.
Therefore, when our argument is based on the void, we deny
the existence of both the temporary and the middle, since we

---

[8] These names are derived from the verse of the *Mādhyamika* which
we quoted above. See Section 2, *Historical*.

consider the void as transcending all. Thus, the three will all be void. The same will be the case when we argue by means of the temporary truth or the middle truth. Therefore, when one is void, all will be void ; when one is temporary, all will be temporary ; when one is middle, all will be middle. They are otherwise called the identical void, identical temporary and identical middle. It is also said to be the perfectly harmonious triple truth or the absolute triple truth.

We should not consider the three truths as separate because the three penetrate one another and are found perfectly harmonized and united together. A thing is void but is also temporarily existent. It is temporary because it is void, and the fact that everything is void and at the same time temporary is the middle truth.

Non-existence and temporary existence may be regarded as contrasts. The middle does not mean that it is between the two. It is over and above the two ; nay, it is identical with the two, because the true state means that the middle is the very state of being void and temporary. The three truths are found ever united and harmonious. In fact, they are mutually inclusive. The Middle Path (madhyama pratipād), the True State (svalakṣaṇa) and Thusness (tathatā) are here synonymous and identical in every way. Here one must bear in mind that though the word 'void' is used, it does not mean 'nothingness' but 'devoid of any thinking or feeling' or 'free from attachment.' Even the idea of void is negated ; it is altogether a negation. Then any existence ought to be temporary because all dharmas are 'established' in mind or exist by causal combinations. They exist only in name, not in reality ; that is, they have 'nominal existence.' Any permanent existence should be negated, but temporary existence should be admitted. That all things are void and temporary is the middle truth, i.e., the absolute.

The ultimate truth taught in the Tendai School is Thusness (Tathatā), not thisness (tattva). Thusness means the true state of things in themselves, the phenomenal world being the state of things manifested before us. The true state of things cannot be seen directly or immediately. We must see it in the phenomena which are ever changing and becoming. Thus the true state is dynamic. The phenomena themselves *are identical with* the true state of things. The true state of things is Thusness, i.e., things as they are manifested, just as moving waves are not different from the still water. We generally contrast the still water with the moving waves, but moving or staying they are only the manifestation of one and the same water. What is being manifested or shown outwardly is nothing but the thing itself. There is no difference between the two.

This is the theory of the true state of all *dharmas* ; that is, all elements manifested are the elements in their own state (*sarva-dharma-svalakṣaṇa-tā*). Or, to use another expression, the 'worldly state (phenomenal) is permanent' (*lokalakṣaṇa-nityatā*).

According to the Tendai doctrine any *dharma* expresses itself in all three truths. All existences are thus mutually permeating in all three truths.

The whole universe is said to have the constituency of three thousands,' but the theory is quite different from other pluralistic systems. It is not an enumeration of all *dharmas* ; nor is it the world system of three chiliocosms. What is it then ? We must explain these 'three thousands.' The expression 'three thousands' does not indicate a numerical or substantial immensity, but is intended to show the inter-permeation of all *dharmas* and the ultimate unity of the whole universe.

As the basis of 'three thousands' the school sets forth a world-system of ten realms. That is to say, the world of living beings is divided into ten realms, of which the higher four are saintly and the lower six are ordinary :

1. The realm of Buddhas. A Buddha is not inside the circle of ten, but as he advents among men to preach his doctrine he is now partially included in it.

2. A *bodhisattva* : a would-be-Buddha.

3. *Pratyeka-buddha* : a Buddha for himself, not teaching others.

4. *Śrāvaka* : a direct disciple of the Buddha.

Ten Realms of Beings

The above four are classed as the saintly stages.

5. *Heavenly Beings* : superhuman as they are, they cannot get perfectly enlightened without the teaching of the Buddha.

6. *Asura* : fighting spirits. Though partially heavenly, they are placed in the lower half of the realm.

7. *Men* : neutral in nature.

8. *Preta* : departed beings, otherwise called ' hungry spirits.'

9. Beasts : innocent in nature, including the whole animal kingdom.

10. Depraved men : ' hellish beings ' who are in the lowest stage.

These ten realms are mutually immanent and mutually inclusive, each one having in it the remaining nine realms. For example, the realm of men will include the other nine from Buddha to Hell, and so will any of the ten realms. Even the realm of Buddhas includes the nature of hell and all the rest, because a Buddha, though not hellish himself, intends to save the depraved or hellish beings, and therefore also has hell in his mind. In this sense, the realm of the Buddhas, too, includes the other nine realms.

This immanence of each of the ten worlds in all of them accounts for 100 worlds. Further, each of these realms has ten different features as we have seen above, i.e., form, nature, substance, force, action, cause, circumstance, effect, remuneration and the ultimate state. These are the ten features of Thusness. By discovering these ten features in the 100 worlds, this school arrives at the doctrine of 1,000 realms.

Moreover, each realm consists of three divisions : the species of living beings, the species of space-region or vessel to live in and the species of five aggregates (*skandhas*) taken separately from living beings—form (=matter), perception, conception (idea), volition (will) and consciousness. Thus there are three thousand realms, constituting the whole of manifested reality.

In Buddhism, ' three thousands ' usually refers to the great chiliocosm consisting of 1,000 small, 1,000 middle and 1,000 large worlds.[9] With the Tendai School, however, it is not such a world-system, but is the universe of all beings and things, i.e., the whole world of dynamic becoming.

It is not Buddhistic to seek the original principle or to consider the absolute as separate or independent. Here the Tendai School at once comes back to the ideation theory but expresses it somewhat differently. It is set forth that a conscious-instant or a moment of thought has 3,000 worlds immanent in it. This is a theory special to this school and is called ' three thousand originally immanent,' or ' three

---

[9] For example, in the Realistic (Kusha) School where an extensive world-system is elaborated along these lines: -

thousand immanent in principle,' or 'three thousand immanent in nature' or sometimes 'three thousand perfectly immanent.' The immanency, either original, theoretical, natural or perfect, conveys one and the same idea ; namely, that the one moment of thought is itself 3,000 worlds. Some consider this to be the nearest approach to the idea of the Absolute, but if you consider the Absolute to be the source of all creation it is not exactly the Absolute. Or, it may be considered to be a form of ideation theory, but if one thinks that ideation manifests the outer world by the process of dichotomy it is quite different, for it does not mean that one instant of thought produces the 3,000 worlds, because a production is the beginning of a lengthwise motion, i.e., timely production. Nor does it mean that the 3,000 worlds are included in one instant of thought because an inclusion is a crosswise existence, i.e., existence in space.

Although here the 3,000-world doctrine is expounded on the basis of ideation, it is not mere ideation, for all the *dharmas* of the universe are immanent in one thought-instant but are not reduced to thought or ideation.

That the world is immanent in one moment of thought is the philosophy of immanence, phenomena being identical with conscious action. It may be called 'phenomenology,' each phenomenon, matter or mind, expressing its own principle or nature.

The principle each phenomenon expresses is the triple truth of harmony (as void, as temporary and as mean), i.e., noumenon originally immanent, perfectly immanent, immanency in principle and immanency in nature. This means simply that a thing or being itself is the true state. Hence the phrase : " Everything, even the color or fragrance, is identical with the Middle Path, the Truth."

The Threefold Body (*Trikāya*) of the Buddha is mentioned as Buddhahood ; its representative theory is held by the Tendai School. Every Buddha of Perfect Enlightenment is supposed to possess three bodies. Although the original names of *Dharma-kāya*, *Saṃbhoga-kāya*, and *Nirmāṇa-kāya* mean literally 'Principle-body,' 'Enjoyment-body' and 'Transformation-body,' the term 'body' in the ordinary sense is rather misleading because it conveys the idea of a bodily existence. The Principle-body or Truth-body is the Ideal or the Principle or Truth itself without any personal existence. It is identical with the Middle Path Truth. The Enjoyment- or Reward-body is the person embodied with real insight, i.e., the body attained as the value of a long causal action. It is twofold : (a) The body for self-enjoyment, i.e., the person when he is enjoying his own enlightenment. (b) The body manifested for the enjoyment of others, i.e., *bodhisattvas* above the primary stage of saintly perfection. The Transformation-body is a body variously appearing to save people. It is also twofold : (a) The body exclusively for *bodhisattvas* of the primary stage, that is, a superior body of Transformation. (b) The body for those who are prior to the primary stage.

Every Buddha has these three aspects. While a Buddha represents the Principle or Truth which he himself has realized, he is, on the one hand, the realizer of the ideal or the enjoyer of his Enlightenment and, on the other hand, the giver of the ideal or the deliverer of all who are suffering or perplexed. Thus the Buddha is viewed as the ideal (Enlightenment) itself, the enjoyer of it (the Enlightened), the giver of it to others (the Enlightener). The Enjoyment-body is obtained by the Buddha as a reward for long effort, while the Transformation-body is freely assumed by him in order to meet the needs of others and the world.

The Three Bodies of the Buddha are further divided into four, five, six or ten, but the above stated Threefold Body of the Tendai School may be regarded as the fundamental theory of Buddhahood.

X. THE SHINGON SCHOOL
(THE TRUE WORD SCHOOL)[1]
(Mantra)

(Mysticism)
[Mahāyānistic]

(1) PRELIMINARY

Shingon or 'true word' is a translation of the Sanskrit
mantra' which means a 'mystic doctrine' that cannot be
expressed in ordinary words. The doctrine which has been
expressed in the Buddha's words should be distinguished from
the ideal which was conceived in the Buddha's mind but not
expressed in words. The Shingon School aims at the Buddha's
own ideal not expressed in any way. An organization of
Buddhists something like a Mantrayāna seems to have existed
at Nālandā at the time of I-ching in the 7th century, for he
mentions the existence of a bulk of Mantra literature there and
he himself is said to have been trained in the esoteric doctrine
though he could not master it satisfactorily. The center of
learning of mysticism, however, seems to have moved to the
Vikramaśīlā University farther down the Ganges, for Tibetan
Buddhism had special connections with the University.

It is a well-known fact that in India as early as the Vedic
period there existed the Atharva practice of sorcery, which had
four kinds of the Homa cult (burnt sacrifice) in an exact
coincidence with those of the Buddhist practice. Such a cult
might have been the practice of Indian aborigines or at any
rate of earlier immigrants. Through a prolonged practice it
eventually amalgamated into what we call 'Tantrism,' which
is often erroneously confused with the Buddhist Diamond
Vehicle Vajrayāna. If it is in any way connected with

[1] Chên-yen.

obnoxious practices, it cannot be called Diamond Vehicle, for that is a name given to a higher mystic doctrine, transcending all Hīnayāna and Mahāyāna doctrines. Such Diamond Vehicle is only represented by Kōbō Daishi [2] to whom the completion of the Mantra doctrine is due.

The critical classification of the Buddha's teaching proposed by Kōbō Daishi is in reality the Ten Stages of spiritual development : [3] (1) Various paths of blind life driven by the instinctive impulse (the stage of common people) ; (2) The Vehicle of human beings striving to have a moral life (the stage of Confucianism) ; (3) The Vehicle of heavenly beings striving to have a supernatural power (the stage of Taoism and Brahmanism)—these three are the worldly Vehicles ; (4) The Vehicle of the direct pupils of the Buddha (śrāvaka) striving for a higher spiritual life as in Hīnayāna schools, Kusha, and Jōjitsu (stage of direct disciples) ; (5) The Vehicle of the self-enlightened ones (pratyeka-buddha) enjoying self-enlightenment yet falling into egoism ; (6-7) The doctrine of Three Vehicles, holding the three Vehicles as real (the stages of the Sanron and Hossō Schools) ; (8-9) The doctrine of One Vehicle holding the one Vehicle as real (the stages of the Kegon and Tendai Schools) ; (10) The Diamond Vehicle as held by the Shingon School. These stages, coming one above the other, show the timely progress of the human mind, while those which stand co-ordinated at one time show the state of the progressive world.

Of these ten, the first is not to be classed as a Vehicle, but since the group of beings is on the way to a Vehicle it is included in the classification of Vehicles. According to the Shingon idea the Diamond Vehicle stands above all others ; it is the supreme Vehicle of mysticism.

One must not forget that there exist two forms of the mystic doctrine, namely, the Taimitsu and Tōmitsu. The former is the mysticism handed down by the Tendai School and the latter transmitted in the Tōji Monastery of the Shingon

[2] Kūkai, 774-835.

School. They are not altogether different, but in practice the Tōmitsu is a special school for it seems to be much more thorough-going than the Taimitsu, while in theory neither side seems to concede in any way. For example, they agree in their treatment of the Buddhas, Śākyamuni and Mahāvairocana, and further in the application of it to the Shintō, 'the Way of Gods,' of Japan. Those who would study the relation of Buddhism with Shintō should clear up this point, for the Shintō names of Ryōbu ('Double Aspect') and Ichijitsu ('One True') originate from the difference of ideas in these two mystic schools.

(2) HISTORICAL

.What we generally call the ' Miscellaneous Mystic '[4] was translated early in the 4th century A.D. Śrīmītra of Pai (Kucha, a Central Asian state inhabited by a white race) translated some texts into Chinese. These were charms, cures and other sorts of sorcery, often containing some *mantra* prayers and praises of gods or saints of higher grades, but generally speaking they could not be regarded as expressing a high aspiration.

What we can designate as ' Pure Mystics ' begins with the three able Indian teachers who arrived in China during the august T'ang period (713-765). The first arrival was Śubhakarasiṃha (637-735) who had been king of Orissa. He joined the priesthood and went to the Nālandā University over which Dharmagupta presided. Well versed in Buddhist concentration (*yoga*), mystical verses (*dhāraṇī*) and fingers inter-twining (*mudrā*), he started for Kashmir and Tibet, and at last came to Ch'angan in 716, where he was well received by the Emperor Hsüan-tsung (685-762).

Wu-hsing, a learned Chinese, who traveled in India, met I-ching at Nālandā and collected various Sanskrit texts. He died on his way home, but his collection reached Hua-yen

---

[4] 'Miscellaneous Mystics' texts are Nanjio Nos. 167, 309, 310.

Monastery in Ch'angan. On hearing this Śubhakarasimha together with I-ching selected some of the important texts and in 725 translated the 'Great Sun' text (*Mahāvairocana*)[5] and others. He wanted to return to India, but was not allowed to depart and died in 735.

The second arrival was Vajrabodhi (663-723) who, coming from South India, became a novice at Nālandā. At the age of fifteen he went to West India and studied logic for four years under Dharmakīrti, but came again to Nālandā where he received full ordination at twenty. For six years he devoted himself to the study of the *Vinaya* (Discipline) text and the Middle (Mādhyamika) Doctrine under Śāntabodhi ; for three years he studied the *Yogācāra* by Asaṅga, the *Vijñaptimātra* by Vasubandhu and the *Madhyānta-vibhanga* by Sthiramati under Jinabhadra, at Kapilavastu, North India ; and for seven years he studied the *Vajra-śekhara* (Diamond Head) and other mystical texts under Nāgabodhi, in South India. At last, he sailed to the southern sea and reached Loyang, China, in 720. He translated several important mystical texts, such as the *Vajra-śekhara*.[6] In 741, while in Ch'angan, he obtained permission to return to India, but on his way died in Loyang.

Amoghavajra (705-774), an able pupil of Vajrabodhi, was from North India. He became a novice at the age of fifteen and arrived in Kuangtung together with his teacher whom he followed as far as Loyang, and received ordination at twenty. In twelve years he mastered all the mystical doctrines and practices. When his teacher died he went to Ceylon together with his fellow pupils, thirty-seven in all, and visited a teacher, Samantabhadra, from whom he learned the doctrines of the *Vajra-śekhara-yoga* and *Mahā-vairocana-garbhakośa*. With his rich collections he returned to Ch'angan in 746.

Amoghavajra was an instructor of Hsüan-tsung, Su-tsung and Tai-tsung, the three successive Emperors. He translated 110 different texts, in 143 Chinese volumes (*chüans*). Among them was the most important text *Rita-saṅgraha* or *Tattva-saṅgraha* (i.e., *Vajra-śekhara*),[7] 'Diamond Head' which, it is

---

[5] *Taishō*, No. 848.   [6] *Taishō*, No. 932.   [7] *Taishō*, No. 865.

interesting to note, was incidentally discovered at the same time by Professor Tucci of Italy and Professor Ono of Japan. The former found in Tibet the Sanskrit text and the latter discovered in Japan the pictorial annotation of the text, which was brought back from China by Enchin (Chishō Daishi) in 853. The happy coincidence of discovery of the two distinguished professors will contribute much to the history of the mystical school of India, Tibet, China and Japan.

Ichigyō (I-hsing, 683-727), a pupil of Śubhakarasimha, who was well versed in the Sanron, the Zen, the Tendai, and the calendar, assisted Śubhakarasimha in his translation of the ' Great Sun ' text. On hearing the lecture from his teacher, Ichigyō compiled a commentary on the ' Sun ' text called *Ta-jih Ching Su.* Since he was a savant, of the Tendai doctrine, his commentary is said to contain some of the Tendai tenets. The commentary, as it was left in an unrevised manuscript, was afterward revised by Chih-yen, a pupil of Śubhakarasimha, and Wên-ku, a pupil of Vajrabodhi, and was called by a new name *Ta-jih Ching I-shih.* The Tōmitsu follows the former revision while the Taimitsu adopts the latter. Ichigyō studied under the two Indian teachers, Śubhakara and Vajrabodhi, and received the cults of both the Realm of 'Matrix Repository' (*Vajra-dhātu*) and the Realm of Diamond Elements (*Garbha-kośa* or *Garbha-kukṣi*), but he is said to have held the latter as the more important of the two.[8] To show the line of transmission we will give here a table of succession :

1. Śubhakarasimha, 637-735
    |
    I-hsing (Ichigyō), 683-727
    |

(Taimitsu)   Tōmitsu
    |

2. Śubhakarasimha, 637-735
    |

For explanation of the two Realms, see below.

I-lin (Girin)
|
Shun-hsiao (Jungyō)
|
Saichō, Taimitsu, First transmission.
|
3. Śubhakarasiṃha, 637-735
|
Hsüan-ch'ao
|
Hui-kuo (Keikwa), 746-805
|
Kūkai, Tōmitsu, Matrix Repository transmission.
|
4. Amoghavajra, 705-774
|
Hui-kuo (Keikwa), 746-805
|
Kūkai, Tōmitsu, Diamond Element transmission.
|

1. Amoghavajra, 705-774	6. Amoghavajra, 705-774
I-ts'ao (Gisō) Gishin	Hui-tse (Esoku)
	Genshō

|
Ennin (Jikaku Daishi), Taimitsu, Second transmission.

During the Hui-ch'ang period (845) in China when there was destruction of Buddhism, Ennin (Jikaku Daishi) of the Tendai School was in China. He encountered troubles in this period but because of the disorder was able to collect valuable materials of mystic Buddhism.

Fortunately the mystical doctrine and practices were brought home by the four Daishis (Great Masters) and others, and were once and for all organized and systematized by the able hand of Kōbō Daishi (Kūkai). The Kōyasan, the center of learning of mystic doctrine, is said to have had 990 monasteries during its flourishing period.

Kōbō Daishi, the founder of the Shingon School in Japan, was the first and foremost artist in sculpture and in calligraphy. His literary style was admired in China as well as in Japan. He founded a private school of arts as an educational center of common people in Kyoto. Although it was dropped soon after his demise, his influence in primary education remained forever in Japan. It is but reasonable that the verse *Iroha* (alphabet) attributed to him was popularized and perpetuated in Japan.

At present the Shingon School has two branches, old and new ; the monasteries under it number 10,000 in all.

(3) PHILOSOPHICAL

The Shingon School claims to be the only esoteric doctrine whereas all other schools are considered exoteric. The distinction of the two doctrines is found in the treatment of the spiritual body (*Dharmakāya*) of the Buddha. The spiritual body is the body of principle and therefore is colorless, formless and speechless, according to the exoteric doctrine ; whereas according to the esoteric doctrine of the mystic school the preaching Buddha himself is of spiritual body and is with form, color and speech. His speech is found in the *Great Sun* (*Mahāvairocana*) text and the *Diamond Head* (*Vajra-śekhara*). Again, the exoteric schools recognize that the state of cause of Buddhahood is explicable in parts, but the state of effect of it can in no way be explained. This state of the inexplicable Buddhahood has been explained in the above mystic texts. As to the time occupied before the attainment of Buddhahood the exoteric schools hold it to be three long periods (*kalpas*), while the esoteric school regards it as merely one thought-moment or at any rate the one life, and asserts that this body of ours becomes Buddha. In the one school the Tripiṭaka literature is depended upon, but in the other schools the rituals (*kalpa* or *vidhi*) are regarded as authoritative.

A mystic hymn (*mantra*) is the source of obtaining the enfolding power of Buddha. If we speak of the preaching of the spiritual body and the explicability of the state of effect, we can speak so because we presume that all speeches are the real speeches issuing from the Buddha's own will, or, we should say, a voiceless speech for his own enjoyment of the taste of *Dharma*.

According to the exoteric schools the Buddha's preachings are all for others' enjoyment, and the spiritual body itself is unknowable and the state of Buddhahood is altogether inexplicable. Thus no preaching of the spiritual body will be recognized. The Shingon School, on the other hand, asserts that the Buddha had no 'secret fist,' which he demonstrated by his own hand, and was preaching the truth perpetually, but the listeners had no ear to hear and no mind to understand.

The three mysteries of the body, speech and thought of the Buddha will remain mysteries forever if there is no means of communion. Such a means of communion should come from the mystic power (*adhiṣṭhāna*, enfolding power) of the Buddha but not from the limited effort of an aspirant. The means itself is nothing but the manifestation of the mystic power, which can be expressed through the three activities of men, i.e., our body, speech and thought. According to the ritualistic prescription (*vidhi* or *kalpa*), the means of communion has three aspects : 'finger-intertwining' (*mudrā*) and other attitudes of one's body, 'mystical verse' (*dhāraṇi*) and other words of prayer, and *yoga* concentration, corresponding to our three activities. So through the prescribed ritual we can realize the perfect communion between the Buddha and the aspirant, thus attaining the result of the 'Buddha-in-me. I-in-Buddha' ; hence, the theory of Buddhahood as attainable in this corporeal life.

The Mahāvairocana, as the Great Sun Buddha is called in Sanskrit, is apparently different from the Buddha Śākyamuni, but if mystically considered, the latter himself will be the former, and the Bodhisattva Samantabhadra who is attending Śākyamuni will be Vajrapāṇi under the mystical Buddha. Even the mystical Buddha is of two aspects, generally represented as two separate Buddhas.

In Buddhism, a Buddha, however remote in age or however great in origin, will be individual, for the perfection of knowledge and wisdom is the perfection of personality and that is a Buddha. A. personal perfection embellished by the three mysteries is the spiritual body of knowledge and wisdom. The static nature of the Buddha is potentially perfected like the great luminary (Diamond Element), and is the Mahāvairocana (Great Sun) of the Diamond Element.- To us it is not yet clear that the all-illumining dynamic force, like warmth or mercy, is to enfold all beings which are in the realm of natural principle (Matrix Repository). Therefore, the spiritual body of principle is depicted as if the world of nature, i.e., universe itself, should become illumined and assume a splendor of perfect wisdom. This Buddha is possessed of the perfect harmony of the sixfold greatness ; i.e., earth, water, fire, air, space and consciousness and is the Buddha Mahāvairocana of the Matrix Repository. These curious names of the worlds of 'Diamond Element' and 'Matrix Repository' indicate the indestructible character of personal wisdom, otherwise called the realm of effect and the natural source of beings (sometimes called the realm of cause).

These two aspects of the Buddha are strictly distinguished. I used the word 'static' or 'dynamic' with regard to the person of the Buddha on the basis of the manifestation of his enfolding power. Seen from the attainment of his perfect wisdom, the Buddha of the realm of nature is static and therefore has the sign (*mudrā*) of 'meditation,' while the Buddha of the realm of wisdom is dynamic owing to the vivid realization of his ideals and has the sign of 'wisdom-fist.' Suppose an individual develops himself and attains enlightenment and advances so far as to conform to the universal principle ; he will then be the Buddha Mahāvairocana of the individual realm (Diamond Element). In sculpture he is represented with the left hand grasping the index finger of the right hand, the sign of 'wisdom-fist.'

On the other hand, when the universe itself becomes illumined and assumes a splendor of wisdom, he then will be the Buddha Mahāvairocana of the natural realm (Matrix Repository). In sculpture he is represented as having the sign of meditation on the universe, with the right hand on the left, the thumbs touching each other.

Thus there are two Buddhas with one and the same name, different in manifestation but identical in quality. "They are two and yet not two." When the six great elements (earth, water, fire, air, space and consciousness) are coordinated crosswise (according to space) we get the universe, i.e., the universal body of the Buddha of the Matrix Realm. When the six elements are arranged lengthwise or vertically (according to time), we get the individual of five aggregates, i.e., the personal body of the Buddha of the Diamond Realm. Mystically speaking, the two persons of ultimate perfection would be of one and the same width and height.

To illustrate the sphere of activity of the two Buddhas a diagram-like circle (*Maṇḍala*) was invented for each, having the whole show of saintly beings with the Buddha at the center.

The Realm of Matrix Repository*

Each of the four quarters has a Buddha, and each of the four corners has a *Bodhisattva*, thus making up the party of nine with the central one. Saintly beings represented are 1,461 in all.

1,461

---

* This chart and the one on p. 158 have been transposed from the positions they occupy in earlier editions of this volume. This has been done in order to produce agreement between the symbols in the charts and the descriptions given by Dr. Takakusu.—*Eds.*

The Realm of Diamond Element

414

This has the central party of nine representing the Diamond Realm. Figures represented here amount to 414.

The circle is of four kinds :

1. The Great Circle (*Mahā-maṇḍala*) is the circle of the Buddha and his companions represented by pictures or painted figures, i.e., a plane representation.
2. The Symbol Circle (*Samaya-maṇḍala*) is the circle of the same assembly represented by symbols or an article possessed by each. *Samaya* in Sanskrit means the ' original vow ' but here it is represented by an article borne by each.
3. The Law Circle (*Dharma-maṇḍala*) is the circle of letters (*bīja-akṣara*) representing all the saintly beings.
4. The 'Artcraft Circle (*Karma-maṇḍala*) is the circle of sculptured figures.

In Japan we have no circle of sculptural representation. The multitude of Buddhistic images of Java is said to be of this kind. *Karma* in Sanskrit means ' action ' or ' work '; here it especially means the artistic work of solid representation.

The fourfold circle indicates the efficacious power of the three mysteries. The figures, painted or sculptured, show the mystery of the body of the Buddha ; the letters show the mystery of speech of the Buddha ; and the symbol indicates the ' original vow,' the thought of the Buddha.

The Shingon School has the ritual of anointment

(*abhiṣeka*) as well as the ordination ceremony. The area of anointment must be decked with the Circles of the two realms ; all ritual requirements must be fulfilled. Sometimes the Circles are spread out and thereby the ritual area is formed. So the area is called ' Circle.' Only the adequate performance of the ritual can make the evoking of any enfolding power of Buddha effective.

According to tradition, Śubhakarasiṃha and his pupil, I-hsing, transmitted the Matrix doctrine, while Vajrabodhi and his pupil, Amoghavajra, taught the Diamond doctrine. Thus we must presume that there were two traditions of transmission, both being only partial or one-sided.

However, the recent discovery of the *Tattva-saṅgraha* in Tibet by Professor Tucci and the *Vajra-śekhara* (*Rita-saṅgraha*) in Japan by Professor Ono make the old traditions entirely untenable, because the *Vajra-śekhara* represented in the *Five Assemblies* was kept in secret in the Mii Monastery in Ōmi and Shōrenin in Kyoto. The ' Five Assemblies ' are *Buddha, Padma, Ratna, Vajra* and *Karma.* These being originally the divisions of the Diamond Realm, it is clear that we had from the beginning the text of the ' Diamond ' doctrine brought by Śubhakarasiṃha. They were actually the transmission by Śubhakarasiṃha. From this it will be seen that at the time of Śubhakarasiṃha both the ' Diamond ' and ' Matrix ' doctrines were existing in China. Tucci's text is Sanskrit and Ono's is a pictorial explanation without which a perusal of the Sanskrit original often becomes impossible. Students of mysticism may expect a real contribution from the study of these texts.

XI. THE ZEN SCHOOL
(THE MEDITATION SCHOOL)[1]
(Dhyāna)

(Pure Intuitionism)
[Mahāyānistic]

(1) BUDDHIST SCHOOLS OF THE KAMAKURA PERIOD (1185-1335 A.D.)

Buddhism in the Nara period (710-794 A.D.) was a philosophy of investigation and speculation, while that of the Heian period (794-1185 A.D.) was externally an eclecticism or syncretism of Shintoistic and Buddhistic ideas and internally a unification of the theory of universal immanence (exoteric). Buddhism in this later period greatly influenced the social life and culture on all sides by its doctrine of enfolding power (esoteric). In the Kamakura period (1185-1335 A.D.) the specific character of Buddhism was pre-eminently practical, national and markedly enthusiastic in preaching, exclusive in doctrine, more simplified and specific than ever, but extensive in the application or the realization of the ideal, since all Buddhist schools in the period preached salvation—i.e., the way of enlightenment—for all, that is, pansophism.

The religious activity of this period was, in a way, a strong protest against the previous orthodox schools which seemed to end in an exhibition of either speculative achievement or ritualistic efficacy, betraying in their aristocratic pomp and ceremonial display the fast degenerating tendency of philosophical-religious life in general. The importance of a reversion to the monistic and practical religion of Prince Shōtoku[2] was strongly felt. The consensus of the leading ideas and the necessity of spiritual reform among the populace

---

[1] Ch'an.   [2] 574-622 A.D.

brought about the uniformity of the religious type of the time. Certainly the memory of Prince Shōtoku was greatly awakened and a considerable increase in his images, sanctuaries, memorial services and even guilds of artisans connected with him was conspicuous during the period. One of the Buddhist schools founded at the time enshrined him as the patriarch of Japan.

Kamakura Buddhism, the Buddhism of ' All-Enlightenment,' may be summarized into seven schools :

1. The Zen School of meditative intuitionism
   a. Rinzai Sect founded by Eisai (1141-1215)
   b. Sōtō Sect founded by Dōgen (1200-1253)
2. The Fuke School of introspective asceticism, founded by Kakushin in 1255
3. The Jōdo School of Amita-pietism, founded by Hōnen (1133-1212)
4. The Shin School of Amita-pietism, founded by Shinran (1173-1262)
5. The Ji School of Amita-pietism, founded by Ippen (1239-1289)
6. The Nichiren School of Lotus-pietism, founded by Nichiren (1222-1282)
7. The Shin-Ritsu Sect, the reformed school of self-vow discipline, founded by Eison (1201-1290), the restorer of the disciplinary school

(2) PRELIMINARY

As an inheritance from the ancient Aryan race, India has had the habit of meditation practiced in all schools of philosophy as well as in religion. There are six systems of Indian philosophy (darśana, ' view '), one of which, called Yoga, is especially devoted to meditation or concentration.

The Yoga system is the practical side of the Sāṅkhya philosophy, which is dualistic. In Sāṅkhya, Self (Ātman) and Nature (Prakṛti), one blind as it were, and the other lame, cannot function without being united. Self has the intellec-

B.—11

tual function, but cannot move without the physical function of Nature. When the two combine together, they see the way and move at will. Self, like the promoter of a theatrical play, simply looks on his mate's acting and moving but curiously thinks that he himself is acting in the moving, though in reality only Nature is moving and achieving. Only self-culture brings about freedom, that is, independence of Self. The method of self-culture is practically the Yoga system of Patañjali (second century B.C.). The Sāṅkhya system, originally heterodox since it was atheistic, asserted only the existence of the individual *Ātman* (Self) and not of *Mahātman* (Universal Self, *Brahman*). But in the practice of abstract meditation an object of self-concentration was necessary and so the doctrine assumes the form of deism (but not theism). At the end of meditation, when the absolute separation of Self from Nature has been effected, the object of meditation, *Brahman, Parama-ātman* or God, whatever it is, is no longer used.

The constituents of Yoga abstraction (concentration) are generally eight : 1. restraint (*yama*) ; 2. minor restraint (*niyama*) ; 3. sitting (*āsana*) ; 4. restraint of breaths (*prā-ṇāyāma*) ; 5. withdrawal of senses (*pratyāhāra*) ; 6. retention of mind (*dhāraṇā*) ; 7. concentration of mind (*dhyāna*) ; 8. concentration of thought (*samādhi*). These practices of the Yogin are actually similar to those of the Yogācāra School of Buddhism.[3] Yogācāra means 'practice of self-concentration' and has several things in common with the Yoga philosophy. The Yogācāra School is Buddhist idealism taught by Asaṅga,[4] systematized by his brother Vasubandhu [5] as the Theory of Mere Ideation (Vijñaptimātratā), and introduced to China by Hiuen-tsang[6] as the Fa-hsiang (Hossō) School. According to I-tsing,[7] famous traveler in India, it was one of the only two Mahāyāna schools in India (Mādhyamika and Yogācāra).[8]

---

[3] See Ch. VI.   [4] c. 410-500 A.D.   [5] c. 420-500 A.D.
[6] Hsüan-tsang, 596-664.   [7] I-ching, 635-713.
[8] See my translation, *A Record of the Buddhist Religion as Practiced in India and the Malay Archipelago by I-tsing* (A.D. 671-695), Oxford, 1896, p. 15.

This fact is fully confirmed by Sāyaṇa's commentary on the *Vedānta Sūtra,* in which these two are treated as the only existing Buddhist systems.

The meditation (*dhyāna*) practiced in the Zen School consisted of twelve ways of meditation, three grades and four kinds in each ; namely, four form-realm-meditations (*rūpa-dhātu*), four formless-realm-meditations (*ārūpya-dhātu*) and four measureless-meditations (*apramāṇa-dhyāna*). The last, the measureless-meditations, are exactly identical with those of the Yoga system. Which one is indebted to the other we cannot say, though they look quite Buddhistic. They are : 1. benevolence (*maitrī,* to give joy to others); 2. cheerfulness (*muditā,* to keep oneself happy) ; 3. mercy (*karuṇā,* to remove the suffering of others) ; 4. indifference (*upekṣā,* to transcend the above three). These, though subjective, have all beings as their objective, whereas the four form-realm-meditations and four formless-realm-meditations have the form-heaven and the formless-heaven as their objectives. It is a well-known fact that in the Buddha's career he practiced the formless *dhyāna* with Ārāḍa Kālāma, an ascetic who attained the mental state of boundless consciousness, and Udraka Rāmaputra, another ascetic who reached the highest stage of being neither conscious nor unconscious. Finally, the would-be Buddha surpassed his teachers and, having found no more to learn from them, went his own way in spite of their eager requests to stay and train their respective pupils.

The importance of the abstract meditation of the Yoga system is laid upon the evolution and reversion of the dual principles and upon the final liberation of Self from Nature, while that of the idealistic Yogācāra School of Buddhism is centered on the unification of the world within and without, on the synthesizing of our causal and illusory existences, and thus negatively discovering the state of Thusness (*Tathatā*).

Buddhism has, of course, a special doctrine of meditation. Although the depth and width of contemplation depend upon one's personal character, the methods or contents of meditation taught by the Buddha are similar in Hīnayāna and Mahāyāna. This special meditation is generally called 'Tathāgata meditation,' as it forms one part of the sacred teaching. The highest development of it is seen in the perfect 'calmness and insight' (*samathavipaśyana*) of the Tendai School and in the mystical *yogācāra* of the Shingon School.

(3) HISTORICAL

To understand Tathāgata meditation, one must study the history of the meditative teaching of the Buddha. When we speak of the Tathāgata meditation, we presuppose the rise of patriarchal meditation by the advent of Bodhidharma in China in 520 A.D.

Tathāgata Meditation

The Buddha first taught the Threefold Basis of Learning (*trisikṣa*) : Higher Discipline (*adhi-śīla*), Higher Meditation (*adhi-citta*) and Higher Wisdom (*adhi-prajñā*). In the six-fold perfection of wisdom, concentration (*samādhi*) is one of the most important factors. He further taught meditation as the 'basis of action' (*karma-sthāna*), such as meditation on the ten universal objects, on impurity, on impermanence, on breaths, etc. The object of meditation with the Buddha seems to have been to attain first, tranquillity of mind, and then activity of insight. This idea is common to both Hīnayāna and Mahāyāna. To intensify the original idea and to apply it extensively, each school seems to have introduced detailed items of contemplation.

Generally speaking, the mental cultivation of Buddhism is divided into three : 1. 'effort' stage ; 2. 'view-path' stage ; 3. 'practice-path' stage. The adjustment of one's self so as to proceed to the path, that is, the beginner's undertaking, comes first. The first path one treads is the 'effort' stage in which there is the practice of calmness and insight. One must practice :

Calmness

A. Fivefold restraint of mind
   1. Meditation on impurity of the worldly life to adjust the mind with regard to passion and avarice. (individual)
   2. Meditation on mercy to cultivate the idea of sympathy to others and to stop the tendency of anger. (universal)
   3. Meditation on causation to get rid of ignorance. (individual)
   4. Meditation on diversity of realms to see the difference of standpoints and to get rid of selfish views. (universal)
   5. Meditation on breathing leading to concentration so as to correct the tendency of mental dispersion. (individual)

When one's faulty mind has been adjusted and calmness has been obtained, one proceeds to the next.

Insight

B. Fourfold retention of mind
   1. The impurity of body is meditated upon and fully realized.
   2. The evils of sensations are meditated upon and fully realized.
   3. The evanescence or impermanence of mind and thoughts is meditated upon and fully realized.
   4. The transiency of all elements or selflessness is meditated upon and fully realized.

Hīnayāna Buddhism calls these practices 'basis of action' (*kammatthāna*) which is one of the modes of analytical meditation. Some forty such meditations are given in the *Visuddhi Magga* : four 'measureless meditations'; ten 'impurities'; four 'formless states'; ten 'universals'; ten 'remembrances'; one 'sign';

and one 'mental reflex.' We need not go into the detail of all these meditations.

The ordinary way of meditation is as follows :

> Arrange your seat properly, sit erect, cross-legged, and have your eyes neither quite closed nor quite open, looking ten or twenty feet ahead. You should sit properly but your body will move on account of your breaths. To correct such movement, count your in-breath and out-breath as one and slowly count as far as ten, never beyond.
>
> Although your body may become upright and calm, your thought will move about. You must therefore meditate upon the impurity of human beings in illness, death and after death.
>
> When you are well prepared to contemplate, you will begin to train yourself by concentration on the ten universals. This is a meditative unification of diverse phenomena into one of the ten universals, that is, blue, yellow, red, white, earth, water, fire, air, space, consciousness. In this you must meditate upon the universe until it becomes to your eyes one wash of a color or one aspect of an element. If you meditate upon water, the world around you will become only running water.

Such a process of meditation is common to all Buddhist schools, Hīnayāna as well as Mahāyāna, and is the feature of the Tathāgata meditation.

Patriarchal Meditation

The history of Zen is mythical. It is said that one day Brahmā came to the Buddha who was living at the Vulture peak, offered a Kumbhala flower, and requested him to preach the Law. The Buddha ascended the Lion seat and taking that flower touched it with his fingers without saying a word. No one in the assembly could understand the meaning. The venerable Mahākaśyapa alone smiled with joy. The World-Honored One said : "The doctrine of the Eye of the True Law is hereby entrusted to you, Oh Mahākaśyapa ! Accept and hand it down to posterity." Once when Ānanda asked him what the Buddha's transmission was, Mahākaśyapa said : "Go and take the banner-stick down !"[9] Ānanda understood him at once. Thus the mind-sign was handed down successively. The teaching was called the 'school of the Buddha-mind.'

The 28th patriarch was Bodhidharma.[10] He was the third son of the King of Kañcīpura, South India. Obeying the instruction of Prajñātara, his teacher, Bodhidharma started for the East and arrived in China in 520 A.D. The Emperor Wu-ti invited him to Nanking for an audience. The Emperor said : "Since my enthronement, I have built many monasteries, copied many holy writings and invested many priests and nuns. How great is the merit due to me ?" "No merit at all," was the answer. "What is the Noble Truth in its highest sense ?" "It is empty, no nobility whatever." "Who is it then that is facing me ?" "I do not know, Sire." The Emperor could not understand him. Bodhidharma went away, crossed the Yangtze River and reached the capital, Loyang, of Northern Wei. After a sojourn there he went to Mount Wu-t'ai and resided in the Shao-lin Temple where he remained and for nine years, facing a cliff behind the edifice, meditated in silence.

A strong-minded Confucian scholar, Hui-k'o,[11] came to Bodhidharma and asked for instruction. He obtained no reply. Thereupon he stood in the snow and cut off his left arm, thereby showing his sincerity and eagerness. Bodhidharma then made him a pupil and gave him a robe and a bowl as a sign of transmission. This is the line of the patriarchal meditation. The fifth patriarch, Hung-jên,[12] had two able pupils. The regular succession fell on one of them, Hui-nêng,[13] who became the founder of the Southern Meditation School. His aim was an abrupt attainment of enlightenment and his school is called the Southern School of Abrupt Enlightenment.

[9] The presence of the banner outside the temple was indicative of preaching of the Law. To take the banner down means to do away with word-preaching.

[10] c. 470-534.   [11] Eka.   [12] Gunin.   [13] Enō, 638-713.

He is the sixth patriarch of Zen. The other able pupil was Shên-hsiu[14] who remained in the north and propagated the Zen of patriarchal meditation earnestly. His school was called the Northern School of Zen. His teaching was a gradual attainment of enlightenment and named the Northern School of Gradual Enlightenment. Since the Northern School taught the Tathāgata meditation as well, Dengyō Daishi is said to have belonged to it. All of the Japanese sects belong to the Southern School.

Japanese Zen

Zen was introduced to Japan several times. Hiuen-tsang's pupil, Dōshō,[15] who went to China in 654 A.D., introduced and taught it for the first time in the Zen Hall of Gangōji, Nara. Next, Tao-hsüan,[16] a Chinese *vinaya* (discipline) master, came to Nara in 710 A.D. and taught the Zen of the Northern School. He transmitted it to Gyōhyō in 733 A.D., who in turn taught it to Saichō (Dengyō Daishi).

A special Zen instructor of the Southern School, Gikū, a pupil of Ch'i-an,[17] came to Kyoto and taught Zen from 851 to 858 A.D. in the Danrinji Temple built by the Empress Danrin. He was successful in his teaching. In all the above cases the propagation was assisted by the Court but did not continue long. The last-mentioned teacher went home disappointed in 858 A.D., leaving a monument at the Rashōmon, Kyoto, inscribed : "A record of the propagation of Zen in Japan."

The watchword of Zen in China was "not to pay respect even to king or prince." Such an attitude did not appeal to the nationalistic mind of Japan. In the Kamakura period several Chinese teachers were invited or welcomed by the Shogunate government. Tao-lung Lan-hsi (Dōryū Rankei, founder of the Kenchōji Temple in 1249), Tsu-yüan W'u-hsüeh (Sogen Mugaku, founder of the Engakuji Temple in 1273) and I-ning I-shan (Ichinei Issan, who though not invited, came to the Shuzenji Temple in 1299) came to Kamakura and busied themselves in the instruction of Zen. We must remem-

---

[14] Jinshū, 605-706.   [15] 629-700.   [16] Dōsen.   [17] Enkwan Saian.

ber, however, that it was only after the able founders of
Japanese Zen, Eisai and Dōgen, had opened and brilliantly
led the way, that these Chinese teachers made their appearance
on the scene. Eisai, who built the Kenninji Temple in Kyoto,
wrote a treatise, "Kōzen Gokoku-ron" (Propagation of Zen as
the Protection of the Nation), in which he asserted that the
propagation of the Zen practice would serve to protect the
prosperity of the Empire. He was right in his view, as the new
religion greatly helped to pacify and strengthen the hearts of
the warriors. Zen taught that even fighters must introspect
and think of morality and responsibility. Dōgen wanted to
rectify the abnormal system of government and went so far as
to advise Tokiyori, then the *de facto* ruler, to restore the
regime to the Throne. As the proposal was not complied
with, he left at once and retired to the Eiheiji Monastery which
he bulit in the province of Echizen. This deepened the ruler's
respect for him and one of Dōgen's pupils in Kamakura was
persuaded to take the document of a generous grant of land
to his teacher. The priest gladly did so. Upon receiving it,
Dōgen was so enraged that he at once drove his pupil away.
He ordered the chair the priest sat on destroyed, the ground
under the chair dug three feet deep and the earth thrown away.
After this incident he was admired more than ever, and the
Zen practice became popular among the people.

   The second Zen school, Fuke, was founded by Kakushin
who, like Dōgen and Eisai, went to China in 1249 and received
the Zen training under Fu-yen (Butsugen), a great teacher of
the school. On his return home in 1255 he founded the school
of homeless mendicancy, commonly called 'community of
nothingness,' in which the members were said to be 'lying on
dew and feeding on air.' The school eventually became a
community of *rōnin* ('lordless warriors') and as such helped
the government and the people in various respects. This was
abolished after the Great Restoration in 1868.

   In the Zen School we have at present three principal sects :
1. Rinzai Sect, first introduced from China by Eisai in 1191
and then by Benen in 1235 ; 2. Sōtō Sect, introduced by Dōgen
in 1127 ; 3. Ōbaku Sect, introduced by Ingen in 1654. This

last sect, though of late introduction, has 640 monasteries.

(4) PHILOSOPHICAL AND RELIGIOUS

Zen has much philosophy but is not a philosophy in the strict sense of the term. It is the most religious school of all and yet not a religion in the ordinary sense of the word. It has no scripture of the Buddha, nor does it hold any discipline set forth by the Buddha.

Without a *sūtra* (discourse) or a *vinaya* (discipline) text no school or sect would seem to be Buddhistic. However, according to the ideas of Zen, those who cling to words, letters or rules can never fully comprehend the speaker's true idea. The ideal or truth conceived by the Buddha should be different from those taught by him because the teaching was necessarily conditioned by the language he used, by the hearers whom he was addressing, and by the environment in which the speaker and hearers were placed. What Zen aims at is the Buddha's ideal, pure and unconditioned. The school is otherwise called 'the School of the Buddha's Mind.' The Buddha's mind is after all a human mind. An introspection of the human mind alone can bring an aspirant to a perfect enlightenment. But how ?

The general purport of Buddhism is to let one see rightly and walk rightly. The way of viewing (*darśana-mārga*) is different from the way of walking (*bhāvanā-mārga*). People walk often without seeing the way. Religions generally lay importance on practice, that is, how to walk, but neglect teaching the intellectual activity with which to determine the right way, that is, how to see. To judge whether the path we are going to take is right or not, first of all, science is important, but, as we go on, we discover that philosophy is much more important than anything else. In case science and philosophy do not give a satisfactory result, we must resort to the meditative method of Zen in order to get insight into any given problem.

First, find out your way and begin to walk on it. The foot acquired by meditation can carry you across the wave-

flux of human life, and over and above the air region of the
heavenly world and finally make you perfect and enlightened
like the Buddha. Contemplation is the eye which gives insight, and, at the same time, the foot which procures a proper
walk. Zen (meditation and concentration) is the lens on
which diverse objects outside will be concentrated and again
dispersed and impressed on the surface of the negative plates
inside. The concentration on the lens itself is concentration
(*samādhi*) and the deeper the concentration is, the quicker
the awakening of intuitive intellect. The further impression
on the negative film is wisdom (*prajñā*) and this is the basis
of intellectual activity. Through the light of reflection
(*prajñā*) outwardly, i.e., insight, we see and review the outer
world of diversity once again so as to function or act appropriately toward actual life.

The meditation of the patriarchal Zen, therefore, was not
an analytical method like science nor was it a synthetical
method like philosophy. It was a method of thinking without
ordinary thinking, transcending all methods of logical argument.
To think without any method of thinking is to give opportunity
for the awakening of an intuitional knowledge or wisdom. All
methods of meditation as taught by Hīnayāna, by Yogācāra
(quasi-Mahāyāna), by the abrupt method of calmness and
insight (*samathavipaśyana*) of Tendai, or by the mystical *yoga*
of Shingon can be used if the aspirant likes, but are in no way
necessary.

The ideas peculiar to Zen may be summarized as follows :
"From mind to mind it was transmitted," "not expressed in
words or written in letters"; "it was a special transmission
apart from the sacred teaching." "Directly point to the human
mind, see one's real nature and become an enlightened Buddha."
Or, "the very body or the very mind is the Buddha." The idea
was very well expressed in Hakuin's hymn on sitting and
meditating : "All beings are fundamentally Buddhas ; it is like
ice (which represents our actual condition) and water (which
represents an underlying Buddha-nature) ; without water there
will be no ice. . . . This very earth is the lotus-land and this
body is Buddha."

The basic idea of Zen is the identity of *ens* and non-*ens*. "The true state is no (special) state"; "the gate of *Dharma* is no gate"; "holy knowledge is no knowledge." The mutual identification of two opposed ideas, such as black and white, good and evil, pure and impure, or the like, results from deep meditation. "The ideal body has no form, yet any form may come out of it." "The golden mouth has no word, yet any word may come out of it." Ideas of a similar nature are often encountered.

There is, however, a peculiar process in Zen. To concentrate one's mind in silent meditation, a *kōan* ('public theme') is given to an aspirant to test his qualification for progress towards enlightenment. On receiving a theme, one sits in silence in the Zen hall. One must sit at ease, cross-legged and well-posed with upright body, with his hands in the meditating sign, and with his eyes neither quite open nor quite closed. This is called sitting and meditating, which may go on for several days and nights. So the daily life, lodging, eating, sleeping, swimming or bathing should be regulated properly. Silence is strictly required and kept; that is, while meditating, dining or bathing, no word should be uttered and no noise should be made. Sometimes a public dialogue called 'question and answer' (*mordō*) takes place where the 'cloud or water'—the name used for traveling students—ask questions of the teacher who gives answers, hints or scoldings. When a student or any aspirant thinks that he is prepared on the problem, he pays a private visit to the teacher's retreat, explains what he understands and proposes to resolve the question. When the teacher is satisfied, he will give sanction; if not, the candidate must continue meditation.

Zen, which is generally practiced in a forest retreat seems to be far away from the real world, but the general trend of mind of the Zen people is always towards a strict observance of rules and a minute accomplishment of discipline. Their ideals are immediately expressed in their daily life and in personal experiences. They are generally very practical. The famous words of the Zen patriarchs, such as "no work, no food" ("one day without work, one day without food"), "every day, good day (to work)," "daily mind the way," "the living, the teaching" ("going, staying, sitting, or lying are the sacred teaching"), exemplify their practical application of ideals. We can say without hesitation that it requires training to hear a voice in silence, to find action in inaction, motion in absence of motion or to have preparedness in peace and fearlessness in death. Such a tendency must have appealed to the warrior class, thus eventually producing the way of knightly behavior (*bushidō*).

Besides, when we see the Zen influence so conspicuously discernible in literature (poetry, short poems, etc.), drama (*Nō*, ballad-drama), painting (monochrome, portraiture), architecture (temple-building, paper windows, tea houses), industrial arts (lacquer, etc.), and the social life (tea ceremony, vegetable cookery, flower arrangement, interior decoration), and at present in the educational training of Japan the Zen ideas can be regarded as almost inseparable from the Japanese national life. Probably the national ideal of simplicity, purity and sincerity can find its expression most appropriately in the Zen practice of Buddhism.

XII. THE JŌDO SCHOOL
(THE PURE LAND SCHOOL)[1]
(Sukhāvatī)

(Amita-pietism)
[Mahāyānistic]

(1) PRELIMINARY

The general Japanese name for Amita-pietism is Jōdo meaning 'Pure Land,' which is a translation of *Sukhāvatī* ('Land of Bliss'). Those who believe in Amita Buddha will be born in the 'Pure Land' to become a Buddha.

The idea of being 'saved' is generally considered new in Buddhism. But King Milinda (Menandros, a Greek ruler in Sagara, about 115 B.C.) questioned a learned priest Nāgasena, saying that it was unreasonable that a man of bad conduct could be saved if he believed in a Buddha on the eve of his death. Nāgasena replied : "A stone, however small, will sink into the water, but even a stone weighing hundreds of tons if put on a ship will float." Nāgārjuna[2] again asserted that there were two ways for entering Buddhahood, one difficult and one easy. One was traveling on foot and the other was passage by boat. The idea of boat or vehicle expressed here at least suggested the appellations 'Hīnayāna' and 'Mahāyāna,' the Great and Small Vehicles, even though the terms were not actually designated by Nāgārjuna himself. Amita-pietism will be the greatest of all vehicles to convey those who are in need of such means.

There are two original texts in Sanskrit, a large[3] and a

---

[1] Ching-t'u.   [2] c. 100-200 A.D.

[3] *Taishō*, No. 360. English translation by F. Max Müller : *The Land of Bliss*, in Sacred Books of the East, Vol. XLIX, The Clarendon Press, 1894.

small [4] *Sukhāvatī-vyūha* ('Sūtra of the Land of Bliss'), both
of which were translated into Chinese. Chinese translations
from 147 to 713 A.D. were twelve in number, but at present only
five are in existence.

From the facts just stated one can scarcely doubt the origin
of this doctrine of salvation by Amita. Since the faith seemed
so strange to some people, various ideas and hypotheses have
been proposed regarding this faith. Some have asserted that
it was borrowed from Christianity, chiefly from the legend of
Thomas' mission in India (Dahlmann). Others have pointed
out certain resemblances in the *Avesta* or in Manichaeism
(Eliot). Some have gone so far as to say that it might have
been acquired on the way from Central Asia to the East
(Reischauer).

These authorities generally formed their opinions from
outward resemblances without entering into the internal development of Mahāyānistic ideas. The faith in Amita was
simply the outcome of a far-reaching contemplation of the
Buddha-nature. If you strip away all the external features of
Śākyamuni and all the conditions of his Indian life, you will
find an ideal Buddha to suit his perfect Enlightenment. To be
more definite, if we depict a Buddha on the basis of perfect
Enlightenment we come to the ideal of Buddhahood, i.e., Buddha of Infinite Light and Infinite Life. When the ideal of
Nirvāṇa which is spaceless and timeless, birthless and deathless,
changeless or waveless is realized, it will be nothing but the
Infinite (Amita or Amitābha). The description of the Land
of Bliss, the name of Unbounded Light and Life, and the
illumined person of limitless wisdom and benevolence are simply
interpretations given to the Infinite.

(2) HISTORICAL

Nāgārjuna's *Daśabhūmi Sūtra* and Vasubandhu's [5] com-

---

[4] *Taishō*, No. 362. English translation by F. Max Müller : *The
Smaller Sukhāvatī-vyūha*, in Sacred Books of the East, Vol. XLIX, The
Clarendon Press, 1894.   [5] c. 420-500.

mentary on it are the Indian authorities recognized by the
Jōdo School. The easy way and the 'power of another' are
already indicated and elucidated by them. In China the
authorities of the faith are many, but the following four lines
of transmission are generally recognized :

(1)
Fu-t'u-ch'êng, an Indian in
China between 310 and 348
A.D.
:
Tao-an (Dōan, 584-708)
:
Hui-yüan (Eon)

(2)
Bodhiruci, an Indian in China
between 503 and 535 A.D.
:
Hui-ch'ung (Eryū)
:
Tao-ch'ang (Dōjō)
:
T'an-luan (Donran, 476-542)
:
Ta-hai (Daikai)
:
Fa-shang (Hōjō, 495-580 A.D.)

(3)
Bodhiruci
:
T'an-luan (Donran)
:
Tao-ch'o (Dōshaku, c. 645)
:
Shan-tao (Zendō, d. 681)
:
Huai-kan (Ekan)
:
Shao-k'ang (Shōkō)

(4)
Tz'u-min (Jimin), who went
to India during the T'ang
period (618-709 A.D.) and
received the Amita-pietism in
Gāndhāra

The decisive authorities chosen by Shinran (1173-1262)
are T'an-luan, Tao-ch'o and Shan-tao, by whom the details
of the easy way and the perfect reliance on the Buddha's power
are minutely annotated. In Japan there are many authorities
(the history of the faith is very long), though Genshin

(942-1017) [6] and Hōnen (1133-1212) are the pre-eminent promoters of the doctrine. Prince Shōtoku, in the reign of the Empress Suiko (593-628 A.D.), is said to have believed in Amita. At any rate, a reference to the Western Land of Bliss is found in one of his commentaries. Ein, a Korean priest, lectured in 640 A.D. on the *Sūtra of the Land of Bliss* before the Throne. In the Nara period (710-794 A.D.) Gyōgi is said to have traveled about and propagated the faith among the people. Kanjin, a Chinese *vinaya* (discipline) master who came to Nara in 754 A.D., imparted the worship of Amita to his Japanese pupil, Eiei, on the eve of the latter's death near Kuangtung.

But in the Nara period the Amita-pietism was not systematically taught, though there must have been some followers who privately adhered to it. In the Tendai School the Amita worship was taken up and promoted as an all-inclusive faith. It was Jikaku Daishi (Ennin), [7] the third patriarch, who instituted the two forms of repeating the Amita formula, standing and sitting, and introduced music relating to the Land of Bliss. Even now adherents read the smaller *Sukhāvatī* text in the daily service. On that account their protest against Hōnen's founding a new exclusive school of Amita-pietism was exceptionally strong. Prohibition of the Jōdo School did not satisfy them and they attempted to insult Hōnen's corpse although it was already buried. On Mount Hiei there were earnest followers of Amita-pietism who devoted themselves to the study and practice of the School. A brilliant representative was Genshin, otherwise known as Eshin, who wrote, among others, an important treatise for the faith and invented a special pictorial art of paradise and Amita welcoming the pious believers. A learned follower of his line, Ryōnin, [8] founded an eclectic sect of the Tendai and Jōdo Schools called Yūzūnembutsu Sect ('All Permeating Faith of the Buddha Amita') which, in reality, is a compromise between the Lotus doctrine and Amita-pietism. He is said to have been inspired by Amita himself about the truth, "One in all, all in one ; one

---

[6] 1133-1212.   [7] 794-864 A.D.   [8] 1071-1132.

B.—12

acts for all, all act for one." It is the idea of salvation by another's power, mutual help being the basic idea. Accordingly, an act of adoration to the Buddha done by one will be of help to another. Their practice will be not only for one another but also for the salvation of society at large. This faith became extinct soon after Ryōnin's death but was revived by Hōmyō, one of the believers, in 1321. Although it belongs to Amita-pietism, it uses the *Lotus* text and the *Wreath* text as well. Thus we can regard it as belonging to the doctrine of the 'Holy Path' rather than to that of the 'Pure Land.' [9] The headquarters of this school are at the Dainembutsuji Temple, Hirano, near Ōsaka, where it governs some 357 monasteries.

In this respect, we must remember that there is in the Tendai School itself a sub-sect called Shinsei Branch, founded in the Tokugawa period (about 1780), which devotes itself to the worship of Amita and rules over more than 400 monasteries, while the two branches, Sammon and Jimon, govern more than 3,000 and 800 monasteries, respectively. The worship of Amita has prevailed considerably in the Shingon center, Kōyasan, as it has in the Tendai center, Mount Hiei, but we cannot determine how far the school was studied or practiced in the Shingon School at an early period. However, among some sixty-six existing monasteries at Kōyasan, the older edifices have the Buddha Amitābha as the chief object of worship. At the end of the Heian period, Kakuban (Kōkyō Daishi, 1095-1145), a distinguished priest of the Daidenpōin at Kōya and afterwards the founder of the new sect of Shingon, earnestly devoted himself to the faith of Amita and aspired for a birth in the Land of Bliss in the ensuing life. Thus we can presume that the school must have been taken up by influential circles.

Ryōhen,[10] a learned priest of Kongōsammaiin, who was a professed believer of Amita, traveled to Tanabe, Kii, and converted a chief of the fishing village there. According to his

---

[9] See p. 180 for the distinction of the two doctrines.
[10] About 1200.

teacher's instruction, the new convert went to Kōyasan and built the Karukaya Hall ('Grass-thatched Hall') which became the headquarters of the Amita faith. Almost all of the Hijiri class (sage) at Kōyasan were Amita-pietists who traveled throughout the district and worked for Kōyasan as propagandists. "Whenever we go the voice of the Amita-formula is heard," is recorded in one of the memorials presented to the Government. "In front of and behind the monasteries, under the roofs, and by the waysides the sacred place is getting so noisy that no one can quietly meditate and concentrate one's mind." Iyeyasu finally ordered that the Amita formula should be repeated only in the Karukaya Hall.

Kūya [11] was the earliest Amita-pietist who publicly worked for the propagation of the faith. He is said to have been a son of Emperor Daigo, or at any rate a scion of the Imperial family. He traveled to the country places, built bridges and dug wells for the people whenever needed. In 938 A.D. he came to the capital (Kyoto) and strolled through the streets loudly reciting the Amita hymns specially composed by himself, modulating the voice to music, beating a bowl and dancing as he went on. The people called him 'sage of the streets.' He built the Rokuhara Monastery in which he enshrined a large statue of the Eleven-faced Kwannon (Avalokiteśvara) and a copy of the Tripiṭaka literature. Taira no Sadamori followed him from a deep admiration of his personality. He traveled farther to the Ainu district and the Buddhist teaching was for the time accepted by the aborigines. The Amita-formula recited according to his style was called *Kūyanembutsu* and the dance was called *hachi-tataki* ('beating a bowl'). His school was famed as the School of Kūya. The Kōshō Monastery (one of Kūya's priestly names was Kōshō), commonly called Kūya Hall, still exists in Shijō, Kyoto, and the street itself is named Takaki-chō after his dancing style *hachi-tataki*. After his death his school became extinct, though the Ji School of Amita-pietism revived it,

[11] 903-972 A.D.

honoring Kūya as the remote founder of the Ji School, which rules over 486 monasteries at present.

(3) PHILOSOPHICAL AND RELIGIOUS

Amita-pietism, as represented by the Jōdo School of Hōnen, the Shin School of Shinran and the Ji School of Ippen, shows a unique aspect of Buddhism. While all other schools of Mahāyāna insist on self-enlightenment, these schools teach sole reliance on the Buddha's power. The Buddha of all other exoteric schools is Śākyamuni while the Buddha of these schools is Amita or Amitābha ('Infinite Light') or Amitāyus ('Infinite Life') whose Land of Bliss (*Sukhāvatī*) is laid in the Western Quarter, often designated as the Pure Land (Jōdo).

The critical division of the Buddha's teaching adopted by Hōnen was into the two doctrines of the Holy Path and the Pure Land, originally proposed by Tao-ch'o (Dōshaku) of China, c. 645. The former is the difficult way to traverse while the latter is the easy way to travel defined by Nāgārjuna. There is another division which was proposed by Vasubandhu and elucidated by Tao-ch'o, that is, the ways of self-power and of another's power. Another's power here means the power of the Buddha Amitābha, not any other's power like that of Yūzūnembutsu. Those who pursue the Holy Path can attain Buddhahood in this world, if they are qualified, while those who aspire for the Pure Land can attain Buddhahood only in *Sukhāvatī*, the Pure Land.

Now what is *Sukhāvatī* and who is Amitābha or Amitāyus ? We have seen that the Amitābha or Amitāyus ('Infinite Light' or 'Infinite Life') is a Buddha idealized from the historical Buddha Śākyamuni. If the Buddha is purely idealized he will be simply the Infinite in principle. The Infinite will then be identical with Thusness. The Infinite, if depicted in reference to space, will be the Infinite Light, and if depicted in reference to time, the Infinite Life. This is *Dharma-kāya* (ideal). This *Dharma-kāya* is the *Sambhoga-kāya* (the 'Reward-body' or 'body of enjoyment'), if the Buddha is viewed as a Buddha 'coming down to the world.' If he is viewed as a *Bodhisattva* going up to the Buddhahood, he is a would-be Buddha like the toiling *Bodhisattva* (Śākyamuni). It is Śākyamuni himself who describes in the *Sukhāvatī-vyūha* the activities of the would-be Buddha, *Dharmakāra,* as if it had been his former existence.

The vow, original to the would-be Buddha or even to Śākyamuni himself, is fully expressed in forty-eight items in the text. Items Nos. 12 and 13 refer to the Infinite Light and the Infinite Life. " If he cannot get such aspects of Infinite Light and Life he will not be a Buddha." If he becomes a Buddha he can constitute a Buddha Land as he likes. A Buddha, of course, lives in the 'Nirvāṇa of No Abode,' and hence he can live anywhere and everywhere. His vow is to establish the Land of Bliss for the sake of all beings. An ideal land with adornments, ideal plants, ideal lakes or whatnot is all for receiving pious aspirants. The eighteenth vow which is regarded as most important, promises a birth in his Land of Bliss to those who have a perfect reliance on the Buddha, believing with serene heart and repeating the Buddha's name. The nineteenth vow promises a welcome by the Buddha himself on the eve of death to those who perform meritorious deeds. The twentieth vow further indicates that anyone who repeats his name with the object of winning a birth in his Land will also be received.

As to the interpretation of these three vows, there are certain differences among the schools. Generally speaking, the Jōdo School takes the vows as literally as possible, while the Shin School elucidates the intent of them rather freely to suit all parts of the text. According to the Jōdo School these three vows should be taken separately as they are independent vows, though there are some differences in importance.

To the Shin School, however, they are interdependent. The eighteenth is the fundamental vow. The nineteenth and the twentieth are subordinate vows. Though the eighteenth vow expects sole reliance on the Buddha, the followers of the nineteenth and twentieth vows depend on their own actions, the former on meritorious deeds and the latter on repetition of the Buddha's name. They have no complete reliance on the Buddha's power. So their destiny cannot be the Pure Land itself. They must, according to Shinran, go through some purgatory which is called the 'secluded place' or the 'realm of neglect' referred to in other sections of the text. But they will be transformed and in the end admitted to the real Land of Bliss.

With regard to the appearance of Amita or Amitābha, their opinions are also at variance. It is said to have been ten *kalpas* (long periods) ago. The Jōdo School takes this literally, while the Shin School holds that the time 'ten *kalpas* ago' is something like 'ages ago,' and may refer to a second or third appearance. The original Buddha may be of much more remote age. Thus the 'Lotus' doctrine is here applied to the Amita-pietism.

The smaller text of *Sukhāvatī-vyūha* is a résumé or abridged text of the larger one. The last of the three texts, the *Amitāyur-dhyāna Sūtra*,[12] tells us the origin of the Pure Land doctrine taught by the Buddha Śākyamuni. Ajātaśatru, the prince heir-apparent of Rājagriha, revolted against his father, King Bimbisāra, and imprisoned him. His consort, Vaidehī, too was confined to a room. Thereupon the Queen asked the Buddha to show her a better place where no such calamities could be encountered. The World-Honored One appeared before her and showed all the Buddha lands and she chose the Land of Amita as the best of all. The Buddha then taught her how to meditate upon it and finally to be admitted there. He instructed her by his own way of teaching and at the same time by the special teaching of Amita. That both teachings were one in the end could be seen from the words he spoke to Ānanda at the conclusion of his sermons. "O Ānanda ! Remember this sermon and rehearse it to the assembly on the Vulture Peak. By this sermon, I mean the name of Amitābha." From this we can infer that the object of the sermon was the adoration of Amita. Thus, we see that

---

[12] *Taishō*, No. 365. See my English translation, *The Sūtra of the Meditation on Amitāyus*, Sacred Books of the East, Vol. XLIX, The Clarendon Press, 1894.

Śākyamuni's teaching was after all not different from that of Amitābha.

The principal difference of the Jōdo School from that of Shin is in the treatment of the repetition of the Buddha's name. With Jōdo the devotional repetition of the Buddha's name is a necessary action of the pious to deepen the faith, without which salvation will never be complete ; while according to the Shin School it is simply an action of gratitude or an expression of thanksgiving, after one's realizing the Buddha's power conferred on one. The Shin School holds the exclusive worship of the Amitābha, not allowing even that of Śākyamuni, the strict prohibition of prayers in any form on account of private interests, and the abolition of all disciplinary rules and the priestly or ecclesiastical life, thus forming a community of purely lay believers, i.e., householders. As the orthodox Jōdo School with all kindred sects still conforms to the old priestly life, it differs extensively from the Shin School.

The Ji School of Amita-pietism is somewhat different. It was founded in 1276 by Ippen (1238-1289). He set forth the rule of reciting the hymns of Shan-tao (Zendō)[13] six times every day, hence the name Ji (time). In theory he derived his idea from the *Lotus* as did Ryōnin of Yūzūnembutsu, but in practice he followed Kūya who invented a popular dance for the popularization of the Amita-faith. Thus the school has a totally different feature from the other schools of Amita-pietism. Ippen is said to have visited Kumano Shrine in Kii in 1275 where he was inspired by a holy verse of four lines, which he believed to have come from the deity of the shrine. Each of the first three lines was headed by a numeral, 6, 10, 10,000 and the last line by 'people,' altogether making up 'six hundred thousand people.' He at once made up his mind to save that number of people by a propagation of the Amita-faith. Now Amita-pietism with all its kindred schools taken together has more than one-half of the Japanese population as adherents.

[13] d. 681.

Amita-pietism is of four aspects : 1. That of Tendai and Shingon, in which Amita is one of the five Wisdom Buddhas (*Dhyāni*-Buddhas) governing the Western Quarters, having Mahāvairocana (the Great Sun Buddha) at the center; 2. That of Yūzūnembutsu in which the value of one's faith in Amita is transferable to another or vice versa, i.e., religion of mutual help with faith ; 3. That of Jōdo in which Amita's faith is taught exclusively in accordance with the three *Sukhāvatī* texts of the school, especially based on the Buddha's vows ; 4. That of Shin in which the faith is taught strictly in accordance with the eighteenth vow of the Buddha described in the larger *Sukhāvatī* text. In both Jōdo and Shin the Buddha Amita is more than one of the five Buddhas, although his Land is laid in the Western Quarter ; instead, he is the one central Buddha. Of these four aspects, the first originated from mystics, the second was influenced by *Lotus* principles, the third was based chiefly on the three vows, and the fourth centered on one vow of the Amita.

Thus we see the ideas of the Amita schools concerning the Buddhological principle of Mahāyāna. According to the theory of original immanence of Tendai and the duo-homoi-ousian (two essences in one) theory of Shingon, the principle of one-is-all and all-are-one will be readily admitted. Of the five Wisdom Buddhas, Amitābha of the West may be identical with the central Mahāvairocana, the Buddha of homo-cosmic identity. Without reference to mysticism, Amitābha's original vows, his attainment of Buddhahood of Infinite Light and Life, and his establishment of the Land of Bliss are all fully described in the *Sukhāvatī* text. It is but natural that Śākyamuni, who hinted to his pupils in the *Lotus* not to regard him as a Buddha of eighty years of age with a small stature, for he is in reality a Buddha of remote ages and of world-wide pervasions, should be identified with the Buddha of Infinite Light and Life. A complete reliance on such a Buddha's power will be a reason-able outcome of this teaching. Shinran especially represents the last stage of this idea. He insisted on an absolute faith in Amita, not making any effort for enlightenment by oneself. One should rely exclusively and absolutely on Amita, faith alone being the cause of salvation.   According to him, even the believing thought itself is the grace of the Buddha, and one's remembrance or repetition of the name of the Buddha is simply a token of free thanksgiving shown toward the Buddha.

being the cause of salvation. According to him, even the believing thought itself is the grace of the Buddha, and one's remembrance   Buddha is simply a token of free   wn toward the Buddha.

XIII. THE NICHIREN SCHOOL
(NEW LOTUS)

(Lotus-pietism)
[Mahāyānistic]

(1) PRELIMINARY

Since the *Lotus of the Good Law* was translated and expounded by Kumārajīva,[1] it has been one of the most popular subjects of Buddhist study along with the *Prajñā* and *Nirvāṇa* texts. When the philosophy of immanence or the phenomenological doctrine was promulgated on the basis of the *Lotus* by Chih-i,[2] it was generally known as the T'ien-T'ai[3] School. It was Saichō (Dengyō Daishi, 767-822 A.D.) who went to China and received the doctrine from this school and on his return in 804 A.D. founded the school in Japan. His theoretical elucidation of the *Lotus* doctrine may not be much different from the original Chinese school, but his practical application of the doctrine to the national cult and synthetic treatment of all other Buddhist schools subordinate to his school seem to be the new aspects added by virtue of his genius. Besides the *Lotus* doctrine, he professed to teach mystic Shingon, Amita-pietism, contemplative Zen, as well as Mahāyānistic *Vinaya* discipline. To him these were subordinate doctrines to the *Lotus* or at any rate concurrent systems to complete the central doctrine. However, in the course of time, there appeared among his followers some ardent specialists in each of these systems and sometimes the result was separation. In the Heian period (794-1185) the mystic rituals and ceremonial performances promoted by this school in concert with the Shingon School

---

[1] During 383-406 A.D. in China.
[2] Chih-kai, 531-597 A.D.
[3] Tendai in Japanese.

carried the day to satisfy the aristocratic taste of the time. There arose in time a devotional school of Amita-pietism which also flourished in the bosom of the school. Through the influence of the two streams of religious activities a great Buddhist transformation took place in the national life and thought of Japan during the period.

The refinement of vernacular literature, mystification of fine arts, development of national architectural and industrial arts, and the graceful manners and customs of the refined class were all due to the influence of Buddhist culture. Probably the Japanese appreciation of universals, tolerance and thoroughness in research owe a great deal to Buddhist training. But peace often ends in effeminacy. As a rule political corruption and social degeneration in general could not be checked in any way. An opportunity for a military power was now opened and perhaps hatred and struggle among courtiers, clans, territorial lords and partisans were more than we know from history. Already in the closing period of the Heian era all under heaven was weary of war and disorder. By the establishment of the military government at Kamakura, the people in general expected peace and order to be restored, but all in vain. Intrigues and strifes were going on more than ever. The arrival of the 'latter age' of religion was now felt in the public life of the nation. A general reformation in political as well as religious life seemed to be an urgent need. The authority of the two old schools of Tendai and Shingon was waning, or, at any rate, was suffering the same fate with the aristocratic classes. The new Amita-pietism of Hōnen,[4] though gaining ground among the people at large, had no marked influence over the ruling classes. The Zen School of the time, though it seemed appropriate for the knightly training of military people, had as yet no power over the political affairs. A man of keen observation and strong character like Nichiren (1222-1282), if imbued with a firm religious conviction, could not remain without protesting.

To know Nichiren and his school we must first know the

---

[4] 1133-1212.

Lotus text on which all his ideas and arguments are founded. What is the *Lotus* text ? A text-criticism shows that originally the *Lotus* text consisted of twenty-one sections and was later enlarged into twenty-eight sections by addition and division. The earliest translation was by Dharmarakṣa in 286 A.D., the second by Kumārajīva in 406 A.D., and the third (complete translation) by Jñānagupta and Dharmagupta in 601 A.D. Among them, the second was the best in Chinese composition and regarded as authoritative by the best *Lotus* authorities.[5] In spite of late translation, it represented an earlier form of the text than the first translation, judging from some internal evidences, e.g., a quotation by Nāgārjuna,[6] and the like. Besides, elements of the contents of the added or divided chapters were extant in the original form of twenty-one sections. Anyhow, the existing text in twenty-eight sections (Kumārajīva's translation) was used by Chih-i, Saichō and Nichiren himself. It is the only translation of the text used in Japan, either within or without the Nichiren School. Let us review the contents of the text and the standpoint of Nichiren in the *Lotus* doctrine.

(2) HISTORICAL

What is historical with the other schools of thought is personal with the Nichiren's Lotus-pietism, for it is Nichiren's personality that constitutes the feature of the school. It was not accidental that the school was called after the founder's name. Nichiren was born in 1222, the son of a fisherman of Kominato, Awa, the southeastern coast of Japan. He was sent to Kiyozumi, a hill near his home, to live as a novice in a monastery. He was ordained in his fifteenth year. His early problem, "What was the Truth taught by the Buddha ?" was

---

[5] *Taishō*, No. 262. English translations : *The Lotus of the True Law*, translated by H. Kern, Sacred Books of the East, Vol. XXI, The Clarendon Press, 1884 ; *The Lotus of the Wonderful Law*, translated by W. E. Soothill, Oxford, 1930.

[6] c. 100-200 A.D.

not solved there.   He proceeded to Kamakura and later passed
to Mount Hiei in search of the Truth.   His study of ten years
(1243-1253) on the mountain convinced him that a revival of
Tendai philosophy alone was the nearest approach to the
Truth.

By Tendai philosophy Nichiren meant not what he found
there at hand but what was taught by Dengyō Daishi himself.
The original T'ien-T'ai of Chih-i was chiefly theoretical, whereas
the Japanese Tendai of Dengyō Daishi was practical as well
as theoretical.   But after the two great masters, Jikaku and
Chishō, the practical sides of Tendai were either mystic rituals
or Amita-faith ; that seemed to them most important.   The
fundamental truth of the *Lotus* doctrine seemed to be laid aside
as if it were a philosophical amusement.   Nichiren could not
accept this attitude and so returned in 1253 to his old monastery
at Kiyozumi where he proclaimed his new doctrine that the
Lotus alone could save the people of the depraved age, the
essential formula being "Homage to the Text of the *Lotus* of
the True Ideal."   It is *Dharma-smṛti* (thought on *Dharma*) and
not *Buddha-smṛti* as was the Amita-formula.   *Dharma* is the
ideal realized by the original Buddha.   All beings are saved
through homage to the *Lotus* of Truth, and this alone, he
declared, is the true final message of the Buddha.

The abbot and all others opposed him and he had to
escape to Kamakura where he built a cottage and lived for
a while.   He preached his doctrine in streets or in parks,
attacking the other schools as violently as ever.   He wrote a
treatise on the *Establishment of Righteousness as the Safeguard
of the Nation*, which he presented to the Hōjō Regent in
1260.   His main arguments were against the Amita-pietism of
Hōnen, which he considered to be chiefly responsible for the
evils and calamities within and without the nation.   In the
treatise he condemned Hōnen as the enemy of all Buddhas,
all scriptures, all sages and all people.   It was the duty of the
government, he said, to terminate his heresy even with the
sword.   His idea of the identification of religion with national
life is manifest throughout the work.

Nichiren's classification of 'latter age' began with the year

1050, according to the generally accepted calculation of the date of Nirvāṇa. The last of seven calamities, the foreign invasion, was predicted in it. He contended that national peace and prosperity could be attained only through the unification of all Buddhism by the doctrine of the *Lotus* of Truth. Later, he attacked the religious schools then extant and formulated his views as follows : Jōdo (Amita-pietism) is hell, Zen (meditative intuitionism) is devil, Shingon (mysticism) is national ruin and Ritsu (discipline) is traitorous. These four cover practically all existing schools of his time and were the doctrines that had been subordinate to Tendai.

As Amita-faith propagated by Hōnen, Shinran [6a] and others was most influential among the people at large, the Zen trend of thought, specially appealing to the ruling military class of the time, was probably the second influential doctrine. Owing to the activities of Eisai,[7] Dōgen[8] and Enni[9] in Kyoto, and the Chinese teachers Rankei, Sōgen and Ichinei, in Kamakura, the Zen School was certainly asserting its position in the national life and culture. As to Shingon, the power of mystification which it cherished never lost its hold on the mind of the people ; the Shingon School was influential all over Japan. The Ritsu was a school of discipline reformed by Eison who prayed against the Mongol invasion at the Shinto shrine of Iwashimizu by an Imperial order, when Emperor Kameyama himself was present and vowed to sacrifice his life for the safety of the nation. Thus the Ritsu must have been quite influential at the Court.

Nichiren's attacks against these schools became more violent than ever when he was mobbed, attacked and banished to Izu in 1261. Even after his return to Kamakura and to his native place to see his ailing mother, he did not refrain from his violent protest against the government as well as the religion, and went so far as to say that Tokiyori, the Hōjō Regent who believed in Zen and wore a Buddhist robe, was already in hell and that the succeeding Regent Tokumune was on the way to hell. Upon the arrival of the Mongolian envoys demanding tribute, he again remonstrated with the Regime to

6a 1173-1262.   7 1141-1215.   8 1200-1253.   9 1235.

suppress the heresies and adopt the *Lotus* doctrine as the only way out of national calamities. In 1271 he was arrested, tried and sentenced to death. In a miraculous way he escaped the execution and was banished to the remote island of Sado at the end of the same year.

In spite of the hardships and troubles he experienced there, Nichiren wrote several works. In the *Eye-opener*, his famous vows are found : " I will be the pillar of Japan ; I will be the eyes of Japan ; I will be the vessel of Japan." Here he became conscious of himself being the Bodhisattva Viśiṣṭa-cāritra ('Distinguished Action') with whom the Buddha entrusted the work of protecting the Truth.

After three years he was allowed to return to Kamakura in 1274. No moderation, no compromise and no tolerance could be extracted from him in spite of an ardent effort on the part of the government. He retired to Minobu, west of Mount Fuji, and lived peacefully. He died at Ikegami, near Tokyo, in 1282.

Nichiren's militant spirit was kept alive by his disciples, six of whom were earnest propagandists. One of them, Nichiji, went to Siberia in 1295 but no further report was heard of him. The school, always colored by a fighting attitude, had many disputes with other religious institutions. In 1532, for example, it had a conflict with Tendai, the mother school, called the war of Tembun. One of the Nichiren sects called Fujufuse Sect ('no give or take') refused to comply with the parish rule conventionally set forth by the government and was prohibited in 1614 along with Christianity by the Tokugawa Shogunate. There are at present eight Nichiren sects, two of which are important : 1. The Nichiren School proper with headquarters in Minobu, 3,600 monasteries under it. 2. The Kenpon-Hokke School, otherwise called the Myōmanji School which has 580 monasteries.

(3) PHILOSOPHICAL AND RELIGIOUS

Just as the personality of Nichiren constitutes the Nichi-

ren School, the essence of which is the *Lotus* formula "Homage
to the *Lotus* of Truth," so it is the personality of the Buddha
that constitutes the *Lotus* doctrine. The whole *Lotus* text
may be a drama as Professor Kern imagined, but the Buddha is
not only the hero in the play. The Buddha is also the organizer
or proprietor of the drama. The Truth of the *Lotus* text is
not an impersonal death truth ; it is the ideal, the Truth blooming, fragrant and bearing fruits as the lotus, the Truth active,
the Truth embodied in the Buddha, the Truth-body, the
Enlightenment itself, the Enlightened and Enlightenment
and Enlightener all combined. So the real Buddha of the
text is not that corporeal Buddha who got enlightened
under the *bodhi* tree, preached for the first time at the
Deer Park of Banaras and entered Nirvāṇa at the Sāla
grove of Kuśīnagara at eighty-one years of age. He is
the Buddha of immeasurable ages past, ever acting as
the Enlightener. By enlightening all beings he exercises
benevolence to all. Out of his mercy he teaches the doctrine
of expediency. He is in reality the organizer of the drama,
yet he himself acts as a hero in the play, leading all the dramatic
personnel, even with some of the inferior characters who in time
will be able to play a role. The three Vehicles, of course, as
well as Devadatta the wicked and Nāga the serpent maid,
all come under the Buddha's illumination. The world of
illumination of the remote Buddha is called the 'realm of origin'
and the world of illumination by the incarnate Buddha is called
the ' realm of trace.' I used the word 'realm' but it does not
mean a separate division or place. It simply indicates the 'activity of the Buddha of original position' or 'that of the Buddha
of trace-leaving manifestation.' 'Original position' and 'trace-
manifestation' are the problems long discussed in the *Lotus*
schools and all center on the Buddha's personality, a Buddhological question. When it is applied to the *Lotus* text, the
question at the outset will be, "Which Buddha is revealing the
Truth ?"

It is generally accepted that the first fourteen sections of
the text, with an introduction, a principal portion and a conclusion, refer to the realm of trace, while the last fourteen

sections also with an introduction, a principal portion and a conclusion, relate to the realm of origin. The object of the *Lotus* on the whole is a revelation of Truth. In the former sections, chiefly in the section of *upāya* or 'expediency,' the Buddha reveals that what he taught before the *Lotus*, during forty or more years, was only an expedient; more definitely, the teachings for direct disciples (*śrāvakas*, i.e., *arhat*-teaching), for the enlightened-for-self (*pratyeka-buddha* teaching) and for lesser *bodhisattvas*, i.e., the teaching for the three Vehicles, was for expediency's sake, and indicated clearly that the 'one vehicle for all' (*ekayāna*) is the Truth. In the latter sections, chiefly in the longevity section, the Buddha speaks of his own personality, and reveals that the historical existence which he has now nearly completed is not his real body but shows clearly his Truth-body (*Dharma-kāya*) to be a true realization of remote ages past.

The former sections refer to the doctrine in which the Truth is revealed ; expediency is taught as expediency and Truth as Truth. The latter sections, on the other hand, refer to the personality in which the Buddha himself is revealed ; the recent as the manifested person and the remote as the real original person. So far Nichiren agrees with Dengyō Daishi. Nichiren, however, standing on the doctrine of personality, asserts that all teachings before the *Lotus* and also the former sections of the *Lotus* are the 'trace doctrines of the Trace Buddha' and that only the latter sections are the 'essential original doctrines of the Original Buddha.' He established his school on the basis of the original *Lotus*. Thus his school is called either the Nichiren School after the founder or the Hommon-Hokke School after the doctrine.

The difference of the tenets of Dengyō Daishi and Nichiren is further seen in the treatment of the substance of the *Lotus* text. The *Lotus* doctrine assumes ten regions, ten thus-aspects and three realms. Dengyō Daishi lays importance on the principle of the realm of trace. The realm of trace treats only the nine regions, teaching the causal states of culture and therefore considering mind and thought as important factors of training, and finally attributing all the phenomenal worlds to the mere-ideation theory. The threefold view of one mind and the 3,000 worlds immanent in one thought-instant are taught minutely. According to the Nichiren School, the Tendai is too much inclined to the theoretical side of the Truth, thereby forgetting the practical side of it. Nichiren holds that the realm of origin teaches the effective state of enlightenment and the Buddha's person is the center of Truth ; the reality of the phenomenal worlds centers in the personality of the Buddha ; and all aspirants should be guided to realize the Ideal-body of the Buddha.

The *Lotus* text reveals the original Buddha whose principle and practice are fully explained in the original portions of the text. What the founder holds important is the Buddha's practice, not his principle. One who understands and practices the practical aspects of that Buddha is a devotee or realizer of the *Lotus*, just as the *bodhisattva* of supreme action (Viśiṣṭacāritra) is placed in the highest position in the text. The Buddhahood (perfect enlightenment) of such an adept will be immediate in this very body.

The original Buddha was like the moon in the sky, and all other Buddhas of the *Wreath*, of the *Āgama*, of the *Vaipulya* ('developed'), the *Prajñā* ('wisdom'), the *Gold Light* (*Suvarṇaprabhāsa*), the *Sukhāvatī* (Pure Land) and the *Great Sun* (*Mahāvairocana*) were all moons in various waters, and merely reflections of the one central moon. It is only a fool who would try to catch a reflected moon.

The title of the *Lotus of the Good Law* sums up all these principles and practice of the Buddhas of origin and trace, and, to Nichiren, is the only remedy to procure the reform of the depraved state of the 'latter age,' in spite of all counteractions from existing poisons. The fourfold watchword set forth by Nichiren, as we have seen above, was the renowned object of hatred by all the rest of the Buddhist schools of Japan, for it was against the Amita-pietism of Jōdo, the meditative intuitionism of Zen, the ritual mysticism of Shingon and the formalistic discipline of Ritsu. This was the wholesale denunciation of all existing Buddhist schools except the Tendai School of Dengyō Daishi, which he sought to reform and restore to its original form.

XIV. THE NEW RITSU SCHOOL
(THE REFORMED DISCIPLINARY SCHOOL)[1]
(Vinaya)

(Disciplinary Formalism)
[Mahāyānistic]

(1) PRELIMINARY

Vinaya (discipline) is the moral code of Buddhism and is invariably translated into Japanese 'ritsu' (*discipline*). The whole code containing 250 articles for priests and 348 for nuns existed from the lifetime of the Buddha. A weekly convocation called 'fast' (*upoṣadha*) was held for the purpose of reciting the code, one article after another, to ascertain whether any member of the 'noble' community had committed any crime or sins described in it. Confession, repentance, surveillance, custody, excommunication or any other necessary means was taken after judgment was passed on the person in question. The nature of precepts (*śīla*) was twofold : 1. The positive precepts, the precepts for performance, i.e., the rules that should be performed on such occasions as ordination for a novice (*bhikṣu*), convocation for weekly reading of the code, summer retreat for yearly study and training of the community, graduation ceremony ; rules concerning residence, medicines, leathers ; settlements of disputes in the congregation ; and also the rules of council meetings, judicial court of discussion, voting and decision, treatment of contributions, confiscation of properties or the like. 2. The negative precepts of prohibition, i.e., not to commit any sin or crime. The nature of prohibition was also twofold : (a) prohibition in order to safeguard one from crime or sin, like the prohibition of drinking an intoxicating liquor, which may lead to a sin or crime ; (b) prohibitions of actual crimes, such as killing, stealing, lying, com-

---

[1] Lü.

mitting adultery, etc., which are themselves evil in nature. The entire prohibitive code is as follows : 1. crimes that incur expulsion (for the monks, there are 4 ; for the nuns there are 8) ; 2. crimes that require suspension of priestly right (for the monks, 13 ; for the nuns, 17) ; 3. offences that require confession and ablution (for the monks, 90 ; for the nuns, 178) ; 4. offences requiring public confession (for the monks, 4 ; for the nuns, 8) ; 5. offences requiring forfeiture (for the monks, 30 ; for the nuns, 30) ; 6. actions that are indefinite as to whether they are offences or not (for the monks, 2 ; for the nuns, none) ; 7. minor prohibitive regulations of the order (for the monks, 100 ; for the nuns, 100) ; 8. judicial settlement of disputes (for the monks, 7 ; for the nuns, 7)—total for priests, 250 ; for nuns, 348.

The formalistic Hīnayāna was inclined to hold to letters, words and forms of the *Vinaya* discipline. Consequently, a schism arose as to the legality of the ten allowances (such as receiving money only if used for the order) of the rules, and the council of Vaiśālī met to discuss and decide them. The idealistic Mahāyāna laid more emphasis on the spirit of the rules rather than the letter. Though Mahāyāna seemed to be transgressing the rules, it would harmonize itself with the spirit of the Buddhas who had set forth the rules.

The recipient of a precept had to keep in mind the four aspects of discipline : 1. the elements of discipline ; 2. the essence of discipline ; 3. the action of discipline ; and 4. the form of discipline. Among these, the most important was the essence of discipline, without which the acceptance of discipline would never be complete. The essence of discipline is the conscious energy ever active as a firm impression received at the faithful acceptance of discipline. This is, in fact, the result of the heart-felt vow taken at the solemn occasion of ordination. This energy ought to manifest itself in thought, word, or action whenever a function is needed, and one will therefore act accordingly so as to conform to discipline. The essence of discipline is thus a moral force acting in the mind, like conscience.

There are two ordinations, that for the initiation of a

novice receiving five disciplinary rules and that for a full qualification of a priest receiving ten. Both are the precepts of
common-sense morality (not to kill, steal, lie, commit adultery,
drink liquors, etc.). These two are the formal ordinations
performed by both Hīnayāna and Mahāyāna and may be
called a priest (*bhikṣu*) ordination. There is another informal self-vow ordination performed by the Mahāyāna only,
which is set forth in the *Brahma-jāla Sūtra*, and may be called
a *bodhisattva* (future Buddha) ordination. In the Nara
period (710-794 A.D.) there was only the former, but during
and after the Heian period (794-1183) the latter came to be
generally followed.

(2) HISTORICAL

The Emperor Shōmu (724-748 A.D.) once intended to
invite an able teacher from China in order to train the Japanese
priests and nuns in the Ritsu (*Vinaya*) doctrine. He sent out
two priests, Eiei and Fushō by name, to carry out this purpose.
The then ruling Chinese Emperor, Hsüan-tsung, however,
was much in favor of Taoism and did not wish to send any
Buddhist teacher to Japan. Consequently, negotiation with a
much-famed *vinaya* teacher, Chien-chên (Ganjin),[2] failed.
However, as the need of an instructor was imminent, Tao-
hsüan (Dōsen),[3] one of the pupils of that teacher, was sent
to Nara in advance. He arrived there in 735 A.D. and busied
himself teaching the Ritsu, the Zen and the T'ien-t'ai doctrines
while waiting for his teacher's arrival.

Meanwhile, Ganjin prepared secretly for his departure with
the aid of the two students, Eiei and Fushō. He actually built
ships five times with the help of the former prime minister Li
Lin-fu and others, but each time failed through shipwrecks.
Finally, he embarked on the ship of the Japanese envoys
returning home and arrived at Nara in 754 A.D. He was
welcomed by the Court and a special monastery Tōshōdaiji as

---

[2] 687-763 A.D.   [3] 596-667 A.D.

well as a sacred area for ordination was built for him. All of
the Imperial family, headed by the ruling Empress, the ex-
Emperor and ministers, received the first ordination from him.
His discipline was that of the Four-Division tradition,
(*Dharmaguptiya*), otherwise called the Ritsu School of the
South Mountain founded by Tao-hsüan, a pupil of the famous
Hiuen-tsang.[4]

Dengyō Daishi (Saichō, 767-822 A.D.) received the ordination but afterwards rejected it, and started a new *bodhisattva*
ordination based on the Tendai doctrine which was purely
Mahāyānistic and informal called the discipline based on
'round and abrupt' doctrine which is the *Lotus* doctrine, the
round or perfect doctrine, the effect of which can be obtained
abruptly. A strong protest from Nara was raised against it.
It was only after his death that Imperial permission was given
for the establishment of the new ordination. A sacred hall
of this ordination was built on Mount Hiei and became the
basis of ordinations of all other schools, Zen, Jōdo and their
sub-sects. Even Nichiren intended a special ordination hall
of a similar type but he did not succeed.

In the Nara period there were three sacred areas of ordination : 1. Tōdaiji Temple, Nara ; 2. Kwanzeonji Temple,
Tsukusho ; 3. Yakushiji Temple, Shimozuke. In the
Heian period there was another ordination hall on Mount Hiei,
originally planned by Dengyō Daishi. The Shingon School
of Kōbō Daishi [5] had an anointment hall in Tōji, Kyoto, as
a substitute for the ordination hall. Later, when the followers
of Chishō Daishi [6] at the Mii Temple began to dispute with
the followers of Jikaku Daishi at Mount Hiei, the former could
not receive ordinations on the mount and consequently built
a new hall called Samaya Kaidan. Thus in the Heian period
there were practically five ordination halls in Japan. Of these,
the typical one was the 'round and abrupt' ordination hall
which was based on the 'round and abrupt' doctrine of the
'Lotus Truth.'

The essence of discipline was considered to be an unmani-

---

[4] Hsüan-tsang.   [5] 774-835 A.D.   [6] 814-891 A.D.

fested moral force (*musa*) immanent in the recipient's mind. We can thus realize that importance was here laid upon the spiritual effect of ordination rather than the ceremonial performance of the rite.

The Tōshōdaiji Monastery in Nara was built by the Court and was made the authorized headquarters of all Buddhist training in discipline. The founder of the Ritsu School of the South Mountain, Ganjin, was succeeded by his able pupils, Fa-chin (Hōshin) from China, and Johō [7] from Arsak, East Persia, both of whom lived to the Heian period and took part in the Imperial ordination. The school exists even today as a separate school, but its formal discipline has never been popular in Japan, partly because of the introduction of the new Hīnayānistic doctrine brought home by I-tsing [8] from India and partly because of the rise of the Mahāyānistic discipline of the Tendai School.

(3) PHILOSOPHICAL AND RELIGIOUS

The formality of the Ritsu School lies in the carrying out of the disciplinary code, both positive and negative, in letter rather than in spirit. To keep the discipline to letters and words was the chief concern of the schools of the Nara period when the Four-Division doctrine was introduced by Ganjin. It was Hīnayānistic, but, since there was no other alternative, it was admitted as common to both Hīnayāna and Mahāyāna. Let us call it the Disciplinary School. In Japan, since the time of Prince Shōtoku [9] there has been the idea of a non-formal discipline, to maintain the original spirit of the Buddha's moral code. This non-formal discipline was the chief idea running through all schools of all ages in Japan. While the aspirants of formal discipline were chiefly priests, those of non-formal discipline were *bodhisattvas* or future Buddhas, without distinction of priests or laymen.

Generally speaking, the importance of discipline was laid

---

[7] Ju-pao.   [8] I-ching, 635-713 A.D.   [9] 574-622 A.D.

on what we call the essence of discipline, i.e., spiritual force created in the mind on making a vow and vividly acting always against a violation of that vow. The Realistic (Kusha) School takes this to be one of the forms (*rūpa*, matter), i.e., a substantial element without manifestation (*avijñapti-rūpa*), while the Nihilistic (Jojitsu) School regards it as a special element—neither matter nor mind—in want of a function of both. Further, the Idealistic (Hossō) School treats it as a perceptive form conceived at ordination that really proceeds from the stored seed of thought (*cetanā*). This is the unmanifested mental function that keeps one in accordance with his own pledge. It is the innermost impression which functions like conscience.

Self-vow Discipline

In the formal discipline there should be a private tutor (*upādhyāya*), a ceremonial teacher (*karma-ācārya*) and some witnesses. An ordination should be carried through by a convocation (*saṅgha*). When the article of a disciplinary code is read, the recipient makes a vow of obeisance. But in some cases when such formal requirement cannot be fulfilled, one is entitled to make a self-vow informally. It can be designated as the self-vow discipline, as is gloriously exemplified by Queen Śrīmālā in the *Śrīmālā Sūtra*. Prince Shōtoku lectured twice on this text before the Throne. At the second time the Empress Suiko stood up before the Buddha and loudly repeated the Queen's vows as her own. This was the first example of the self-vow discipline ever practiced in Japan. The self-vow ordination is permitted in the *Brahma-jāla Sūtra*.[10] On failing to obtain the proper instructor in discipline one can accept the precepts by self-vow. It is a kind of *bodhisattva* ordination.

Self-immanent Discipline

In opposition to the formal ordination, an ideal ordination

---

10 *Taishō*, No. 21.

was proposed by Dengyō Daishi. He called it the 'round and abrupt' ordination. As stated before, the 'round and abrupt' was the appellation of the *Lotus* doctrine, the perfect doctrine, the effect of which could be obtained suddenly. It is purely Mahāyānistic and considered by the Tendai School as an ordination only for *bodhisattvas*. According to the *Lotus* doctrine, all the morals of discipline are originally immanent in one's own mind and not the products of a special effort. It can be called the self-immanent discipline and is special to the Tendai School.

Self-nature Discipline

The Zen School of the Kamakura period (1185-1335 A.D.) had an ordination of a similar kind. According to this school the idea of moral discipline is originally innate in human nature. By introspective meditation one can draw it out and put it to practice. The formal side of discipline is now also carefully attended to by the Zen School, but the introspective nature of the Zen training makes the ordination ceremony very impressive and fascinating.

Besides this Zen ordination, there are the anointment ritual of the Shingon School of mysticism and the fivefold transmission of the Jōdo School of Amita-pietism. These take the place of the disciplinary ordination but can be left unnoticed here because of their somewhat different nature.

In the Ritsu School there was a new movement in this period, a departure from the Ritsu School of the South Mountain or the Four-Division School. The movement was started by Eison (1201-1290) on the basis of self-vow discipline. It was a reformed doctrine, called the Reformed or New Ritsu or Reformed Disciplinary School and was, in reality, a revival of the self-vow ordination of Prince Shōtoku, as performed by the Empress Suiko. Eison studied the *Vinaya* literature in the Tōdaiji Temple and, as he became aware of the idea of self-vow running through the *Śrīmālā* and *Brahma-jāla* texts and the Tendai and Zen schools, founded with a fellow-student this Reformed School of Self-vow Formalism. He meant to revert to the original idea of the Buddha and Prince Shōtoku, following the general tendency of Buddhism of the Kamakura age. However, it is regrettable that we do not have the details of his idea of training. His fame as a great Ritsu (*Vinaya*) reformer was far-reaching, and it was due to his influence that this disciplinary school saw the most flourishing age after the time of Ganjin of Nara. In 1281 the Emperor Gouda ordered Eison to pray in the Otokoyama Shrine against the invasion of Kublai Khan. The storm which repelled the 100,000 invaders was believed to have been an answer to his earnest prayer. The title Kōshō Bodhisattva ('promoter of righteousness') was given to Eison in 1300 A.D. by the Court.

During the age of Buddhist Renaissance in the Tokugawa period (1603-1868 A.D.), the two branches of disciplinary formalism, the Myōhō-ritsu (discipline according to the Law) School of Jōgon [11] in Yedo, and the Shōbō-ritsu (discipline of True Law) School of Jiun [12] in Kawachi, had certain connections with Eison's new discipline, either directly or indirectly. The two branches of the Tokugawa period did not prosper much, but the founders of both schools were talented scholars of Sanskrit and revived Indian studies to a great extent.

---

[11] 1641-1704 A.D.   [12] 1718-1804 A.D.

XV. CONCLUSION

In conclusion, I should like to say something more about the metaphysical and dialectical questions of Buddhism, for in the foregoing pages I have been too occupied with describing the historical and technical details of the different Buddhist schools and have somehow neglected to consider the general problems of philosophy which concern special doctrines.

With regard to *cosmogonical* and *cosmological* questions, Buddhism has no special theory of its own and seems to have adopted the then-accepted theory of the world-system of Sumeru (Pāli : *sineru*) and chiliocosm (*sahassi-lokadhātu* ; Skt. : *sāhasri-lokadhātu*). However, it does have a definite theory of the world-periods or aeons (*kalpa*) which is substantially identical with that of the Sāṅkhya and Jaina Schools of India. The Sāṅkhya School might have been the originator of the *kalpa* theory as Garbe thinks,[1] and Buddhism as well as Jainism might have been indebted to it. Although evolution (*samvatta* and *samvatta-tthayi* ; Skt. : *samvarta-sthāyin*) and devolution (*vivatta* and *vivatta-tthayi* ; Skt. : *vivarta-sthāyin*) are equally described in all three schools, Buddhism gives minute details as to the Buddhas who appear and the people who live in each of the four world-periods.

Since the cycle of aeons repeats itself in due course, a story of creation or the Creator does not exist in Buddhism. Practically speaking, Buddhism has no cosmogony, no theology, no divinity. Brahmā as a personal God in Buddhism is only a Being in the 'form-heaven' who comes and receives the Buddha's instruction. Thus a deification of the Buddha, as some suppose, is out of the question.

The universe, according to the Buddhist idea, is not homocentric. It is instead a co-creation of all beings. Moreover, everyone of us is self-created and self-creating. As long

---

[1] Richard Garbe, *Die Sāṅkhya Philosophie*.

as all beings have common purposes, it is but natural that there be groups of similar types of beings. Buddhism does not believe in the doctrine that all have come out of one cause, but holds that everything inevitably comes out of more than one cause ; in other words, all is mutually relative, a product of interdependence.

As to *ontological* questions, Buddhism rarely concerns itself, for 'thatness' (*tattva*, reality), which refers chiefly to matter, is not what Buddhism seeks. The theory of no-substance (selflessness) which Buddhism holds will not permit any discussion about things-in-themselves or real entity. Instead, Buddhism is concerned with 'thusness' (*tathātva, tathatā*, state of being thus), a term which originally referred to form (*rūpa*) or becoming (*saṅskāra*) and not to matter. It is not accidental that Buddhist Realism (Kusha) or Idealism (Hossō) begins with 'form' (*rūpa*) and never speaks of matter or substance in the enumeration of their seventy-five or one hundred elements which 'have become' and 'have not become' (*dharma saṅskṛta* and *asaṅskṛta*). Some may doubt whether 'selfless' was applied to things in general from the beginning, but the phrase 'all things selfless' (*sarva dharma nairātmana*) does not allow any such supposition.

The Realist School (Sarvāstivāda), assuming that all things exist, has an atomic theory, but the existence of the atom is only for a moment and nothing remains the same for two consecutive moments (*sarva saṅskāra anitya*). The theory of momentary destruction (*kṣaṇa-bhanga*) is also held by the Mahāyāna schools, which regard the world as in a constant state of flux.

Whether Buddhism has the idea of the One against the Many or the Absolute against the Relative is extremely doubtful. Buddhism certainly opposes dualistic ideas and often negates a pluralistic diversity in man's ascent of Self-Culture. However, it never advances a monistic view positively. Even the Mahāyāna doctrine of Aśvaghoṣa, as in the *Awakening of Faith*, limits Thusness to the human mind, which ascends if conditioned by a pure cause and descends if polluted by an impure cause. Thusness is therefore something like a neutral state. In reality, the term means 'the state of being thus' or, ultimately speaking, Buddhahood. *Dharma-dhātu* (The Realm of Principle) has a double meaning, signifying the actual universe and the indeterminate world (Nirvāṇa); in the latter case it is identical with the Thusness of the Buddha. Nirvāṇa ('flamelessness') means, on the one hand, the death of the human body and, on the other, the total extinction of life-conditions (negatively) or the perfect freedom of will and action (positively). *Tathāgata-garbha* ('Matrix of Thus-come or Thus-gone') likewise has a twofold meaning : the 'Thus-come' or 'Thus-gone' (Buddha) concealed in the Womb (man's nature) and the Buddha-nature as it is. Buddha-nature, which refers to living beings, and *Dharma*-nature, which concerns chiefly things in general, are practically one as either the state of enlightenment (as a result) or the potentiality of becoming enlightened (as a cause). It is generally known that *Dharma-kāya* has two senses : the 'Scripture-body' means that the Teaching remains as representative of the body after the Buddha's demise, and the 'Ideal-body' means the Enlightenment as a Formless-body. The same twofoldness applies to *Śūnyatā* or 'Void.' 'Void' does not always mean an antithetical nothingness or emptiness. In a higher sense it indicates the state *devoid* of all conditions of life. Hence it is sometimes said that *śūnya* is *aśūnya* (Void is non-void). More precisely, it is not the state in which nothing exists but is the state in which anything can exist. It is the world of perfect freedom of actions unconditioned by life. Exactly alike is the True Reality. It is said that True Reality is no reality ; or we may say that true characteristic is no characteristic. In such cases, the terms 'reality' and 'characteristic' should be interpreted in their ordinary literal sense while the adjective 'true' determines their real meaning.

Thus in Buddhism any word which represents something like the First Principle must always be interpreted in its twofold meaning, for Buddhism admits a worldly or common-sense truth and, by its side, sets forth a higher or absolute truth in order to elevate it.

The terms given above are all expressive, either subjectively or objectively, of the true principle of nature, universe and humanity, and point finally to perfect enlightenment or perfect freedom. Buddhism, after all, does not lose individuality or personality, for the result is nothing but the perfection of personality or the realization of the Life-Ideal. A loss of identity is not the question. One may think that *here exists a world of super-individuality apart from the world of individuality into which one figuratively jumps in due course and all becomes one. The view of such a distinct world of non-individuality is but the assumption of a larger individual world. Such a world is utterly inadmissible in Buddhist thought ; but, religiously speaking, it is possible for the enlightened to speak partially of the world of indeterminateness (Nirvāṇa) in his instructing descent to the world of determinateness.

With regard to the *psychological* question, Buddhism does not admit the existence of a soul that is real and immortal. *Anātma* or non-self refers to all things (*sarva-dharma*), organic and inorganic. In the case of human beings, there will accordingly be no soul, no real self that is immortal, while in the case of things in general, there will be no noumenon, no essence which is unchangeable. Because there is no real self spatially, i.e., no substance, there will be no permanence, i.e., no duration. Therefore no bliss is to be found in the world.

There are no ordinary *eschatological* questions in Buddhism because all beings are in the eternal flux of becoming. One should note, however, that birth incurs death and death again incurs birth. Birth and death are two inevitable phenomena of the cycle of life which ever repeats its course. The end of self-creation is simply the realization of the Life-Ideal, that is, the undoing of all life-conditions, in other words, the attainment of perfect freedom, never more to be conditioned by causation in space-time. Nirvāṇa is the state of perfect freedom.

Concerning *epistemological* questions, Buddhism has much more to say than any other philosophy. As sources of cognition Buddhism recognizes the world of sensation (*pratyakṣa-pramāṇa*), the world of inference (*anumāna*) and the world of pure intuition (*dhyāna*). Thus sense-data, reason and inner experience resulting from intuition will all provide the content of knowledge. Besides these we can appeal in every case to the Word that has been uttered from the world of perfect enlightenment (*bodhi*), i.e., the Buddha (the 'Enlightened').

Without purity of conduct there will be no calm equipoise of thought; without the calm equipoise of thought there will be no completion of insight. The completion of insight (*prajñā*) means the perfection of intellect and wisdom, i.e., perfect enlightenment. It is the result of self-creation and the ideal of the self-creating life.

The Buddha, as a man, taught men how to become perfect men. The central principle of self-creation is the gradual development of intellect and wisdom, the object being the perfection of personality. The realization of the Life-Ideal is Buddhahood. But there will be no objective enlightenment apart from the Enlightened One. There exists only the inner experiencer, no absolute otherness.

The doctrine of the Middle Path means in the first instance the middle path between the two extremes of optimism and pessimism. Such a middle position is a third extreme, tending neither one way nor the other. The Buddha certainly began with this middle as only one step higher than the ordinary extremes. A gradual ascent of the dialectical ladder, however, will bring us higher and higher until a stage is attained wherein the antithetic onesidedness of *ens* and non-*ens* is denied and transcended by an idealistic synthesis. In this case the Middle Path has a similar purport as the Highest Truth.

The above statements refer chiefly to the metaphysical and intuitive problems of Buddhist thought. Now as to the *dialectical* questions. Nāgārjuna's [2] method of argumentation is particularly notable. Following the Buddha's practice, he started from an evaluation of the worldly or common-sense truth and termed it 'closed truth' (*saṃvṛti-satya*). Without denying the common-sense truth he set forth beside it a highest-sense truth (*parama-artha-satya*). 'Highest-sense' does not mean the highest-sense truth at the beginning, but is only the highest at any particular time. It is, in fact, only a higher-sense truth, as the term *lokottara* ('above the world') indicates. Gradually the common-sense world will reach the higher-sense truth then set forth, which latter has now become the common-sense truth. By the side of it Nāgārjuna would set forth a still higher-sense truth which again will become a common-sense truth in time. Thus the standard of common-sense truth will be raised higher and higher until it attains pre-eminently the Highest-sense Truth, which can be taken as the Absolute in the Western sense of the word. But in fact, it is not the Absolute nor is it the One because any one can reach that stage of perfect freedom.

The Highest-sense Truth has been made dialectically and positively by Nāgārjuna without using any antithetic and negative method such as expounded by Hegel. In addition to the six fundamental principles of Buddhist thought which I have described in Chapter III, I might add this Principle of Appreciation of Common-sense Truth. This was the attitude the Buddha himself took during his teaching career and was not altogether Nāgārjuna's invention. A thorough-going negative method was also used by Nāgārjuna in his famous Eight-fold Negation. With it all the phases of becoming or life-conditions have been negated. "Production and extinction, permanence and annihilation, unity and diversity, coming and going" are the refuted examples in four pairs and eight items. If there be any views or attachments he would deny them at once as they come forward. The final result of Nāgārjunals negation is the Void which is not an actual emptiness but is instead the state *devoid of* special conditions of the world of life.

In passing we must not overlook Nāgārjuna s important method of demonstrating Truth from all possible viewpoints. It is called the Discrimination of the Fourfold Thesis, as I have already referred in Ch. VII : 1. positive (*ens*) ; 2. negative (non-*ens*) ; 3. both positive and negative (*both* ens *and non-*ens *together*) ; 4. neither positive nor negative (*both* ens *and non-*ens *negated*). These four are considered to be all the possible viewpoints which can be advocated. The intellectual groups of the Buddha's time were not-satisfied by the simple answer of "yes" or "no," for almost every one of his opponents used this fourfold viewpoint, and the Buddha used it carefully in refuting any erroneous thesis of his opponents. For example, when the First Cause is questioned : 1. Is it caused by self ? 2. Or is it caused by another ? 3. Or is it caused by both ? 4. Or is it caused by neither ? Similarly, if Being is the thesis : the first view will affirm it (*ens*) ; the second will deny it (non-*ens*) ; and the third will conditionally affirm the above two, as does the Buddhist idealist (affirming the inner world but denying the outer world). The fourth view, however, will negate both *ens* and non-*ens*. The application of this method to any disputation will exhaust all possibilities of an argued question. I should like to call it the Principle of Exhaustive Demonstration of Truth, and might add it also to the above-mentioned Fundamental Principles of Buddhist thought.

I shall not discuss here the details of the Buddhist logic of Nāgārjuna, Vasubandhu,[3] and Dignāga (Diṅnāga) for which I shall refer the reader to Stcherbatsky's excellent work, *Buddhist Logic.*[4] Let it suffice here to say that Buddhist logic is not a formal logic of thought, but is rather a logic of dispute or debate which lays stress on the investigation of cause, relations and possibility and is therefore an art of argumentation and refutation. The science of cause (*hetu-vidyā*) is the name given to Buddhist logic ; the Buddha himself was sometimes called '*vibhajya-vāda*' (the 'discriminative'), meaning a logician.

The aim of the Buddha was the establishment of the Kingdom of Truth. The foundation of such a Kingdom was, in case of a sovereign whose title was 'Turning the Wheel' (*cakra-vartin*), laid by throwing a wheel into the air. The golden wheel thus thrown, going around in the sky, would come back to the original place in seven days. The circle-line drawn by the motion of the wheel in seven days would determine the sphere of the Kingdom to be ruled by the sovereign.

---

[3] c. 420-500 A.D.

[4] Th. Stcherbatsky, *Buddhist Logic,* 2 Vols., Leningrad, 1932. Vidyā-bhūṣaṇa's exhaustive work entitled *A History of Indian Logic* should also be consulted among other studies.

'Turning the Wheel of Truth' (*Dharma-cakra-pravartana*) would practically mean 'preaching the Buddha's Ideal' or the 'realization of the Buddha's Ideal in the world,' i.e., the 'foundation of Kingdom of Truth.'

The Buddha's Ideal, that is, the Truth he has conceived, would be difficult to be understood without reference to the fundamental principles of Brahmanism. The attributes of *Brahman*, the universal principle, were, according to the Upaniṣads, '*saccidānandam*,' that is, 'being' (*sat*), 'thinking' (*cit*) and 'joy' (*ānandam*). In the case of *Brahman*, the First Cause, these would be 'Self-extant,' 'All-knowing' and 'Blissful.'

The time-honored Buddhist principle was threefold :

1. *Sarva-dharma-anātmatā*, 'Selflessness of all elements,' i.e., 'No substance.'
2. *Sarva-saṅskāra-anitya-tā*, 'Impermanence of all component beings and things and elements,' i.e., 'No duration.'
3. *Sarvam duḥkham*, 'All in suffering,' i.e., 'No bliss.'

To these sometimes another *Nirvāṇam sukham*, "Nirvāṇa is Bliss,' is added. These are generally called the 'Three or Four Signs' of Buddhism, which distinguish Buddhism from any other school. The Buddha's first theory that all beings have no abiding self is opposed to the Brahmanic theory of 'permanent being' (*sat*) and is against the immortality of an individual soul and the existence of the universal soul or spirit or Creator (*Mahā-ātman*). It is the theory of no real substance. A denial of an immortal being is a denial of immortality. The Buddha's second theory that all beings or things are impermanent is directed at this point. All existence is temporary or transitory. Nothing will remain the same for two consecutive moments. Life is an eternal flux of change, that is, the wave of life. A continuity of flowing waves might give an appearance of permanence but it is an illusion It is the theory of no duration.

Since the world has no abiding substance and no enduring permanence, we shall have no enjoyment in this world. One should accept suffering as suffering and not be deceived by a disguised joy. One should not be optimistic because all ends in suffering ; nor should one try to shun it because there is no final escape. One should go against it with all bravery and perseverance and overcome it. This is the theory of no bliss and is directly opposed to the Brahmanic theory of bliss (*ānandam*).

As to the second Brahmanic theory of 'thinking' or 'knowing' (*cit*) which is later summed up as the 'knowledge' section (*jñāna-kāṇḍa*) of the Upaniṣads, the Buddha proposed his theory of ignorance (*avidyā*), i.e., the 'blind will to live,' as the root-principle of the Twelve-Divisioned Cycle of Causations and Becomings. The way of undoing one's ignorance is his religion of Self-Creation based on knowledge and wisdom. The perfection of fullness of insight is the perfection of personality, i.e., perfect Enlightenment (*Bodhi*).

Accordingly, the Buddha first taught the way of Life-View (*darśana-mārga*) The Four Noble Truths on suffering and its extinction, the Twelve-Divisioned Cycle of Causations and Becomings and the principle of indeterminate nature of beings and things show his view of life The indeterminate nature of men is to be determined by Self-Creation. The Buddha next taught the way of Life-Culture (*bhāvanā-mārga*). Here he trained his pupils either by dialectic argument or by intuitive meditation in order to awaken their intellect or insight. In course of time, Buddhist schools developed their own methods of attaining Enlightenment. Nāgārjuna's negative rationalism [5] and Bodhidharma's pure intuitionism [6] are the most developed examples. As a result of Life-Culture by these methods, the principles of Reciprocal Identification, True Reality and Totality as described in Ch. III are arrived at. Finally, as the way of No More Learning, the principle of Nirvāṇa, that is, perfect freedom, in which the state of undifferentiated indeterminateness is attained. This is the realization of Life-Ideal in Buddhism.

[5] The Sanron School.   [6] The Zen School.

INDEX